finding a middle ground in the immigration debate between proponents of open borders and restrictionism

over-generalizing

Associative obligations based on participation in shared institutions (political membership as basis for "special obligations" to those of our political community)

obligatory vs. discretionary instead of refugee vs. economic migrant

Ethic of membership must be balanced against ethic of universalism.

Qualified (rather than absolute) rights of states to control immigration

Is consent a fiction?

Her concept of peoplehood- participation in shared institutions is what makes us a people, not nationality

Why is self-determination valued over positive rights?

Area of der value over positive rights?

originating to the global world reshaping as it went to current system

OXFORD POLITICAL THEORY

Series Editors: Will Kymlicka, David Miller, and Alan Ryan

Immigration and Democracy

OXFORD POLITICAL THEORY

Oxford Political Theory presents the best new work in contemporary political theory. It is intended to be broad in scope, including original contributions to political philosophy, and also work in applied political theory. The series contains works of outstanding quality with no restriction as to approach or subject matter.

OTHER TITLES IN THIS SERIES

Against Marriage
An Egalitarian Defense of the
Marriage-Free State
Clare Chambers

Civics Beyond Critics
Character Education in a Liberal
Democracy
Ian MacMullen

The Ethics of Immigration
Joseph Carens

Linguistic Justice for Europe and for
the World
Philippe Van Parijs

Critical Republicanism
The Hijab Controversy and Political
Philosophy
Cécile Laborde

National Responsibility and Global
Justice
David Miller

Disadvantage
Jonathan Wolff and Avner de-Shalit

Levelling the Playing Field
The Idea of Equal Opportunity and
its Place in Egalitarian Thought
Andrew Mason

The Liberal Archipelago
A Theory of Diversity and Freedom
Chandran Kukathas

The Civic Minimum
On the Rights and Obligations of
Economic Citizenship
Stuart White

Reflective Democracy
Robert E. Goodin

Multicultural Citizenship
A Liberal Theory of Minority Rights
Will Kymlicka

Deliberate Democracy and Beyond
Liberals, Critics, Contestations
John S. Dryzek

Real Freedom for All
What (if Anything) Can Justify
Capitalism?
Philippe Van Parijs

On Nationality
David Miller

Republicanism
A Theory of Freedom and Government
Philip Pettit

Inclusion and Democracy
Iris Marion Young

Justice as Impartiality
Brian Barry

Immigration
and Democracy

SARAH SONG

OXFORD
UNIVERSITY PRESS

OXFORD
UNIVERSITY PRESS

Oxford University Press is a department of the University of Oxford. It furthers
the University's objective of excellence in research, scholarship, and education
by publishing worldwide. Oxford is a registered trade mark of Oxford University
Press in the UK and certain other countries.

Published in the United States of America by Oxford University Press
198 Madison Avenue, New York, NY 10016, United States of America.

© Oxford University Press 2019

Library of Congress Cataloging-in-Publication Data
Names: Song, Sarah, 1973– author.
Title: Immigration and democracy / Sarah Song.
Description: New York, NY, United States of America :
Oxford University Press, [2019]
Identifiers: LCCN 2018005606 | ISBN 9780190909222 (hardback : alk. paper)
Subjects: LCSH: Emigration and immigration—Government policy—Moral and
ethical aspects. | United States—Emigration and immigration—Government
policy. | Border security—Government policy. | Democracy. | Sovereignty.
Classification: LCC JV6271 .S66 2018 | DDC 325/.1—dc23
LC record available at https://lccn.loc.gov/2018005606

1 3 5 7 9 8 6 4 2
Printed by Sheridan Books, Inc., United States of America

Contents

Preface

I STARTED WRITING this book ten years ago, but I've been thinking about immigration for much longer. I was drawn to the topic as a scholar of law and politics because it raises so many important and challenging questions. My interest in immigration is also motivated by personal experience.

I immigrated to the United States with my parents in 1980, when I was six. My parents were born just before the Korean War and the division of the country into north and south. My father lost his father in the war and eked out an existence with his mother and two siblings by farming a small plot of land. They struggled at farming (my father recalls having to forage in the woods to survive after bad-crop years) and eventually sold the land. They used the money to open a clothing shop, but when the business burned down in a fire, they migrated to Seoul in search of a better life. Despite many gaps in his education, my father was able to go to college, the first in his family to do so, and to attend a Methodist theological seminary founded by American missionaries. My mother came from a better-off family in Seoul; her father had been a city government clerk. She excelled at school but did not go to college. Her eldest brother was the only one of the seven children who got a college education. My parents met at a church in Seoul, where my father was an assistant pastor and my mother was a kindergarten teacher in a program run out of the church. After they married, they moved to a small town south of Seoul to serve a parish there. My earliest memories are of using the outhouse in winter and feeding wood into the fire underneath the two-room parsonage to keep warm.

Neither of my parents had family or friends in the United States, but my father had always wanted to visit the country whose military and missionaries had so greatly influenced Korean society. He went to the United States alone on a student visa and a year later was offered a job as pastor of a church in Kansas City. He was granted a religious-worker visa, which allowed him to sponsor my mother, brother, and me. My mother initially opposed the move; all her family and friends were in Korea and the thought of uprooting to a foreign land whose language and culture she didn't know frightened her. She eventually relented.

Our first home in the United States was a one-bedroom apartment in Raytown, Missouri, the blue-collar suburban town that served as the setting of the TV sitcom *Mama's Family*. I had to repeat first grade at the local public school because I could not speak any English. My parents went on to serve immigrant churches in Kansas City, Missouri; Shiloh, Illinois; and Salem, New Hampshire. In all these places, I made American friends at school and in the neighborhood while socializing with Korean immigrants at church. In all our adopted American hometowns, I witnessed the hardships and opportunities that come with immigration. The immigrants I knew were assembly-line workers, custodians, dry cleaners, and owners of convenience stores. I also witnessed the tensions that arise when immigrants settle in a society divided by racial and economic inequalities.

It was not until I had entered college that I acquired the critical tools for thinking about immigration. I began my freshman year in 1992, shortly after the Los Angeles riots. I was looking for a class that might help me understand what had happened and was fortunate to find a course titled "Race and Ethnic Relations in the U.S." The course gave me a much deeper understanding of the forces that drive immigration and shape the integration of immigrants. Through an interdisciplinary "Social Studies" major, I was able to take a range of courses in economics, history, philosophy, political science, and sociology. It was through the study of political theory that I acquired a much richer normative vocabulary. In reading about justice, freedom, and equality, I was immediately drawn to questions about the scope of these concepts. Do we have special obligations to people in our own country? What do we owe to people in other countries, including prospective migrants who wish to move in search of better opportunities?

I married into a family of immigrants. My husband Gabriel's family came from Mexico, Germany, and Italy. His mother's father, Jose Cruz Perez, was born in California in 1926. Jose's father had come to the United States during World War I to work as a smelter, and Jose was born on the grounds of the Pittsburg Works plant in California, where his father worked. At the age of six, Jose was forced to move to Mexico with his parents during the Mexican Repatriation. Against the wishes of his parents, Jose returned to the United States in 1945, at the age of nineteen, to work at the same plant as his father had. He eventually met and married Esther Rangel, who was also the child of Mexican immigrants. Gabriel's paternal grandmother, Amelia Guidi, had emigrated from Italy as a child, and his paternal grandfather was the son of Hermann Otto Schnitzler, a German immigrant, and Euphemia Fredericks, a Creole woman from New Orleans.

I have told all these stories to my children, Joaquin and Anna, so that they know the diverse origins of our family. I bring them up here to acknowledge that all scholarly work is motivated in part by some personal interest or experience. This book is informed by my experience as an immigrant and from knowing immigrants of diverse backgrounds, but it is not an attempt to build a theory from my own experience. My aim is to clarify and interpret the ideas with which we debate immigration using the tools of political theory. Now that they are older, I talk with my kids, as I do with my students, about the politics of immigration, why the issue provokes such intense and divergent opinions, and the importance of making the effort to understand the sources of our disagreement with others. I have approached these conversations with the same hope with which I have written this book: that we can move beyond an "us versus them" mentality and engage in reasoned debate about immigration.

Acknowledgments

PORTIONS OF THIS manuscript were presented at workshops and conferences over the last ten years. I am grateful to participants at those gatherings for stimulating discussions and suggestions for improvement. The core idea for the book developed out of a paper I wrote for the 2012 meeting of the American Society for Political and Legal Philosophy in New Orleans, which was published in *NOMOS LVIII: Immigration, Emigration, and Migration.* I am grateful to Jack Knight and Andrew Rehfeld for the invitation and to Michael Blake and Adam Cox for their excellent comments.

I had the great pleasure of discussing early versions of several chapters at my home institution. Warm thanks to my Berkeley colleagues Kinch Hoekstra and Eric Rakowski as well as Josh Cohen and Véronique Munoz-Dardé for the opportunity to discuss parts of my manuscript on two separate occasions at the Workshop in Law, Philosophy, and Political Theory, sponsored by Berkeley Law's Kadish Center for Morality, Law, and Public Affairs. I am indebted to Chris Kutz for stimulating and very helpful conversations following these presentations. I am also grateful to Leti Volpp, Marianne Constable, and other members of the Law and Humanities group at the Townsend Center for Humanities for critical feedback, as well as to Wendy Brown, Kathy Abrams, KT Albiston, Irene Bloemraad, Taeku Lee, Meir Dan-Cohen, Dan Lee, Mark Bevir, and Shannon Stimson for their encouragement. The Jurisprudence and Social Policy Program and the Law School at Berkeley have proven to be a wonderful intellectual home, and I thank my deans and associate deans for their support.

My thinking about borders and belonging was greatly aided by presentations at Princeton's Program in Ethics and Public Affairs and the political theory workshops at Washington University, the University of Virginia, and Yale University. Chapters 2 and 3 were presented at the Ethics of Immigration Conference at Washington and Lee University's Roger Mudd

Center for Ethics in November 2015. I am grateful to Angie Smith for the invitation and to the other speakers at the conference, including Joe Carens, Linda Bosniak, David Baluarte, Cybelle Fox, Reyna Grande, Félix Gutiérrez, Lucas Guttentag, Margaret Hu, David Martin, and Shelley Wilcox, for engaging discussion. I presented chapter 3 at the Stanford Political Theory Workshop in January 2016. Thanks to Emilee Chapman and Joshua Ober for the invitation, Brian Coyne for his trenchant comments, and the other workshop participants for a stimulating discussion.

I had the good fortune of discussing a very rough draft of the manuscript at the annual manuscript workshop sponsored by the Jean Beer Blumenfeld Center for Ethics at Georgia State University, in August 2016. I am grateful to Andrew I. Cohen for the invitation and Michael Blake and Margaret Moore for traveling to Atlanta to discuss the manuscript with me, as well as to Andrew Altman, Andrew I. Cohen, Andrew J. Cohen, George Rainbolt, Christie Hartley, and other Georgia State faculty and students who participated in the workshop.

Subsequent presentations helped me develop the main ideas of the book. I am grateful to Jiewuh Song for the opportunity to discuss chapters 3 and 4 at the Seoul National University Political Theory Workshop. Thanks to participants in the Pozen Center Human Rights Workshop at the University of Chicago, especially Emma MacKinnon, Jennifer Pitts, Chiara Cordelli, Susan Gzesh, and Jane Dailey, for their suggestions on how to incorporate aspects of the legal history of the plenary power doctrine into what is primarily a work of contemporary political theory. I am grateful to Bob Pasnau, Adam Hosein, and University of Colorado Boulder's Center for Western Civilization, Thought, and Policy for hosting a forum where I was able to discuss immigration with Adam Cox, Rogers Smith, and Mark Krikorian. Thanks also to David Boonin and other members of the Philosophy Department for engaging with my work at the Center for Values and Social Policy while I was in Boulder.

Several presentations in spring 2017 helped me improve the manuscript. I am grateful to Dirk Hartog and Anne Cheng for the invitation to the Princeton American Studies Workshop and to Margot Canaday, Ying Chan, Desmond Jagmohan, and other participants for their incisive comments and questions. Thanks to Christine Straehle for organizing an excellent symposium on migration for the 2017 APA Pacific meeting that brought together Gillian Brock, Michael Blake, Alex Sager, Didier Zuniga, and Colin Macleod. I am also grateful to Amandine Catala and Margaret Moore for organizing and hosting a conference on territorial rights in Montreal. I thank Patti Lenard and Matt Lister for generously providing written comments on chapter 7.

For excellent research assistance, I thank Mina Barahimi, Kony Kim, Joel Sati, Caitlin Tom, Vasanthi Venkatesh, and Pauline White Meeusen. Caitlin read early drafts of all the chapters and offered incisive suggestions for improvement; she also patiently assisted me with the endnotes. Vasanthi shared insights from her own comparative research on temporary migrant-worker programs. My conversations with Joel challenged me to clarify my notion of peoplehood and what we owe to noncitizens already present in the territory of democratic societies.

I am indebted to Margaret Moore and two other reviewers for their comments on the entire manuscript. Grappling with their suggestions helped me improve the manuscript considerably. I am grateful to Will Kymlicka, David Miller, and Alan Ryan for including my book in the Oxford Political Theory series. Warm thanks to Dave McBride and Emily Mackenzie at Oxford University Press for their support of the project, Ginny Faber for excellent copy editing, and Damian Penfold for shepherding the manuscript through production.

On a more personal note, I want to express my heartfelt thanks to Margot Canaday, Michelle Hoffman, and Jean Ku for their friendship over the years. They have supported me with meals, walks, and good conversation and reminded me of the importance of balancing work with everything else we value in life.

Finally, I am incredibly grateful to my family for their love and encouragement as I worked on this book: the Perez and Schnitzler families, who shared their many stories of immigration with me; my parents Young Il Song and Byoung Hyuk Song, who have always believed in me; my partner Gabriel Schnitzler for his love and good humor, and our children Joaquin and Anna, who bring so much joy to our lives. This book is dedicated to my family.

1

Introduction

IMMIGRATION IS ONE of the most contentious issues in contemporary politics. How should we think about it, and what kinds of policies should we support? This book explores the values and principles that shape and ought to shape public debate about immigration.

Nearly two-thirds of all international migrants live in Europe (76 million) or Asia (75 million). North America hosts the third largest number of migrants (54 million), followed by Africa (21 million), Latin America and the Caribbean (9 million), and Oceania (8 million). As of 2015, the United States is the top migrant destination in the world, with a migrant population of 47 million, 19 percent of the world's total. Germany and the Russian Federation hosted the second and third largest numbers worldwide (12 million each), followed by Saudi Arabia (10 million). The United Kingdom, United Arab Emirates, Canada, France, Australia, and Spain are also in the top ten. The total number of international migrants in the world today is 244 million, roughly 3 percent of the world's population.[1]

Public debate about immigration is often framed in binary terms—you are either for it or against it. On one side are proponents of open borders, who regard borders as unjust and inefficient. Most migrants want little more than to make better lives for themselves. As a writer in the *Atlantic* recently asked, "What moral theory justifies using tools of exclusion to prevent people from exercising their right to vote with their feet?" There is no moral framework, he concluded, that regards foreigners as less entitled to exercise their rights than those "lucky to have been born in the right place at the right time."[2] Global egalitarians and libertarians join with immigrant rights' advocates in arguing for generally open borders. As the opinion pages of the *Wall Street*

Journal put it, "Our greatest heresy is that we believe in people as the great resource of our land . . . so long as we keep our economy free, more people means more growth, the more the merrier."[3]

On the other side of the debate are proponents of immigration restrictions. Cultural nationalists focus on the impact of immigration on national identity. Some conservative nationalists define the nation not only in terms of shared values but also in racial, ethnic, and religious terms—in the American case, as a white Anglo-Saxon Protestant nation.[4] By contrast, progressive nationalists reject ethnoracial definitions of the nation and favor immigration restrictions out of a concern for disadvantaged residents of a country. When Bernie Sanders was asked in a *Vox* interview whether he favored sharply increasing immigration up to a level of open borders, he replied, "Open borders? That's a right-wing proposal, which says essentially there is no United States." It might improve the lives of the global poor, but "it would make everybody in America poorer—you're doing away with the concept of a nation state."[5] Sanders's brand of nationalism seeks to protect domestic workers against the competitive pressures that are said to be generated by immigration. The work of the economist George Borjas, which finds that low-skilled immigration hurts low-skilled domestic workers by depressing their wages, offers empirical support for Sanders's position.[6]

Which side is right? I believe each side of the debate is, at best, incomplete. Open borders proponents have not adequately considered what is at stake for the sending and receiving countries, and restrictionists have not taken the moral claims of migrants seriously. We need a normative theory of immigration that takes seriously both the claims of political community and the claims of migrants. My central contention is that both sides have their rightful claims and that each side must make some accommodations in response to the claims of the other.

The Role of Political Theory

Where one stands on immigration depends on answers to a number of fundamental moral and political questions, combined with honest assessments of the effects of immigration. If people wish to migrate across borders, why shouldn't they be able to? States exercise power over borders, but what, if anything, justifies this power? What are the normative grounds and limits of the state's power over immigration? If the state is justified in excluding some and accepting others, how should it decide whom to admit? This book pursues these questions and considers the implications for immigration policy.

Before pursuing these questions, it is important to clarify what role political theory might play in public debates about immigration in democratic societies. One aim of political theory is to search for values and principles that can serve as guides to public judgment, clarify the sources of our disagreement, and perhaps even reduce the extent of disagreement about specific issues. We may not agree on a single solution to the challenges we face, but the hope is to identify the basic principles that an acceptable solution must satisfy.

Some will take the cynical view that participants in public debate pretend to argue about values and principles when they are really just using lofty rhetoric to mask their quest for power over others. To be sure, politics is about power, but we should be wary about embracing this cynical view as the entirety of democratic politics. When we are engaged in politics as participants, debating questions like what sort of healthcare system or what kind of immigration policy we should have, many of us argue as if these questions have answers and as if we might reach some of those answers through reasoned argument. We appeal to principles underlying our side of the argument and examine the principles of our opponent's position and consider the consequences of both.

This effort at reasoning is especially important in democratic societies, where political power is the collective power of the people who must ultimately authorize the decisions made in our name. Because political power belongs to all members of a democratic society, we owe one another reasons for the exercise of that power. Of course, we don't always argue that way, but that is the democratic promise: to show respect for others by debating issues with reasoned arguments. Understood in this way, political theory is not just an academic enterprise; it is critically engaged with public debate in democratic societies.

The Politics of Immigration

If a normative theory of immigration is to be useful and relevant to public debate, it must be attentive to the politics of immigration. That is, we must engage with the actual circumstances and dynamics of politics. I adopt such an approach in this book; it is an approach that might be characterized as "realistically utopian." It is utopian in offering interpretations of values and principles to which we should aspire, but it is also realistic in taking account of real-world institutions and constraints.[7] Four features are crucial for understanding the politics of immigration in democratic societies: (1) majoritarian politics, (2) nationalism, (3) capitalism, and (4) liberal constitutionalism. The first two features push in favor of restricting immigration, while the latter two features support a more open approach to immigration. Let me briefly elaborate these conflicting dynamics.[8]

Majoritarian politics and discourses of nationalism have worked together to produce a politics of restriction in liberal democratic societies. Public opinion and party competition tend to generate pressure for governments to talk and act tough on immigration. In the United States, public opinion about immigration has shifted over time, becoming more polarized along party lines. According to the Pew Research Center, in 1994, 63 percent of Americans said immigrants "are a burden on our country because they take our jobs, housing and health care," whereas 31 percent said immigrants "strengthen our country because of their hard work and talents." In 2016, opinions were nearly the reverse: 59 percent said immigrants strengthen the country, and 33 percent said they were a burden. There has been an increase in more favorable attitudes toward immigrants, but a striking partisan gap between Republicans and Democrats has emerged. Since 2006, the share of Democrats and Democrat-leaning independents who say immigrants strengthen the country increased from 49 percent to 78 percent, whereas the share of Republicans and Republican-leaning independents holding this view has shown little change, shifting from 34 percent to 35 percent.[9] As the 2016 US presidential election demonstrated, partisan mobilization in favor of immigration restrictions rests on ethnonationalist visions of American identity in which immigration is framed as a threat to national security, and social cohesion.

Immigration is a challenging issue for mainstream parties because it does not align with the classic left-right cleavage based on economic interests. For center-right parties, immigration exposes a divide between free-market liberals (who favor an open approach to immigration) and value conservatives (who favor a restrictive approach). For center-left parties, immigration reveals a tension between cosmopolitans (who favor an open approach to immigration) and welfare-state and labor-market protectionists (who favor a restrictive approach). Considering these tensions, it is not surprising that mainstream political parties have tended to either obfuscate the issue of immigration or avoid it altogether. Obfuscating involves sending different messages to different audiences: talking tough in public while being more accommodating toward pro-immigration lobbyists and donors behind the scenes. The problem with obfuscation is that it amounts to thinly veiled hypocrisy, making it vulnerable to countermobilization. The avoidance strategy may work under some circumstances, such as when all mainstream parties see a common advantage in avoiding an issue, but it is, at best, unstable since some political leaders may see an electoral advantage in speaking out on immigration.

This is indeed what happened with the rise of far-right parties in Europe and with the presidential campaign of Donald Trump. Far-right parties, such as the National Front in France, the Alternative for Germany party in Germany, and the Party for Freedom in the Netherlands, have tapped into anti-immigrant sentiment to gain popularity in the wake of the European migration crisis.[10] Even where there are no significant far-right parties, there have been attempts to mobilize the electorate around opposition to immigration. In the United States, the two-party system is sufficiently heterogeneous to provide opportunities for anti-immigrant mobilization, and the right wing of the Republican Party has provided such an outlet. Mainstream parties in the United States have had few electoral incentives to adopt pro-immigration positions and tended to either avoid the issue or compete on a restrictionist platform. Trump's stunning victory over Hillary Clinton in the 2016 presidential election was due in part to his anti-immigration rhetoric, which included calls for building a wall between the United States and Mexico, a ban on Muslims entering the United States, and mass deportation of undocumented immigrants in the United States. He stoked fears about the effects of immigration not only on national security but also on the economic well-being of Americans, picking up support among working-class Americans in Rust Belt states.

There are, however, two other features that push in favor of a more open approach to immigration: capitalism and liberal constitutionalism. First, immigration has long been considered crucial to the performance of advanced capitalist economies. Immigrants have served as a "flexible" low-wage workforce that can fill labor shortages, serving as a counterinflationary force during periods of sustained economic growth. Migrant labor has become, in economist Gary Freeman's words, a "structural requirement of advanced capitalism."[11] Employers and governments have sought low-skilled migrant laborers through a combination of temporary migrant-labor programs and unauthorized migrant labor. Advanced capitalist economies have also sought to attract highly skilled migrants in a number of sectors, including information technology, engineering, medicine, and scientific research. Organized interest groups have sought to translate the economic demand for migrant labor into more expansionist policies, often prevailing over the restrictionist wishes of the broader public.[12] Liberal democratic states have not simply obeyed the demands of business interests; the states themselves have actively sought to secure the conditions of capital accumulation as part of a broader government agenda of global competitiveness.[13] The interests of liberal democratic states, which are closely aligned with the interests of capital, tend to push in favor of more open immigration policies.

A second source of openness toward immigration are liberal constitutional norms. Liberal democratic states have come to regard certain rights and liberties as fundamental and have institutionalized them through constitutions. Courts have come to be seen as protectors of individual rights against the will of electoral majorities. The interests of capital generate demand for "desirable" economic immigrants, but liberal norms place constraints on what governments can justifiably do in their attempts to restrict "undesirable" immigration.[14] Liberal constitutional constraints help explain some of the openness toward immigration in the areas of asylum and family reunification, where governments have had little economic interest in promoting immigration. Liberal constitutional norms also serve as a check on attempts by political leaders to contravene the due process and equal protection rights of noncitizens currently residing in liberal democratic states.

In sum, immigration is an issue subject to conflicting political dynamics. Public opinion and party competition generate pressures to restrict immigration, and elite and popular discourses make nationalist appeals about who "we" are and how newcomers threaten dominant understandings of this "we-ness." Yet the political pressures toward restriction have not translated into entirely closed-border policies. This is both because immigrant labor is essential to advanced capitalist economies and because liberal norms institutionalized in constitutional orders have constrained how governments may treat migrants.

Consideration of these political and economic dynamics must be a part of any answer to the question of what should be done about immigration. Yet knowledge of these dynamics alone cannot tell us what we should do about immigration. Even if social scientists could achieve broad consensus on the facts of immigration, facts alone are insufficient to make decisions about what to do. As the economist George Borjas says in his recent book on immigration, "The immigration debate is about much more than numbers."[15] It is also about values.

The Need for a Political Theory of Immigration

There is a large and growing empirical literature on immigration across a range of disciplines, including economics, history, law, political science, and sociology, but much of this literature only indirectly engages normative questions about how countries *ought* to respond to migratory pressures. Social scientists have provided explanatory theories about the causes and consequences of immigration, and legal scholars have critically assessed substantive immigration laws and procedures of immigration enforcement, but they tend not to provide a systematic discussion of which norms *should* govern immigration.

The more pressing normative questions about immigration are questions of immigration law and policy: Do states have an obligation to admit people fleeing war and violence, and how should this obligation be distributed among states? What about families separated by borders? How should states prioritize among claims for admission based on refuge from persecution, family ties, shared identity, and economic skills? How should temporary-worker programs be weighed against the admission of migrants for permanent residence? What is the proper response to the situation of unauthorized migrants who are already residing in a country? I take up these questions in final part of the book, but I first lay the groundwork by exploring the normative ideals that shape and ought to shape our thinking about immigration.

Immigration raises questions about the legitimacy of state power, boundaries of territory and political membership, and justice within and across state borders. What are the normative grounds and limits of the state's power over immigration? How should the state's claim to control immigration be weighed against the prospective migrant's claim to enter? Examination of these questions can clarify the normative stakes on which different policy positions are based. Sovereign states exercise power over immigration. That power requires justification, and the justification appropriate to liberal democracies is distinctive.

To offer a justification for something (an act, a policy, or an institution) is to argue that it is morally acceptable. We can justify something by showing its moral and prudential advantages and by comparing it against alternatives. In democratic societies, the task of justification requires engaging with democratic values. Against open borders proponents, I argue that there is a convincing justification for the authority of government power over immigration, rooted in the idea of collective self-determination. Against restrictionists, I argue that humanitarian and democratic values constrain the way a government's immigration power may be exercised.

Balancing Particular and Universal Obligations

One of the strongest moral objections to any regime of immigration control is rooted in the idea of the equal moral worth of all human beings. The idea of moral equality is central to an *ethic of universalism*. If we believe in the moral equality of every human being, why shouldn't people be free to move across borders if they wish? The case for open borders is strengthened by a distributive objection: it is a matter of luck whether one is born a citizen of a wealthy country or a poor country, yet border controls help sustain global inequalities by preventing people from poorer societies from moving to richer societies. As the political theorist Joseph Carens puts it, citizenship is "the modern equivalent of feudal privilege—an inherited status that greatly enhances one's life chances."[16] Like being born into a wealthy family, citizenship acquired by being born in the territory of, or to parents who are citizens of, wealthy liberal democratic countries is a matter of luck. It is, to borrow a phrase from the philosopher John Rawls, "so arbitrary from a moral point of view" and yet so strongly determines our prospects in life.[17] If we take the premise of the moral equality of all human beings seriously and acknowledge the moral arbitrariness of how citizenship gets distributed, then, Carens concludes, "there is little justification for restricting immigration."[18]

I agree that the distribution of citizenship is morally arbitrary, but citizenship is nonetheless morally significant. Indeed, Carens himself acknowledges that we stand in a special moral relationship with fellow members such that we have distinctive obligations toward them that we don't have toward others, but he adds this qualification: since there is no good justification for restricting immigration, anyone can elect to join the political community. I think the vision of political membership suggested by Carens and other proponents of open borders is awfully thin and fails to appreciate how membership-based obligations include partiality toward the interests of members when determining immigration policy. A policy of open borders is also an ineffective and undesirable response to addressing global inequality, for reasons I lay out in chapter 5.

This book develops a normative theory of immigration rooted in an *ethic of membership*. An ethic of membership holds that we have particular obligations in virtue of the particular relationships we have with others. This is the idea of associative obligations.[19] Consider relationships with close friends and family. We value such personal relationships noninstrumentally, and we regard the needs, interests, and desires of our friends and family as providing us with reasons to perform actions that we do not have comparable reasons to perform for others. Associative obligations extend to our membership in groups. We find membership in religious communities, ethnic associations, sports clubs, the Girl Scouts, and the Rotary Club to be not just instrumentally valuable but rewarding in their own right. To value membership in a group is just to regard that membership as giving reasons to do things on behalf of the group and to help sustain the purposes of the group. Group memberships may have more instrumental value than intrinsic value for some of us, but even instrumental value is sufficient to ground associative obligations. In the case of personal relationships with family and friends, we look to their needs, interests, and desires as guides to action. In the case of groups, it is group norms that play the role of communicating the needs, interests, and desires of the group.

The idea of associative obligations extends to membership in a political community. What kind of relationship do compatriots have that could give rise to special obligations? The vast majority of our compatriots are strangers, like passengers who happen to be thrown together on a bus, so how can it be that we have associative obligations to one another? Some argue we should regard political membership and its obligations as grounded on consent, but this runs into the familiar problem that most people haven't given their consent to the countries they happen to have been born citizens of. Another answer comes from theorists of nationalism who contend that political membership is based on a shared national identity. As the political theorist David Miller argues, "With national identity comes a kind of solidarity that is lacking if one looks just at economic and political relationships. People feel emotionally attached to one another because they share this identity."[20] Nationalist conceptions have proven to be a politically potent basis for defining political community. The nationalist view says we have special obligations to fellow compatriots because they are "one of us," like an extended kin network. As I discuss in chapter 3, the nationalist view has troubling exclusionary implications. In chapter 4, I propose an alternative conception of political membership based on participation in shared institutions. According to this participatory model, political membership is valuable because it provides an indispensable scheme of social and economic cooperation and because it enables collective self-determination. Although members of a political community are strangers to one another, they come to identify with the community through a shared history of cooperating together.

Adopting the idea of membership-based obligations does not mean we have no obligations to those outside our circles of membership. We can justifiably prioritize the interests of our compatriots, but our membership-based obligations must be balanced against our universal obligations to all of humanity. In other words, the ethic of membership must be balanced against the ethic of universalism. There is a genuine tension here. The idea of associative obligations applied to political membership provides people who already enjoy the good fortune of citizenship in wealthy countries with additional benefits in the form of special claims to one another's assistance. The tension between the particularist claim about political responsibility and the universalist claim about moral equality may never be eliminated, but it can be managed and reduced by recognizing that they are mutually constraining and that each places limits on how the other value may be pursued. This book offers an account of how we might take seriously both our membership-based obligations and our global obligations on the issue of immigration. I argue that what is required is not open borders or closed borders but *open doors* coupled with robust development assistance to poor countries.

Roadmap of the Book

The book is structured in three main parts. Part I considers the perspective of political communities; Part II explores the perspective of prospective migrants; and Part III considers implications for law and policy. Each chapter stands as an essay in itself and can be read on its own. I provide a roadmap here to help readers navigate through the book.

Part I explores the normative grounds of the modern state's power over immigration. States assert control over immigration, but what, if anything, justifies their claim to control? Today it is widely assumed that the modern state has a virtually unlimited right to restrict immigration in order to advance its interests. To set the stage for the normative discussion that follows, I look to law and examine how one state sought to legitimate its power over borders. The link between sovereignty and immigration control emerged in the late nineteenth century in the United States and elsewhere. When thinking normatively about an area of public policy, we often look to law, not only for policy guidance, but also for articulation of the fundamental values underlying law and policy. As legal scholar Linda Bosniak puts it, "In liberal democratic states, law is a social formation comprised not merely of coercive power but of embedded norms and normative argumentation."[21] The law is a potentially fruitful source of normative arguments about real-world controversies.

Chapter 2 examines where the US Supreme Court located the authority of the federal government's power over immigration. In a series of cases in the late nineteenth century, the court declared the federal government's immigration power to be "inherent in sovereignty," a doctrine that has come to be known as the plenary power doctrine. The court drew upon the influential law of nations theorist Emer de Vattel to establish the federal government's virtually absolute power over immigration. The chapter examines the court's reasoning, as well as Vattel's *Law of Nations*, to explore the connection between sovereignty and immigration control. Absolute control over immigration was said to be at the heart of what it means to be a sovereign state. The turn toward plenary power took place in the era of Chinese exclusion and was rooted in racial doctrines couched in the language of national security. I argue that these judicial opinions provide little more than assertions of absolute state sovereignty and they rest on morally reprehensible views about the racial inferiority of Asian migrants.

Chapter 3 turns to contemporary philosophy and political theory to consider arguments in defense of a qualified, not absolute, right of states to control immigration. I examine four leading contemporary theories based on (1) the value of cultural and national identity,[22] (2) the right to property,[23] (3) the value of freedom of association,[24] and (4) the freedom to avoid unwanted obligations.[25] The first three theories invoke the idea of collective self-determination but interpret it in very different ways. The cultural argument views the subject of self-determination as a cultural group or nation. When it comes to immigration, the fundamental imperative is the preservation of a culturally distinctive way of life. The property argument views the collective as a group of joint-owners of state institutions; the right to control immigration is said to derive from the labor of citizens. The freedom-of-association argument views individual members of the state as parties to associations such as marriage and golf clubs, which have the right to refuse association with nonassociates. The freedom to avoid unwanted obligations does not directly engage with the idea of collective self-determination. I argue that each of these theories fall short of providing a compelling theory of state authority over immigration.

Chapter 4 advances an alternative justification for the state's right to control immigration based on the idea of collective self-determination. Collective self-determination is the idea that a group of people should govern themselves. The chapter begins by discussing the meaning, role, and value of collective self-determination and then elaborates a particular conception of collective self-determination. On my account, the agent of collective self-determination is not the nation, joint-owners of state institutions, or members of a voluntary association but "a people." I offer an argument for why "a people" is the proper agent of collective self-determination and explore the connections between collective self-determination, territorial rights, and immigration control. I consider the distinctive requirements of democratic self-determination and its implications for immigration control in democratic societies.

Part I of the book considers who has the authority to determine immigration policy. I argue that a self-determining people has the right to set its own immigration policy (chapter 4). Proponents of open borders reject this argument. Part II examines the case for open borders. There are two main types of arguments for open borders.

Chapter 5 considers the global distributive justice argument for open borders. I challenge two key assumptions underlying this argument: (1) that global distributive justice requires global equality of opportunity, and (2) that global distributive justice requires open borders. I return to the idea of associative obligations discussed in the introduction and argue that equality and justice are fundamentally relational ideals. Our particular relationships and institutional contexts matter for the types of distributive obligations we have. This does not mean we have no global obligations. I examine different forms of global inequality and identify circumstances in which global inequality does constitute global injustice, but I argue that even in such cases, an open borders policy is a limited response. Alleviating global poverty is the major animating concern of the global distributive justice argument for open borders, but it is typically not the world's poorest who migrate, and the departure of a country's more skilled members tends to deepen, not alleviate, global inequality.

Chapter 6 examines three rights-based arguments for freedom of movement across borders. Residents of Ohio enjoy the right to move to California if they wish. Residents of Ontario or Oaxaca may want to move to California for the very same reasons. Why shouldn't they be able to? According to the first argument, freedom of movement is a fundamental human right in itself. The second argument adopts a "cantilever" strategy, arguing that freedom of international movement is a logical extension of existing fundamental rights, including the right of domestic free movement and the right to exit one's country. The third argument is a libertarian one: international free movement is necessary to respect individual freedom of association and contract. This chapter shows how these arguments fall short of justifying a general right to free movement across the globe. I argue that what is morally required is not a general right of international free movement but an approach that privileges those whose basic human rights are at stake.

Part III considers the substance of immigration policy in democratic societies. What kinds of immigration policies should democratic countries pursue? This part of the book is addressed to members and public officials in democratic societies engaged in public debate about immigration. If states have the right to control immigration, as I argue in chapter 4, how should they exercise this right? The state's right to exercise control in restrictive ways may be overridden by competing reasons advanced on behalf of migrants, but the reasons advanced on behalf of migrants do not justify open borders. Instead, what is required is a policy of *open doors*. The question then becomes, open to whom? We need to consider what is at stake for migrants and what is at stake for the political communities they seek to enter. I argue that in some cases the decision to admit migrants is morally required (obligatory admissions), and in other cases, the decision to admit migrants is not morally required (discretionary admissions).

In chapter 7, I consider the claims of refugees and other necessitous migrants and argue they offer an important qualification on the right of states to restrict immigration. The chapter discusses the grounds of this duty, who should be regarded as a refugee, what the duty requires, and how it might be shared among states.

Chapter 8 examines claims for family reunification, which poses another constraint on the right of states to control immigration. Family-based immigration constitutes most immigrant admissions into many democratic countries and has been criticized by those who favor high-skilled immigration. Why should states privilege family relationships in designing immigration policy, and which relationships have counted as "family" and which relationships should count?

Chapter 9 considers discretionary admissions. I begin by discussing temporary-admissions programs and consider whether they are permissible or whether all migrants must be admitted on a permanent basis. I then assess the kinds of criteria that states are morally permitted to use in selecting immigrants for admission.

Chapter 10 turns from questions of immigrant admissions to the question of what is owed to migrants who are already present in the territory of democratic states. I focus on three groups of noncitizens: (1) those admitted on a temporary basis, (2) those who have been granted permanent residence, and (3) those who have overstayed their temporary visas or entered the territory without authorization. What legal rights are these different groups of noncitizens morally entitled to and in virtue of what?

Chapter 11 provides a brief conclusion.

PART I

The Grounds and Limits of Government Power over Immigration

Governments exercise power over borders, but what, if anything, justifies this power? What are the grounds and limits of the modern state's power over immigration? The next three chapters take up these questions. Chapter 2 begins by looking to law—in particular, the origins of the plenary power doctrine in US immigration jurisprudence. When thinking normatively about what to do about pressing issues of public policy, we often look to constitutional values and legal principles for guidance. I argue that the answers we find there are limited and turn in chapters 3 and 4 to consider what contemporary political philosophy has to offer.

2

Looking to Law

THE PLENARY POWER DOCTRINE IN
US IMMIGRATION JURISPRUDENCE

IF WE LOOK to the law for justifications of government power over immigration, what we find is the idea that virtually absolute power over immigration is essential to the sovereignty of states. This chapter focuses on the emergence of this absolutist view in US law, but this view is not unique to the United States. It can also be found in the law of other countries and in the scholarly literature in political science and international relations. Absolute control over territory, including control over immigration, is regarded as a defining feature of state sovereignty. It is what makes a state a state.

In the United States, it was the 1889 case *Chae Chan Ping v. the United States,* also known as the *Chinese Exclusion Case*, in which the US Supreme Court first declared the national government's power over immigration to be "inherent in sovereignty."[1] The case marked, in political scientist Rogers Smith's words, a "significantly novel and momentous" shift toward viewing immigration regulations as acts of virtually unbridled national sovereignty, not exercises of the police powers of state governments or the federal commerce power, as had been the case for much of the nineteenth century.[2] Prior to this case, when state governments challenged federal authority over immigration, the court had located the federal government's immigration authority in the enumerated clauses of the US Constitution, especially the Commerce Clause.[3] In two subsequent cases, *Nishimura Ekiu v. United States* (1892) and *Fong Yue Ting v. United States* (1893), the Supreme Court consolidated the authority of the federal government's power over immigration. In all three cases, the court appealed to the ideas of the leading law of nations theorist of the day, Emer de Vattel.[4]

This view that state control over immigration is "inherent in sovereignty" has come to be known as the *plenary power doctrine* in US immigration law. It survives to this day as well-established precedent. As the legal scholar Stephen Legomsky puts it, "From the 1960s on, the Supreme Court has only infrequently addressed constitutional challenges to immigration legislation, probably because the plenary power doctrine has left little room in which to litigate such issues. But on those few occasions when the Supreme Court did discuss the previous plenary power doctrine cases, the Court consistently reaffirmed it."[5] Legal historian Matthew Lindsay characterizes the plenary power doctrine as "one of the most enduring constructs in American public law," having largely survived Congress's liberalization of immigration policy in 1965 and the civil rights and due process revolutions of the 1960s and 1970s.[6]

How and why did the plenary power doctrine come to be incorporated into US law? As we'll see, the turn to plenary power was motivated by and intimately connected to racism. Given this fundamental flaw in the jurisprudence, why should we look to law at all? It is by diagnosing the problems with the plenary power doctrine that we can begin to identify what a compelling normative justification of government power over immigration might look like.

Chinese Exclusion and the Turn to Plenary Power

Chae Chan Ping was a laborer who came to the United States in 1876, during a period when the Burlingame Treaty between the United States and China, signed in 1868, seemed to permit unrestricted immigration from China. Asian laborers had begun arriving in the United States in the mid-1800s to construct the transcontinental railroad. The California gold rush of 1849 had attracted Chinese laborers to the West Coast, many already under contract to their employers. Anti-Chinese sentiment grew, however, especially on the West Coast, as racial antagonism intertwined with economic depression during the 1870s. White labor groups increasingly opposed Chinese immigration, and cities and states adopted a number of anti-immigrant provisions designed to restrain the growing Asian immigrant population.[7]

In 1882, Congress enacted what is commonly known as the Chinese Exclusion Act,[8] which banned the immigration of Chinese laborers for ten years and prohibited people of Chinese origin from becoming US citizens.. It also required people of Chinese origin to carry identification certificates or face deportation. In signing the Act, US president Chester A. Arthur announced that the "experiment in blending" the "habits and mutual race idiosyncracies" of Chinese laborers with Americans had proven "unwise, impolitic, and injurious to both nations." The law thus closed the doors on both the regulation of immigration by state governments and "race-blind, largely nonexclusionary immigration policies."[9]

In 1884, Congress modified the 1882 Chinese Exclusion Act to provide that a customs certificate would be the only evidence accepted for re-entry.[10] After residing in the United States for over a decade, Chae Chan Ping obtained such a certificate in 1887 and returned to his native China. The following year, while he was still abroad, Congress made further amendments to restrict Chinese migration. It adopted the 1888 Act, which barred the return of Chinese laborers whether they had certificates or not. He returned to San Francisco harbor just six days after the act had been passed and was denied entry. His case provided the Supreme Court with its first opportunity to directly consider the federal government's power to exclude foreigners.

Chae Chan Ping's attorneys made both enumerated-powers and individual rights arguments. They argued the Constitution did not delegate any power to Congress to expel lawful resident aliens and denied that Chae's exclusion had anything to do with commerce. They denied that the Act could be upheld under the treaty power since it expressly violated the treaties with China. They also advanced an individual rights argument: that the Constitution applied to resident aliens as "persons within the jurisdiction of the United States" and prohibited their exclusion from the United States without due process.[11]

Writing for a unanimous court, Justice Stephen J. Field began by characterizing Chinese immigration as "an Oriental invasion" and "a menace to our civilization."[12] He acknowledged the conflict between the Burlingame Treaty and the 1888 Act but found that although they were on an equal footing, the statute prevailed because it had been more recently enacted. The opinion departs from the enumerated powers of the Constitution in favor of maxims of international law as the basis for federal authority over immigration:

> That the government of the United States, through the action of the legislative department, can exclude aliens from its territory is a proposition which we do not think open to controversy. Jurisdiction over its own territory to that extent is an incident of every independent nation. It is a part of its independence. If it could not exclude aliens it would be to that extent subject to the control of another power.[13]

Justice Field makes no attempt to explain how the government's power over immigration had been incorporated into the enumerated powers of the US Constitution. Instead, he established that power by a simple declaration:

> To preserve its independence, and give security against foreign aggression and encroachment, is the highest duty of every nation, and to attain these ends nearly all other considerations are to be subordinated . . . The government, possessing the powers which are to be exercised for protection and security, is *clothed with authority* to determine the occasion on which the powers shall be called forth; and its determinations, so far as the subjects affected are concerned, are necessarily conclusive upon all its departments and officers . . . If, therefore, the government of the United States, through its legislative department, considers the presence of foreigners of a different race in this country, who will not assimilate with us, to be dangerous to its peace and security, their exclusion is not to be stayed because at the time there are no actual hostilities with the nation of which the foreigners are subjects.[14]

The court sought to legitimate the national government's immigration power by pronouncing it "clothed with authority."[15] The power of Congress to exclude foreigners is "conclusive," including its decision to exclude "foreigners of a different race" deemed dangerous to national security.

The court did not address the constitutional due process claim brought by Chae Chan Ping. Instead, Justice Field simply denied that the certificate, statutes, or treaties gave him the right to re-enter. Drawing on Vattel, Justice Field declared the national government's immigration power to be an "incident of sovereignty":

> The power of exclusion of foreigners being an incident of sovereignty belonging to the government of the United States, as part of those sovereign powers delegated by the Constitution, the right to its exercise at any time when, in the judgment of the government, the interests of the country require it, cannot be granted away or restrained on behalf of any one . . . Whatever license, therefore, Chinese laborers may have obtained, previous to the act of October 1, 1888, to return to the United States after their departure, is held at the will of the government, revocable at any time, at its pleasure.[16]

The *Chinese Exclusion Case* set forth the key elements of the plenary power doctrine in US law: that the government's power over immigration is "inherent in sovereignty" and that judicial review of Congress's immigration power is limited. The court's main concern was to establish the federal government's immigration power, not to question whether the rights of individual noncitizens might constrain that power.[17]

The court solidified the plenary power doctrine in the 1892 case *Nishimura Ekiu v. United States*.[18] Nishimura Ekiu was a Japanese national who had traveled to the United States to join her husband. The California immigration commissioner prohibited her from landing and detained her in custody pending her return to Japan. The federal district court in San Francisco then issued a writ of habeas corpus. The federal inspector for San Francisco intervened in opposition to the writ, arguing that Nishimura was excludable under the 1882 Immigration Act, amended in 1891, as a person "liable to become a public charge." The circuit court excluded from the hearing the petition evidence Nishimura offered in support of her right to land and held that the inspector's decision was final under the 1891 Act and not subject to judicial review. Writing for the majority, Justice Horace Gray upheld Nishimura's exclusion. He cited Vattel as Justice Field had done in *Chae Chan Ping*:

> It is an accepted maxim of international law, that every sovereign nation has the power, as inherent in sovereignty, and essential to self-preservation, to forbid the entrance of foreigners within its dominions, or to admit them only in such cases and upon such conditions as it may see fit to prescribe.[19]

Justice Gray acknowledged that aliens prevented from landing were deprived of liberty and entitled to review under a writ of habeas corpus. An administrative officer had declared that once in the country Nishimura was likely to become a public charge, which made her excludable under the statute. She argued that due process required a judicial proceeding, but Justice Gray held that in the case of noncitizens who had not yet entered the United States, a court could inquire into the facts on habeas only if the statute so authorized. He concluded that due process had not been violated in her case, and the habeas review of the facts found by the immigration officer was not allowed.

Nishimura Ekiu expanded the plenary power doctrine in two ways. First, it broadened its scope by applying it to the procedures Congress used in the enforcement of immigration laws, not just the substantive rules for admission and exclusion, as in the *Chinese Exclusion Case*. Second, the court rejected a challenge based on the claim of an individual constitutional right.[20] The court located the immigration power in the international law maxim of "powers inherent in sovereignty," as in the *Chinese Exclusion Case*, and authorized virtually absolute discretion over immigration to Congress and the executive. One question that remained unanswered had to do with the scope of federal immigration power over noncitizens who were already present in the territory of the United States.

This question was taken up a year later in *Fong Yue Ting v. United States* (1893).[21] In 1892, Congress had passed the Geary Act, which extended the 1882 ban on Chinese immigration for another ten years.[22] The act also required Chinese laborers already residing in the United States to register for a certificate of residence. To obtain a certificate of residence, one had to get a white witness to testify to one's pre-1892 residency. Chinese laborers would be subject to deportation unless they could establish to a reviewing court, based on the testimony of a "credible white witness," that they had been resident in the United States when the Geary Act was passed. *Fong Yue Ting* involved three plaintiffs, each of whom had been lawful residents of the United States for more than ten years. Fong Yue Ting and Wong Quan had decided not to apply for certificates and were arrested in New York and ordered deported. The third petitioner, Lee Joe, who had resided in the United States for nearly twenty years, had applied for a certificate but was unable to produce a white witness.

Writing for the majority five-to-three opinion, Justice Gray upheld the Geary Act. Citing *Chae Chan Ping* and *Nishimura Ekiu,* Justice Gray again emphasized the national government's "power to forbid the entrance of foreigners" as being "inherent in sovereignty." As he put it, "The power to exclude aliens and the power to expel them rest upon one foundation, are derived from one source, are supported by the same reasons, and are in truth but parts of one and the same power."[23] Justice Gray cited the following passages from Vattel, whom he called "the leading commentator on the law of nations":

> [E]very nation has a right to *refuse admitting* a foreigner into her territory, when he cannot enter it without exposing the nation to evident danger, or doing her a manifest injury. What she owes to herself, the care of her own safety, gives her this right; and in virtue of her natural liberty, it belongs to the nation to judge, whether her circumstances will or will not justify the admission of that foreigner.
>
> Thus also it has a *right to send* them [Vattel uses the word "asylees"] elsewhere, if it has just cause to fear that they will corrupt the manners

of the citizens, that they will create religious disturbances, or occasion any other disorder, contrary to the public safety. In a word, it has a right, and is even obliged, to follow, in this respect, the suggestions of prudence.[24]

It is striking that, in contrast to the decisions in the *Chinese Exclusion Case* and *Nishimura Ekiu*, which had at least mentioned the Constitution, Justice Gray's argument that Congress has the power to exclude relies exclusively on principles of international law and English practice and makes no reference whatsoever to the Constitution. He declares that the "Constitution of the United States speaks with no uncertain sound on this subject" and asserts that immigration control is an inherent right of every sovereign nation:

> The right to exclude or expel all aliens, or any class of aliens, absolutely or upon certain conditions, in war or in peace, [is] an inherent and inalienable right of every sovereign and independent nation, essential to its safety, its independence and its welfare.[25]

The only question remaining before the court, he says, is whether the way Congress exercised its right in the Geary Act by requiring a system of registration based on white witnesses "is consistent with the Constitution." Justice Gray held that it was: Chinese migrants were not denied due process or equal protection by the Geary Act's white-witness requirement. Since they were neither citizens nor legal residents, they had no right to be in the country at all. Deportation was not a criminal punishment but a means to restore public safety. The fact that only Chinese migrants had to prove their citizenship or legal status in order to re-enter the country was not decisive.[26]

Justice David Josiah Brewer dissented, joined by Chief Justice Melville Fuller and Justice Field, the author of the majority opinion in the *Chinese Exclusion Case*. All stressed the liberties and procedural rights of *persons*, not only citizens, present in US territory. Justice Brewer argued against the focus on "powers inherent in sovereignty," which Justice Field had introduced, calling it "indefinite and dangerous" and suggesting the authority for "the expulsion of a race" is something "within the inherent powers of despotism." He also insisted that "deportation is punishment," arguing that the penalty for unlawful presence could not be constitutionally ordered without a trial involving procedural protections. By contrast, Justice Field affirmed the majority opinion's view on sovereignty, but he argued that the immigration power "inherent in sovereignty" included the power to exclude but not the power to expel persons possessing "our common humanity." The Chinese were entitled to procedural protections instead of "brutality" and "cruelty." He pointed out the disturbing implications of the majority opinion:

> According to this theory, Congress might have ordered executive officers to take the Chinese laborers to the ocean and put them into a boat and set them adrift; or to take them to the borders of Mexico and turn them loose there; and in both cases without any means of support; indeed, it might have sanctioned towards these laborers the most shocking brutality conceivable.[27]

Justice Field's sympathetic approach to *Fong Yue Ting*, in contrast to the *Chinese Exclusion Case*, was based on his belief that the former involved deporting a noncitizen who was inside the territory, whereas the latter involved excluding a noncitizen who was outside the territory.[28]

Through this trilogy of cases—the *Chinese Exclusion Case, Nishimura Ekiu,* and *Fong Yue Ting*—the US Supreme Court located the national government's exclusive and virtually absolute power over immigration in maxims of international law. Prior to these cases, the court had resolved a half-century of debate by locating the source of the immigration power in the Commerce Clause. With these three cases, the court gave up on efforts to ground the national government's immigration power in the Constitution. That immigration had implications for foreign affairs and national security was the primary justification the court cited in relinquishing ordinary constitutional analysis in this area.

Why did the court embrace the plenary power doctrine? Legal scholar Sarah Cleveland suggests the court seems to have concluded that the immigration power was too broad to be justified under the Commerce Clause.[29] Even as the national government was seeking to expand its powers over noncitizens and Native Americans in the name of commerce, the court was moving to narrow the scope of the Commerce Clause. The exclusion of lawful noncitizen residents like Chae Chang Ping was less obviously related to commerce than, say, a head tax on newly arriving aliens. In addition, the immigration power in this case did not merely preclude action by a state government but also nullified previous federal actions. To defend the 1888 Act, the court had to uphold Congress's abrogation of the Burlingame Treaty with China, the power to forbid new arrivals, and the revocation of a legal resident's certificate. The court had acknowledged in the *Head Money Cases* that treaties could establish legally vested rights for private individuals, and if Chae was correct that his right to return under the treaty and prior federal statutes was analogous to property rights, he was likely to prevail.[30] But by asserting that the immigration power was "inherent in sovereignty," Justice Field could reject Chae's claim that the certificate permitted his return without distorting the commerce power.

The turn toward plenary power was also fueled by anti-Chinese racism and a racialized vision of American national identity. Rogers Smith situates the shift from viewing immigration as primarily an economic issue to an issue of inherent national power in the broader context of "Americanism, expounded in the conventional tropes of late nineteenth-century discourse on race and nationality."[31] Many federal judges embraced doctrines of human liberties, including economic liberties, but they viewed them within ascriptive ideologies that extended full rights only to those deemed to belong to "superior" races and nations. Congress had already endorsed such ascriptive ideologies through the 1882 Chinese Exclusion Act. The court, in the *Chinese Exclusion Case,* had declared that if the government determines "the presence of foreigners of a different race in this country, who will not assimilate with us, to be dangerous to its peace and security," the exclusion of such foreigners is justified.[32] The "us" here refers to white Americans. Preservation of a white national identity is offered up as a legitimate ground for exclusion.

What are the implications of this historical discussion for contemporary attempts to justify government power over immigration? The historical role of race and other ascriptive ideologies in such attempts suggests one important challenge for any attempt to justify government power over immigration: Does it have the resources to guard against such exclusions? Second, we need more than declarations that the government's immigration power is "clothed with authority"; we need an argument that clarifies and elaborates the relationship between sovereignty and immigration control. I turn now to consider the author who served as a key source of the US Supreme Court's assertion that the national government's immigration power is "inherent in sovereignty."

Vattel on Sovereignty

Emer de Vattel's *Le Droit des Gens* (*Law of Nations,* 1758) was "the first recognizably modern book on international law." Its influence extended beyond the academy to legal and political practitioners. The French government was referring to it in the 1760s. The US government used it as a guide from the time of the American Revolution. It came to be similarly regarded by British politicians from that time onward. By 1789, Vattel's book had begun its long service in most of the foreign offices of Europe, where it was "generally assumed for the first time that there was a well-known international law, the public law of Europe, and that Vattel had collected and digested it."[33]

Vattel's influence has been attributed to several factors: the need for a systematic reference book on international law at a time when there was a rapid increase in international legal problems, the outdated nature of Grotius's seventeenth-century work, the fact that "the spirit of [Vattel's] work" was "well in accord with the principles of the Declaration of Independence," and "the ambiguity of Vattel's propositions—indeed, the ambiguity of an oracle" that made *Law of Nations* a handy reference in diplomatic correspondence. Vattel could be used to support a variety of positions, and his recognition of both natural law and positive law as sources of the law of nations allowed for flexible interpretations.[34]

Vattel claimed to be developing and extending the German philosopher Christian Wolff's *Jus Gentium Method Scientifica Pertractatum* (*The Law of Nations Treated according to Scientific Method*, 1749).[35] Wolff derived the duty of mutual assistance by way of an analogy between the law of nature among individuals and the law of nature among states.[36] The law of nations was simply the law of nature of *individual persons* in the state of nature as applied to *states*. Vattel adopts the analogy between persons and states: "a political society" is "a moral person" with "an understanding and a will of which it makes use for the conduct of its affairs." When a people confer sovereignty on any one person, they thereby "invest him with their understanding and will, and make over to him their obligations and rights, so far as relates to the administration of the state, and to the exercise of the public authority" (bk. 1, ch. 4, § 40).[37] As with persons, the primary duties of states are (1) to preserve and perfect themselves, and (2) to assist each other in fulfilling those duties each state owes to itself. States should "cultivate human society," primarily through trade so long as the pursuit of commerce did not conflict with their primary duties to themselves. Yet states, like real persons, should remain free and independent, constrained by the rules necessary for their common society but otherwise autonomous (bk. 1, ch. 2, § 23).

Wolff and Vattel were the first to provide explicit articulations of the principle of nonintervention, the key element of Westphalian sovereignty. The fundamental norm of Westphalian sovereignty is that "states exist in specific territories, within which domestic political authorities are the sole arbiters of legitimate behavior."[38] Vattel argues that no state has the right to intervene in the "domestic affairs" of other states, which in his view include the right to enter into commerce and questions of religion and property (bk. 1, ch. 3, § 37). Vattel views nations (*gentes*) as sovereign states (*états souverains*) that constitute an international system based on a balance of power.[39] Vattel emphasized that though nations, like individuals, have a general duty of assistance to others, it is limited by the perfect right of a state to its own self-preservation and self-perfection. A state's duty to self-preservation and self-perfection is "perfect": it outweighs the obligation to assist other states in their efforts to preserve and perfect themselves. The state's duty to other states is "imperfect": it does not create an obligation to do anything in particular, nor can another state claim to have been injured by an alleged violation of it (bk. 1, ch. 2, §§ 13, 14).[40]

Vattel's views of a nation's perfect duties to itself and imperfect duties to others has implications for both trade and immigration. Although a state ought to enter into mutually advantageous trade relations with other states and sell its products at a "fair price," considerations of self-preservation allow it to limit trade or even reject commerce with other states altogether. Each nation is "the sole judge" of whether it is advantageous to engage in commerce (bk. 2, ch. 2, § 24). As for immigration, a state could decide to close off its borders entirely to foreigners, including those seeking a right of passage to "escape from imminent danger" or "procur[e] the means of subsistence," if their entry was deemed contrary to the welfare of the nation (bk. 2, ch. 9, § 123). In considering whether the "exiled or banished" have a "right to dwell somewhere on earth," Vattel defends the state's right to exclude when its self-preservation is threatened:

> Every nation has a right to refuse admitting a foreigner into her territory, when he cannot enter it without exposing the nation to evident danger, or doing her a manifest injury. What she owes to herself, the care of her own safety, gives her this right; and in virtue of her natural liberty, it belongs to the nation to judge, whether her circumstances will or will not justify the admission of that foreigner. (bk. 1., ch. 19, § 230)

This is the passage the US Supreme Court quoted in the *Fong Yue Ting* decision to justify the national government's power to deport noncitizens, the "evident danger" in this case being the racial threat to American identity posed by Chinese migrants.

It is important to look more closely at how Vattel himself viewed the connection between immigration control and sovereignty. How does he understand sovereign power? As I discuss in chapter 3, contemporary

justifications of the modern state's power over immigration have been made
in the name of sovereignty and collective self-determination. Such accounts
bear the burden of elaborating the nature of the sovereign state and its relationship to individual members.

One answer comes from the traditional conception of collective self-
determination that emerges from the line of natural law theorists that extends
from Grotius to Pufendorf, Wolff, and Vattel, a tradition that Hedley Bull has
called the "society of states" view of the global normative order.[41] Vattel's view
is that states have the right of self-determination because states, like persons,
are moral entities with the capacity to realize their nature in the pursuit of
ends. This view is explicitly based on what is called the "domestic analogy,"
described by Wolff as follows:

> Nations are regarded as individual free persons living in a state of na-
> ture . . . Since by nature all nations are equal, since moreover all men
> are equal in a moral sense whose rights and obligations are the same;
> the rights and obligations of all nations are also by nature the same.[42]

Vattel adopts the domestic analogy as well: "A political society is a moral
person" (bk. 1, ch. 4, §§ 40–42).

The problem, though, is that individual persons are different in important
respects from nations and states. As Charles Beitz puts it, "[S]tates, unlike
persons, lack the unity of consciousness and the rational will that constitute
the identity of persons"; they are not "organic wholes with the unity and integrity that attaches to persons qua persons. It should come as no surprise that
this lack of analogy leads to a lack of analogy on the matter of autonomy."[43]
We can derive a person's right to autonomy from the nature of the person,
but we cannot derive the state's right to self-determination from an account
of the state as a moral person. Another challenge, then, for any attempt to
justify the modern state's control over immigration is to go beyond domestic
analogies and provide an account of the nature of the collective and its relationship to individual members in a way that respects the freedom of individual members.

Conclusion

Looking to law does not provide convincing answers to the question of what
justifies government power over immigration. The US Supreme Court sought
to establish the authority of the federal government's power over immigration

by declaring that power to be "inherent in sovereignty," invoking Vattel as the central authority. The pivotal legal cases offer more assertion than argument. More troubling still, the turn toward plenary power was intimately connected with racism. Virtually absolute control over immigration was justified in the name of protecting white Americans from racialized others deemed "dangerous" to national security. Another troubling feature is the near absolute power granted to Congress and the president to regulate immigration. The plenary power doctrine suggests that sovereignty resides in these branches of government rather than in the people they are supposed to represent.

What lessons can we draw from this analysis? We can identify at least three challenges that any attempt to justify government power over immigration must satisfy. First, it must provide an argument, not assertions, about the relationship between sovereignty and immigration control. Why exactly is immigration control important for sovereign political communities? Second, it cannot rely on domestic analogies between the state and the individual; we need an account of the relationship between the state and its individual members, an account of political membership. Finally, it must distinguish between absolute and qualified control over immigration. A defense of government power over immigration need not be a defense of *absolute* control over immigration. Instead, as I will argue in these pages, control over immigration should be regarded as a *qualified* right of states to control immigration, in which the qualifications are defined by humanitarian values and for democratic political communities, by democratic values. The next chapter turns to examine arguments from contemporary political philosophy to see whether they meet these challenges.

3

Philosophical Justifications of State Power over Immigration

IT IS WIDELY assumed that immigration control is essential to the sovereignty of states. This chapter explores the normative foundations of this idea as articulated in recent philosophical work on immigration and territorial rights. Many scholars studying immigration bracket this question and turn their attention to more pressing questions about immigration law and policy. The reason for this is partly pragmatic. After all, states exercise power over borders whether there is a good normative justification for doing so or not. Among the scholars who have taken up this question, many say there is no good justification for state power over borders. They argue that borders should be open as a matter of principle and that people should generally be free to move across borders as they wish. I examine these arguments in Part II, "Why Not Open Borders?" In this chapter and the next, I consider what might be said in defense of state control over immigration.

This chapter analyzes the leading contemporary theories of the state's right to control immigration on offer. Some of these theories are developed as part of broader theories of territorial rights; some simply assume state sovereignty includes rights of territorial jurisdiction and focus on immigration control. Most appeal to the value of collective self-determination, but they ultimately rest their arguments on other values, including (1) the value of culture and national identity, (2) the right to private property, and (3) the value of freedom of association. A fourth account does not engage the idea of collective self-determination, resting instead on (4) the right of individuals to be free from unwanted obligations.

Culture and National Identity

Michael Walzer was one of the first contemporary political theorists to explicitly theorize the issue of membership in a political community instead of
simply taking such membership for granted. In developing his theory of distributive justice in *Spheres of Justice,* the first social good he discusses is "membership," which he suggests is "conceivably the most important good" because
it has historically determined access to other fundamental goods. One way it
is distinct from other goods is that it can only be distributed by taking people
in: "They must be physically admitted and politically received." For Walzer, it
is obvious who should decide how the good of membership should be distributed: "We who are already members do the choosing."[1]

Who are the "we" that makes up the membership? Walzer suggests it
is a group of people who share a cultural identity. Consider one of his key
examples:

> Greeks driven from Turkey and Turks from Greece, after the wars
> and revolutions of the early twentieth century, had to be taken in by
> the states that bore their collective names. What else are such states
> for? They don't only preside over a piece of territory and a random
> collection of inhabitants; they are also the political expression of a
> common life and (most often) of a national "family" that is never en-
> tirely enclosed within their legal boundaries.[2]

Walzer analogizes the political community to a "national 'family'" and goes
on to say that countries are also "territorial states," which possess jurisdiction
over territory. Unlike a national family, the territorial state has the right to
control the physical location and movement of members and nonmembers.
Yet, as with a national family, a fundamental imperative of the territorial
state is the preservation of a culturally distinctive way of life. The following
passages suggest Walzer's argument for state authority over immigration rests
on this cultural imperative:

> The distinctiveness of cultures and groups depends upon closure and,
> without it, cannot be conceived as a stable feature of human life. If this
> distinctiveness is a value, as most people . . . seem to believe, then clo-
> sure must be permitted somewhere. At some level of political organiza-
> tion, something like the sovereign state must take shape and claim the

authority to make its own admissions policy, to control and sometimes restrain the flow of immigrants.[3]

Admission and exclusion are at the core of communal independence. They suggest the deepest meaning of self-determination. Without them, there could not be *communities of character*, historically stable, ongoing associations of men and women with some special commitment to one another and some special sense of their common life.[4]

Walzer grounds state authority over immigration on the value of culturally distinctive communities. It is culturally distinctive communities that are the agents of self-determination exercising power over admission and ex-clusion. In discussing the concept of self-determination in *Just and Unjust Wars,* Walzer suggests, following John Stuart Mill, that self-determination is "the right of a people 'to become free by their own efforts' if they can."[5] In responding to critics of his just-war theory, Walzer writes, "The real subject of my argument is not the state at all but the political community that (usually) underlies it." He defines the political community in cultural terms: "The idea of communal integrity derives its moral and political force from the rights of contemporary men and women to live as members of a historic community and to express their inherited culture through polit-ical forms worked out among themselves."[6] The fundamental constituents of global society are cultural communities, and the role of states is to offer a political embodiment of a process by which cultural communities can di-rect their futures.[7]

David Miller has developed the cultural argument for territorial rights more fully.[8] On his view, the state's right to control immigration is part of the collective right of a *nation* to control its territory and its collective way of life. The nation contains five elements: it is "a community (1) constituted by shared belief and mutual commitment, (2) extended in history, (3) active in character, (4) connected to a particular territory, and (5) marked off from other communities by its distinct public culture."[9] It is the fifth element that makes Miller's account a nationalist one. The distinct public culture of the nation—its national identity—is expressed in part through the labor of people residing in the territory.

On Miller's theory of territorial rights, culture plays a crucial role in explaining the connection between members of a nation and the land they re-side on. As the people make their lives upon the land, they adapt their culture to the territory. For example, whether the climate is hot or cold or whether the territory landlocked or open to the sea will encourage the development of certain customs and discourage others. The people will also transform the territory according to their "cultural values": "Living on and shaping a piece of land means not only increasing its value in an economic sense, but also (typically) endowing it with meaning by virtue of significant events that have occurred there, monuments that have been built, poems, novels, and paintings that capture particular places or types of landscape."[10]

Miller's argument is quasi-Lockean; he draws on the Lockean labor theory of value and adds a nationalist twist. The labor of the nation not only adds economic value; it also endows the land with cultural meaning. The cultural dimension of human labor—acts of "transformation" expressing a particular national identity—is crucial. Because the value added by the nation's labor is, in Miller's words, "*embodied* in cultivated fields, buildings, roads, waterways, and all the rest," there is no way for the nation to retain that enhanced value without also retaining the territory. In order to secure that value over time, the nation needs to maintain control over the territory and "for that it needs rights of jurisdiction such as those normally exercised by a state."[11] The nation's right to territory is justified because it "gives members of the nation continuing access to places that are especially significant to them, and it allows choices to be made over how these sites are to be protected and managed."[12]

In his book on immigration, Miller argues for state control over immigration in terms of *national* self-determination. Self-determination matters because "it gives us, as citizens, some degree of control over what happens to our political community in the future."[13] As in his earlier work, Miller favors viewing the political community as a nation: compatriots are not only involved in a scheme of economic cooperation or subject to a coercive legal regime; "they also relate to one another as fellow nationals, people who share a broadly similar set of cultural values and a sense of belonging to a particular place. They think of themselves as a distinct community of people with historical roots that exists as one such community among others."[14] The national self-determination account gives rise to distinct reasons for state authority over immigration that have to do with its effects on trust within the nation. Immigration increases ethnic and religious diversity in a host society, which some social scientists have suggested may reduce interpersonal trust and trust in political institutions. Lower levels of trust may, in turn, make it harder to gain support for policies involving economic redistribution and for democratic institutions to operate in a deliberative manner. On Miller's account, states are justified in restricting immigration in order to protect the national culture.[15]

Cultural and nationalist theories of immigration control are appealing in a number of ways. They avoid the circularity of some statist accounts that hold a group can have territorial rights only if it is already a state but then define the state as a jurisdictional entity with territorial rights. They also offer a plausible account of why a group of people is connected to a piece of land. On the nationalist view, when a group of people develop their culture on a piece of land through tilling the fields, building monuments, and acting in other culturally expressive ways, they have a rightful claim to control that territory.

Yet there are a number of problems with the cultural and national theories that undermine their appeal. First, by defining political community in terms of a shared national culture, they offer a limited framework for the many multicultural and multiracial political communities in the world. They have limited resources for preventing racial and ethnic exclusions where certain racial and ethnic identities are regarded as central to the national culture. Miller himself says that "immigration need not pose problems, provided only that the immigrants come to share in a common national identity, to which they may contribute their own distinctive ingredients."[16] He explicitly rejects racial exclusions in immigration policy: "To be told that they [immigrants] belong to the wrong race or sex (or have the wrong color) is insulting, given that these features do not connect to anything of real significance to the society they want to join."[17] But what if particular racial and ethnic identities are considered significant to dominant narratives of national identity? Visions of national identity have always been contested, and race and ethnicity have historically played a central role in shaping what it means to be American, British, French, Australian, and so on. Think of the 1882 Chinese Exclusion Act discussed in chapter 2, the National Origins Act that restricted immigration from southern and eastern Europe, and the many other immigration and citizenship policies shaped by racial, ethnic, and other ascriptive ideologies.[18]

In contrast to Miller, Walzer bites the bullet on the exclusionary implications of a cultural theory of immigration control. In discussing the White Australia policy, Walzer notes that Australians in the early twentieth century faced one of two choices with respect to nonwhite refugees seeking admission: they could discharge the duty of mutual aid to "necessitous men and women, clamoring for entry" either by admitting them or by yielding some of their land to the needy strangers so they can establish a separate community, thereby preserving a "white Australia."[19] While Walzer gives weight to the refugees' claim to enter, he takes just as seriously Australians' claim to keep Australia white. It is not surprising that an account of self-determination based on the preservation of distinctive cultural and national identities would include claims for prioritizing specific *racial* identities considering the historical salience of race to shared understandings of national identity. Racial and xenophobic sentiments are not relics of the past. According to cross-national survey data, support for exclusionary conceptions of nationhood has been relatively stable over the past twenty years.[20] They are evident today in the rise of far-right parties in Europe and the white nationalists who helped usher Donald Trump into the White House. Insofar as racial and ethnic identities continue to play a salient role in discourses of national identity, a theory of immigration control centered on the value of national identity may be limited in blocking racial and ethnic exclusions. Liberal nationalists have sought to set racial and xenophobic elements outside their concept of national culture, emphasizing linguistic and cultural elements that are consistent with liberal democratic values. Miller might reply that his theory defines national identity capaciously, to include not only languages, religions, modes of dress, and distinctive cultural practices but also political values and principles. Yet, the challenge for the nationalist view remains what to do when a nation's commitment to racial, ethnic, and religious visions of national identity overtakes its commitment to liberal democratic principles. In the next chapter, I develop an alternative account of self-determination that defines the collective in terms of participation in shared institutions, not possession of a cultural identity.

A second problem with cultural/nationalist accounts has to do with who is doing the laboring, which grounds a claim to control over the territory. The work is performed by individuals, not the nation, so why should the nation gain rights over the territory, and not the individuals who performed the labor? To attribute territorial rights to the nation, more needs to be said about the relationship between the collective entity of the nation and its individual members. If only some members of the nation have labored to construct and maintain national institutions, why is it not only those individuals, not the entire nation, who can claim the right to exclude others from access to those institutions? National institutions do put individuals in a position to labor on collective projects, such as building infrastructure, but the relationship between the nation and the individuals who do the laboring needs to be elaborated. In particular, it seems necessary for the laboring individuals to hold some collective consciousness or intention that they are laboring in ways that are expressive of a national identity. What if the individuals performing the labor do not share this collective intention or possess the requisite attributes of national identity? In many places around the world, it is noncitizen migrant laborers, who don't share the national identity, who work the land and build the infrastructure, which poses a challenge to the nationalist argument that members of the nation possess territorial rights by virtue of their labor.

Finally, the nationalist account seems to extend territorial rights to any group that transforms the land in ways that are expressive of its culture. Think of Koreatown in Los Angeles. Many Korean immigrants in the United States did not enter the country already speaking the English language or possessing other attributes of American national culture, but they did build businesses, community centers, and monuments in Los Angeles. Did they thereby acquire territorial rights, including the right to determine immigration policy, over the parts of Los Angeles they transformed? Nationalists might say their theory applies to nations, not immigrants. Immigrants may have legitimate claims to private-property rights over the products of their labor, but this does not extend to territorial rights because they live and work in the national territory with the nation's consent, and what the nation has consented to is that their labor may ground claims to property, not territorial rights. But such a response would diminish the role of culturally expressive labor at the core of the nationalist account. If culturally expressive labor is what grounds a group's claim to a piece of land, it is not clear why immigrant groups are not also entitled to territorial rights.

Property

Another line of justification for the state's right to control immigration draws more directly on Locke's theory of property. In his *Second Treatise*, Locke advances the idea of a natural right to private property. He begins from the theological premise that God gave the earth to humankind in common and argues that individuals come to hold private property rights in certain parcels of land by virtue of mixing their labor with and adding value to that land.[21] Contemporary Lockeans have set aside the theological premises and developed the labor theory of value. As A. John Simmons puts it,

> There has been no more widespread or enduring intuition about property rights than that labor in creating or improving a thing gives one special claim to it. We feel that those who innocently work to discover, make, or usefully employ some unowned good ought to be allowed to keep it (if in so doing they harm no others) . . . [I]t would be wrong for others to take it away.[22]

From this Lockean intuition, some contemporary Lockeans derive a theory of territorial rights based on the consent of individual property owners who agree to establish a government. Other contemporary Lockeans conceive of the state as a collective agent that acquires territorial rights in the same way that individuals acquire property rights. I examine both individualist and collectivist Lockean theories to see whether they offer convincing arguments for state authority over immigration.

Consider first an *individualistic* Lockean account. Locke himself moves from a group of individuals with a natural right of private property over parcels of land to the collective entity of the state with territorial rights by way of consent: individual property owners make a voluntary agreement with one another to form a state with territorial jurisdiction. As Locke puts it,

> By the same act therefore, whereby any one unites his person, which was before free, to any commonwealth, by the same he unites his possessions, which were before free, to it also; and they become, both of them, person and possession, subject to the government and dominion of that common-wealth, as long as it hath a being.[23]

Consent serves to establish not only political authority over persons but also political authority over territory. When individuals who legitimately own or occupy a piece of land choose to join the social contract, they consent to subject both their persons and their private parcels of land to the state's authority. On the Lockean account, the state's authority over persons derives from the actual consent of those persons.

The individualist Lockean account is appealing in a number of ways. Like the nationalist account, it offers a way of explaining why a certain group is connected to a certain piece of land. As Simmons has emphasized in developing a Lockean account of territorial rights, it can explain why the territories states claim are the ones over which they have authority: those territories are the ones on which the willing members of the community live and labor.[24] The state comes to have jurisdictional rights over individuals and their land by virtue of their consent. In addition, Lockean accounts capture a crucial insight about territorial rights: the history of how the people who reside in a geographic area came to occupy it or acquire ownership matters to the state's claim to jurisdiction over that area. In other words, a state's claim to control territory rests in part on a prior claim of rightful occupancy by those who inhabit the territory and over whom the state asserts its authority.[25]

There are several problems with the individualist Lockean account that undermine its plausibility.[26] First, though individualist Lockeans can explain the creation of legitimate jurisdictional authority over particular pieces of land, they have a harder time justifying contiguous jurisdictional authority of territorial states. On the individualistic Lockean account, a piece of land can become subject to the state's authority only through the consent of individual property owners. However, as the well-known critique of consent-based theories of political authority goes, many individual property owners have never given their consent, rendering consent a shaky basis on which to ground the jurisdictional authority of actual states. Individualistic Lockeans face a serious difficulty: to have a government that can fulfill its aims, including the uniform application of the law, there must be continuity of territorial jurisdiction. What is to be done about individuals who explicitly refuse consent?

The way Lockeans have dealt with this problem is to assume either that jurisdiction is already continuous or that there are strong incentives for anarchists to submit to the state's authority. In *Anarchy, State, Utopia*, Robert Nozick adopted the second move:

> We have discharged our task of explaining how a state would arise from a state of nature without anyone's rights being violated. The moral objections of the individualist anarchist to the minimal state are overcome. It is not an unjust imposition of a monopoly; the *de facto* monopoly grows by an invisible-hand process and by morally permissible means, without anyone's rights being violated and without any claims being made to a special right that others do not possess.[27]

How does the minimal state's monopoly on the use of force become legitimate in the face of recalcitrant anarchists? The anarchist's objection is that the state's claim to a monopoly on the use of force within the state's territory violates her rights not only because the state claims to be the exclusive holder of the right to punish and exact reparations but also because it forces her to pay for protection that she would rather provide herself. Nozick suggests anarchists can be compelled to join the state in exchange for adequate compensation for the loss of utility they experience by having to join. Adopting the concept of compensation from welfare economics, he argues that the loss of autonomy for the independents is justified by the security gained by those who voluntarily joined the state. The appropriate price of compensation is the amount that would return anarchists' utility to what it had been before they were compelled to join, but rather than ask them to determine the price themselves, the state would determine a fair price by some other process, based on interpersonal comparisons and trade-offs between the needs of independents and the needs of everyone else.[28]

But this move is vulnerable to the objection Nozick makes about utilitarianism: it fails to take the rights of each and every individual seriously. Drawing on Rawls's idea of the separateness of persons, Nozick argues against violating the rights of some persons "for the sake of the overall social good": "To use a person in this way does not sufficiently respect and take account of the fact that he is a separate person."[29] Nozick's claim that individuals who initially refuse to consent can be compelled to join the state for some adequate state-determined compensation also fails to respect the separateness of persons.

In contrast to Nozick, Hillel Steiner takes the freedom of individuals very seriously, arguing that individuals have the right to exit the state with their property whenever they wish. As he puts it, "Precisely because a nation's territory is legitimately composed of the real estate of its members, the decision of any of them to resign that membership and, as it were, to take their real estate with them is a decision that must be respected."[30] The problem with Steiner's approach is that it requires us to abandon any conception of territorial rights as securing stable borders within which a state has a legitimate monopoly on the use of force and the right to establish justice.[31]

In contrast to Nozick and Steiner, Simmons avoids the contiguity problem by interpreting Locke differently. The reason individuals join the social contract is, in Locke's words, "for their comfortable, safe, and peaceable living one amongst another, in a secure enjoyment of their properties."[32] If some members of every generation could secede if they wanted to, the political community could not last. Simmons argues that when people consent to make or join a political society, they are consenting to "whatever arrangements are necessary for a peaceful, stable society."[33] This includes establishing a regime of jurisdictional rights that protects and governs property rights but which is distinct from property rights. Political authority can limit the ability of property owners to exit or sell their land to people who do not accept the jurisdictional authority of the state. When they join a political community, property owners agree that "subjects will not bequeath, sell or otherwise alienate land incorporated into that state's territories except on the condition that subsequent holders of that land will also be bound by the obligations of membership, including subjection of the land to state jurisdiction."[34] The problem here, though, is the familiar problem with consent-based theories: very few individual property owners have actually consented to the jurisdictional authority of states, rendering all states illegitimate. Philosophical anarchists like

Simmons are not troubled by this conclusion, but as Margaret Moore has argued, Simmons's account sets the standard for state legitimacy so high that no actual states can meet it, rendering all states lacking rights of territorial jurisdiction.[35]

Do *collectivist* Lockean accounts do better? I focus on Ryan Pevnick's collectivist Lockean theory of immigration control. He takes the basic Lockean intuition—that we are entitled to the fruits of our labor so long as we do not harm others—to explain why a voluntary association has the right to make its own decisions about its future, including whom to admit as future members. His account is collectivist in that he does not seek to derive the state's right to control immigration from the consent of individual property owners; instead, the state is understood as the collective that holds property rights in public institutions. He justifies the self-determination of the collective by appealing to "the group's *ownership* of goods produced through the labor and contribution of members."[36] He extends the Lockean intuition underlying the ownership claims of individuals and voluntary groups to states themselves. Pevnick regards citizens as "joint owners" of state institutions, analogous to owners of the family farm:

> Like the family farm, the construction of state institutions is a historical project that extends across generations and into which individuals are born. Just as the value of a farm very largely comes from the improvements made on it, so too the value of membership in a state is very largely a result of the labor and investment of the community. The citizenry raises resources through taxation and invests those resources in valuable public goods: basic infrastructure, defense, the establishment and maintenance of an effective market, a system of education, and the like . . . these are goods that only exist as a result of the labor and investment of community members.[37]

It is the labor of the citizenry, who constitute the state, which grounds the state's claim of joint ownership over public institutions. Joint ownership grounds the state's right to "at least some discretion in making future decisions about how those resources will be used," including whether and to whom the good of membership will be given in the future.[38]

Pevnick's theory has several problems. The first is that, in contrast to Simmon's individualist Lockean account, Pevnick intentionally conflates property rights and rights of territorial jurisdiction. He defines "jurisdiction" as the authority to administer a system of rights, including private property rights, within a given territory, but also says that "jurisdiction" can be understood as a claim about property writ large. He adopts a broad conception of property as "rules that govern people's access to and control of things," such as land, natural resources, the means of production, and manufactured goods, as well as of some ideas, inventions, and other intellectual products. When he calls someone an "owner" of a resource, he is simply saying that she has some bundle of rights over it. We still need an account of the nature of those rights. Pevnick concludes that we should view *jurisdiction* as a kind of *collective property*:

> The community as a whole determines how important resources are to be used. These determinations are made on the basis of the social interest through mechanisms of collective decision-making—anything from a leisurely debate among the elders of a tribe to the forming and implementing of a Soviet-style "Five-Year Plan."[39]

Instead of blurring the distinctions between property rights and jurisdictional rights, we need a theory that can distinguish between property rights in the strict sense (the right to control, use, and benefit from a particular resource) and rights of jurisdiction (the right to make first-order rules that define property rights and other rights and to interpret and enforce those rules).[40] Consider the example of my backyard. As the owner of this plot of land, I can use and benefit from it; I can also exclude people from entering it. But my ownership claim does not determine who has the right to make the rules governing my backyard and the backyards of my fellow citizens. We need a way of distinguishing between private property rights and territorial rights that captures the distinct sources and nature of these rights.[41]

A theory that distinguishes between property rights and territorial rights allows us to recognize differences between principles governing property and principles governing territory. For example, territorial rights tend to prohibit certain activities that property rights permit, such as destroying religious objects or other objects of great significance to people or evicting all people who do not own their land. Furthermore, territorial rights include the access to and use of airspace and waterways that are not typically susceptible to ownership through "mixing one's labor" with something in a pre-political state. Lockeans might respond to these examples by building in more assumptions about the content of pre-political property rights. For example, one might include airspace and waterways in a pre-political conception of property rights or deny that any state has rights over such things. But these moves would put more pressure on the Lockean view, either by reducing the explanatory power of Lockean property theory or by widening the gap between Lockean theory and settled judgments about the legitimate claims of legitimate states.[42]

A second problem with Pevnick's account has to do with the relationship between the state and individual members. He argues that the labor of individual citizens confers ownership on the citizenry as a whole, but he does not explain how we get from labor performed by individuals to ownership by the state. Why should the state, and not the citizens who performed the labor, gain jurisdictional rights over the territory? How do we get from an aggregation of individual property owners to a collective of citizens with jurisdictional rights? Pevnick suggests individual consent is necessary for membership in the joint ownership association when he discusses the implications of "associative ownership" for long-settled unauthorized migrants. Migrants' contributions to constructing and maintaining public institutions and goods are not sufficient. Consent is necessary: "In the case of illegal immigrants, by entering the country illicitly such individuals took their place in their community without the consent of the citizenry." He acknowledges that unauthorized migrants make contributions through working and paying taxes, but he contends that citizens have no obligation "to pass ownership of their institutions to illegal immigrants" because the migrants have "put themselves in this situation without the consent of the citizenry."[43] On Pevnick's account, value-enhancing labor and fair exchange are insufficient to ground migrants' claims to be included in the project of joint ownership.[44] Citizens must give their consent before migrants' labor can ground a claim to joint ownership. But we could apply this very same critique to Pevnick's application of the consent standard to native-born citizens: very few of them have literally given their consent to the joint ownership project.

Third, Pevnick invokes the idea of self-determination but leaves unanswered important questions about the nature of self-determination. He views the right to self-determination as the right to *democratic* self-determination: the right of members to have an *equal* say in the making of the laws to which they are subject. To elaborate the idea of self-determination, Pevnick relies on an analogy between the state and voluntary associations, but voluntary associations use a range of decision-making procedures. For example, the Rotary Club or a student club may make decisions democratically, but religious or business organizations may concentrate decision-making power in the hands of a few. This suggests that the collective ownership claims of members support a right to self-determination that is consistent with a range of decision-making procedures, only some of which are democratic. In other words, the fact of collective ownership alone cannot entail a right to democratic self-determination.[45] Our intuitions about collective ownership suggest owners are entitled to *some* say in decisions regarding their collective property but not necessarily an *equal* say. How, then, do the collective ownership claims of citizens generate a right to *democratic* self-determination? Pevnick might reply that the citizens' ownership claims over public institutions they have built are special and thus give them a right of democratic self-determination, but this begs the question of how the right of self-determination is to be justified. I explore the grounds of the right of collective self-determination in the next chapter.

Freedom of Association

Christopher Health Wellman's case for the state's right to control immigration also appeals to the value of collective self-determination. He begins with this premise:

1. Legitimate states are entitled to political self-determination.

He does not say much about self-determination, resting his argument instead on the value of freedom of association. His argument rests on two additional premises:

2. Freedom of association is an integral component of self-determination.
3. Freedom of association includes not only the right to associate with others but also the right to dissociate.[46]

Wellman emphasizes that freedom of association includes both the right to *include* and the right to *exclude* potential associates. He quotes Stuart White on this point: "With the freedom to associate, however, there comes the freedom to refuse association. When a group of people gets together to form an association of some kind (e.g., a religious association, a trade union, a sports club), they will frequently wish to exclude some people from joining their association. What makes it *their* association, serving their purposes, is that they can exercise this 'right to exclude.' "[47] White's discussion focuses on intimate and religious associations within one state.

Wellman extends the value of freedom of association to the state itself, arguing by way of analogy with small-scale associations. We would vehemently object if an individual were forced to marry someone against her will.

We would also object if a golf club were forced to admit new members against its will. Wellman concludes:

> [J]ust as an individual may permissibly choose whom (if anyone) to marry, and a golf club may choose whom (if anyone) to admit as new members, a group of fellow citizens is entitled to determine whom (if anyone) to admit into their country.[48]

For the same reason individuals are entitled to reject a suitor, citizens have a presumptive right to reject foreigners who seek to enter. Wellman acknowledges this presumptive right can be overridden by competing considerations, but all things considered, he concludes, "even if egalitarians are right that those of us in wealthy societies have stringent duties of global distributive justice, and even if libertarians are correct that individuals have rights both to freedom of movement and to control their private property, legitimate states are entitled to reject all potential immigrants, even those desperately seeking asylum from incompetent or corrupt political regimes that are either unable or unwilling to protect their citizens' basic moral rights."[49] Among existing theories of immigration control, Wellman's comes closest to a position of closed borders.

Wellman's argument falls short in a few ways. First, he blurs the difference between the right to exclude those who want to be admitted to the state's *territory* and the right to exclude those who want to be admitted to *citizenship*. There are distinctive considerations that apply to each. In analogizing countries with small-scale associations, Wellman seems to rely on a property-based account of territorial rights: "My right to freedom of movement does not entitle me to enter your house without your permission . . . so why think this right gives me a valid claim to enter a foreign country without that country's permission?"[50] Just as individual property owners are entitled to exclude outsiders from their houses, members of a country are entitled to exclude outsiders from entering their country. Yet, like the Lockean accounts discussed in the previous section, Wellman's analogy runs together two types of rights that need to be distinguished: rights of private property and rights of territorial jurisdiction.[51]

Second, Wellman's club analogy does not hold up and it leads him to ignore what is distinctive about the state. Wellman's argument by analogy is reminiscent of Vattel's "domestic analogy," which emphasizes the ways in which states are like individuals. But the state is not an intimate or small-scale association. I do not share a home, place of worship, or clubhouse with all my compatriots. States are typically large enough that one need not have intimate or regular contact with citizens one doesn't know. Wellman acknowledges that our interest in not being forced into association with others applies most clearly in the case of intimate associations, but he maintains that this objection does not defeat the presumptive right of free association of large-scale associations, such as the state. To make his case, Wellman draws on White's discussion of intimate and religious associations, but what is at stake in White's discussion of intimate and religious associations is unique to those associations:

> [I]f the formation of a specific association is essential to the individual's ability to exercise properly his/her *liberties of conscience and expression*, or to his/her *ability to form intimate attachments*, then exclusion rules which are genuinely necessary to protect the association's primary purposes have an especially strong presumption of legitimacy.[52]

The case for freedom of association rests in part on the nature of the association's purpose. We respect freedom of association in the marital context because of the intimate purpose of such associations. We respect freedom of association in the religious context out of respect for freedom of conscience and expression. But the liberal state is neither an intimate nor a religious association. As Sarah Fine has argued, though liberal democratic states are committed to certain values (e.g., toleration, individual liberty, equality before the law), there is reasonable disagreement about the list and ranking of shared values.[53] Even if there were a consensus on a list and ranking, the state is importantly different from religious associations in that the latter are based on shared comprehensive religious doctrines. What is objectionable about forcing religious associations to admit new members against the wishes of the association is that it threatens the very purpose of their association. If I were forced to marry someone I didn't want to or if my church were forced to admit members it didn't want, it would undermine the intimate or religious purpose of these associations. Would the purpose of states be undermined if they did not have control over who may become a member?

Wellman responds with another analogy, between golf clubs and the state:

> [I]f no one doubts that golf clubs have a presumptive right to exclude others, then there seems no reason to suspect that a group of citizens cannot also have the right to freedom of association, even if control over membership in a country is not nearly as significant as control regarding one's spouse.[54]

But the state can be distinguished from a golf club in at least two normatively important respects. First, the state is not a voluntary association. We typically gain citizenship by being born in the territory or born to parents who are citizens. As Rawls puts it, "Political society is not, and cannot be, an association. We do not enter it voluntarily."[55] The nonvoluntary nature of political membership raises the stakes of membership. Exclusion from a particular state can be hugely consequential in a way that exclusion from a golf club typically is not.[56] Outsiders have significant interests in becoming members of that state and exclusion brings nonmembers high costs (and not just costs associated with expressive or intimate purposes). Second, states, unlike golf clubs, do not exist in a competitive environment conducive to market entrants. If a golf club refuses to admit me, I can join another or form my own. If a state refuses to admit me, I can neither form my own nor easily join another. If no golf club will admit me, the consequences are nowhere near as dire as the consequences of being a stateless person.[57]

Considering these differences, the burden rests on proponents of the free association argument to elaborate why freedom of association remains so fundamental for states even if citizens will typically never have anything approaching face-to-face relations with the vast majority of their compatriots. Wellman suggests two reasons. First, the sheer size of the group dramatically shapes the experience of being a member. For example, as a private golf club increases its membership, there will be more wear and tear on the golf course. Similarly, as a political state increases the number of new members, citizens' lives will be affected by population density. This concern about "wear and tear" depends on empirical considerations, and current levels of immigration to wealthy countries far fall short of the "wear and tear" threshold, undercutting Wellman's case for the state's virtually absolute right to exclude. Moreover, the "wear and tear" argument does not deliver the deontological justification that Wellman claims to provide.

A second reason has to do with the power to shape the association's future. Control over rules of admission and membership are significant in part because new members will subsequently have a say in determining the future course of the association. In other words, freedom of association flows from the value of collective self-determination, a point that Wellman acknowledges but does not develop in his writing on immigration. Rather than relying on problematic analogies, we need an account that elaborates the relationship between collective self-determination and immigration control and which recognizes what is distinctive about membership in *political* associations.

We are not at capacity

Freedom from Unwanted Obligations

The fourth and final account of state control over immigration I consider is Michael Blake's argument, which combines a compelling individual rights argument with a Kantian functionalist account of territorial rights. In contrast to Wellman, he derives the state's right to exclude not from freedom of association but from "a presumptive right to be free from others imposing obligations on us without our consent."[58] In contrast to nationalist and property theories, Blake begins with the idea of the state as a fundamentally jurisdictional entity rather than trying to derive the state from a cultural group or a group of property-owners.

Blake begins with two key assumptions. First, he assumes that human beings have certain human rights. He is less concerned with the substance of human rights than with their structure. He adopts the standard tripartite distinction of obligations under human rights: to respect, to protect, and to fulfill human rights.[59] States have an obligation to *respect* human rights; this obligation applies universally to all humans, regardless of whether they are inside or outside their territorial jurisdiction. States also have an obligation to *protect* and to *fulfill* human rights through creating novel forms of political institutions and measures to vindicate rights. The latter two obligations are "emphatically local"—states only have an obligation to protect and fulfill the rights of those who are present in its territorial jurisdiction. There are different ways of grounding the claim that the state has distinctive obligations to those who are physically present in its territorial jurisdiction. Drawing on his earlier work, Blake suggests the coercion principle: all those present in a state's jurisdiction are subject to the coercive power of the state and thereby owed a justification for that subjection, which takes the form of protecting subjects' rights and other obligations of distributive justice.[60] He also suggests the principle of fair play in discussing the example of those "who participate in the American system" as being "authorized and obligated to help support this system's ability to protect and fulfill human rights" of all those who are physically present. For these reasons, Blake argues "the mere fact of her presence within the jurisdiction is sufficient to place these institutions under an obligation to act in defense of these rights."[61]

A second assumption is the definition of states as fundamentally jurisdictional entities. Drawing on international law, Blake lays out three constitutive features of the state: a government capable of exerting coercive control, a particular geographic area over which that control is exerted, and a particular group of people over whom that control is exercised. His definition of jurisdictional control includes not only effective rule over land and resources within the territory but also "all individuals who happen to find themselves within a particular territorial jurisdiction."[62] Blake simply assumes that sovereign states have territorial rights. However, as theorists of territorial rights have emphasized, this claim requires defense.

Blake's definition of the state seems to reflect a Kantian functionalist theory of territorial rights.[63] On the Kantian view, territorial rights are justified in terms of justice, not culture, property, or freedom of association. As Kant puts it, "When you cannot avoid living side by side with all others, you ought to leave the state of nature and proceed with them into a rightful condition, that is, a condition of distributive justice."[64] People who find themselves in conflict over the just use of resources are morally required to enter into political community with one another. As Jeremy Waldron has argued, the frequency and density of disputes that arise in a given territory makes the legal arrangement of the territorial state particularly appropriate: "In the modern world, it makes most sense to adopt a pragmatic and generally respectful stance toward existing territorial demarcations."[65] Without the legal system of the territorial state, individuals in a given area would disagree about what rights they have and when rights are violated. The public law of the territorial state establishes a common view of the rights of individuals, and the state has the coercive means to enforce that view in a clearly demarcated jurisdiction and to adjudicate conflicts among individuals.

Kantian theories of territorial rights suffer from several weaknesses. They have limited capacity to explain how particular states have authority over particular territories. As Moore has argued, the logic of the Kantian account is cosmopolitan: we all have a duty to establish and maintain just institutions, but not any particular set of institutions. The theory offers no internal reason why territorial jurisdiction should not be universal, why we should not end up with a global state.[66] In addition, Kantian accounts set the standard of legitimacy very high, leading to counterintuitive results: most past and current states do not meet any standard of justice, which means they lack any territorial rights here and now. In the case of failed states, Kantian theory seems to rule out any alternative collective agent that might be said to hold territorial rights, leaving the citizens of failed states without any claim to territorial rights. This suggests the need to explore nonstatist accounts of the agent of collective self-determination. Insofar as Blake relies on Kantian assumptions about the foundations of a state's territorial rights, he is vulnerable to these criticisms.

Assuming legitimate states have territorial rights, Blake's focus is on justifying state control over immigration. He offers an elegantly simple normative principle: "we have a presumptive right to be free from others imposing obligations on us without our consent."[67] This principle stems from taking the idea of freedom seriously. If you impose an obligation on me, it infringes on my freedom. I should not be obliged to act in ways that impinge on my freedom without my consent. Applying this to immigration, Blake argues that when a newcomer enters the jurisdiction, she imposes a "new obligation" on current residents "to create and support institutions capable of protecting and fulfilling the rights of the newcomer."[68] These obligations constrain the freedom of current residents by placing them under standing obligations to act in ways to defend immigrant's rights. In response, Blake argues, "legitimate states may refuse to allow immigrants to come in, because the residents of those states have the right to refuse to become obliged to those would-be immigrants."[69] Would-be immigrants face the burden of offering a reason why these residents have an obligation to become obligated to them. Blake is open to the possibility that prospective migrants might offer reasons that may override the claim of citizens to be free from unwanted obligation—for example, that migrants' human rights are not being protected and fulfilled in their home states. In the absence of such a reason, however, the state has the right to exclude migrants. Blake argues that the state has the discretion to decide on the purposes for which this right is to be invoked. For example, it may choose to use this right to protect cultural distinctiveness or solidarity or any other particular good.

Blake's account is attractive in several respects. It recognizes a general right of states to restrict immigration without suggesting all restrictions are permissible. His account also allows us to distinguish between different reasons underlying a migrant's claims to entry. For example, we can distinguish between an individual whose human rights are not being protected in his home state and Blake's own immigration story in which he says he had no right to enter the United States from Canada and there would have been no injustice if the United States had chosen to exclude him. Nonetheless, there are some limits to his account, and discussing them will help set the stage for the alternative account I present in chapter 4.

The first has to do with the deontic grounds of Blake's defense of the state's right to exclude. Blake suggests that the issue of immigration involves a conflict of freedoms. On the one hand, there are the freedoms of migrants—the freedom to migrate to be reunited with family, pursue an occupation of their choosing, and worship with fellow believers. On the other hand, there are

the freedoms of current residents that may be constrained by the arrival of
new immigrants, but exactly how their freedoms are constrained by the arrival of new immigrants is not entirely clear. Blake speaks of new arrivals imposing "new obligations" on current residents, but these are not new *types*
of obligations since current residents already support institutions that protect and fulfill the human rights of fellow residents, such as paying taxes and
serving on juries. They appear to be what Michael Kates and Ryan Pevnick
call new *tokens* of obligation from already existing types: with the birth of
new citizens in the territory or the arrival of new immigrants from outside the
territory, current residents are obligated to support these institutions with respect to a greater number of individuals than before.[70] On Blake's account, it
appears that the primary way that immigration affects the freedom of current
residents is by increasing the *costs* of upholding certain existing institutions.
The greater the number of people whose human rights we must protect and
fulfill, the greater the burden to create and support effective institutions
that aim toward that goal. It is important to emphasize that immigrants not
only impose costs on existing schemes of social cooperation but they also
contribute fiscally by working and paying taxes. Yet Blake rejects such cost-
benefit-analysis grounds for the state's right to exclude; his argument, he says,
is "not one about *costs*, but about *obligations*."[71] The problem for Blake is that
if current residents incur only new tokens (not new types) of obligations with
the arrival of new immigrants, it appears that all that has changed for current
residents is the *costs* of fulfilling obligations that citizens already have to fulfill
for one another.

Blake could respond in one of two ways. First, he could concede the con-
sequentialist point that the weighing of the costs and benefits of immigration is relevant to determining whether the migrants' claim to entry or the
state's right to exclude should trump. But this would shift his theory away
from deontic considerations about rights to considerations about the promo-
tion of a particular good. A second option, which is in keeping with his deontic approach, is to flesh out the nature of the freedom of current residents
that is constrained by the arrival of new immigrants. He might respond that
each new token involves a new relationship, which one has a right to be free
from. The implication for immigration is that each new migrant who enters
the territory generates a new relationship with the current citizenry, one to
which every citizen has an obligation. I think a stronger argument can be developed by looking, not just from an individual point of view, but also at the
collective freedom at stake. As I argue in the next chapter, the freedom at
stake for current residents is the collective right of self-determination.

A second limitation of Blake's defense has to do with the connection between the collective entity of the state and individual members. Blake derives the *state's* right to exclude from the general right of *individuals* to be free from unwanted obligations without their consent. What if a bare majority of the citizenry, say 51 percent, expressed a preference for more open immigration policies but the other 49 percent favored highly restrictive immigration policies. On Blake's normative principle—the presumptive right of *individuals* to be free from unwanted obligations to which they did not *consent*—why couldn't the 49 percent claim their presumptive right has been violated because they never consented to the more expansive immigration policy? To respond, Blake would need to provide an account of the relationship between the state and its individual members. In other words, what is required is an account of collective self-determination that says something about the nature of the *collective* that is the bearer of self-determination and its relationship to individual members.

Conclusion

This chapter has provided a critical assessment of four theories of the state's right to control immigration. Several appeal to the value of collective self-determination, conceiving of the agent of collective self-determination in different ways. The nationalist view derives the state's right to control immigration from the nation and the imperative of cultural protection. The Lockean view derives the right from individuals who consent to subject themselves to the state in order to protect their rights. Kantians view territorial rights, including the right to control immigration, as originally belonging to the state itself, which is necessary for securing justice. In the next chapter, I advance an alternative conception of collective self-determination that I believe avoids the problems identified in this chapter.

4

Collective Self-Determination and Immigration Control

WHAT, IF ANYTHING, justifies the state's power over immigration? Political theorists and philosophers have appealed to the idea of collective self-determination to defend the state's right to control immigration, but their arguments have tended to rest ultimately on other values, such as the value of cultural and national identity, the right to private property, and freedom of association. Building on the critique offered in chapter 3, this chapter develops an alternative account of the state's right to control immigration based on the idea of collective self-determination. In contrast to the absolutist view of state sovereignty analyzed in chapter 2, I argue for a qualified, not absolute, right of states to control immigration.[1] This chapter provides reasons based on collective self-determination for the state's pro tanto right to control immigration. I take up competing considerations that constrain this right in later chapters.

Before presenting my argument, I want to clarify the relationship between collective self-determination and compatriot partiality, the idea that we have special rights and obligations by virtue of our membership in a political community. In the introductory chapter, I advanced the particularist claim that we have special obligations by virtue of our particular relationships and group memberships. The account of peoplehood offered here is intended to elaborate a particularist vision of political membership. Some will reject my particularist approach to obligation in favor of a universalist approach.

Although I do not develop such an approach, I believe the value of collective self-determination also plays an important role in a universalist approach to obligation. Consider the global standpoint of say, a representative individual who does not know her citizenship and must choose principles to structure the international system. She will want a system that protects her basic interests, including a basic interest in collective self-determination. Collective self-determination provides a reason for favoring a system of separate states over a world state because the former allows political order to be established in a way that respects people's judgments about how they should be ruled. In other words, the value of collective self-determination grounds a territorial division of responsibility among states. This means the state has special duties toward those within its territorial jurisdiction that it does not have toward outsiders. If we take the value of collective self-determination seriously, we see that the power to shape the future of one's political community is not a brute, amoral power or a mere convention but a legitimate power of a people aspiring to govern itself.

I begin by discussing the idea of collective self-determination—its meaning, role, and value—and then develop a particular conception of the idea. On my account, the agent of collective self-determination is not a nation, the joint owners of state institutions, or members of a voluntary association but "a people" engaged in the shared political project of collective self-governance. The chapter elaborates and defends the idea of peoplehood. I then explore the connections between collective self-determination, territorial rights, and immigration control. I also consider the relationship between collective self-determination and democracy and discuss the distinctive requirements of democratic self-determination and its implications for immigration control in democratic societies. I conclude by responding to two objections.

The Idea of Collective Self-Determination

Collective self-determination is the moral claim of a collective to rule itself. It is recognized as a fundamental right in United Nations charters and covenants. Article 1 of the UN Charter states that one central purpose of the UN is "to develop friendly relations among nations based on respect for the principle of equal rights and self-determination of peoples."[2] The right of self-determination is further enunciated in article 1 of the International Covenant on Civil and Political Rights: "All peoples have the right of self-determination. By virtue of that right they freely determine their political status and freely pursue their economic, social and cultural development."[3] Collective self-determination is widely understood to be a plausible element of any conception of human rights. It stands for the proposition that "peoples" have the right to significant independent control over their collective life.

As background, I want to highlight four general features of the idea of collective self-determination. First, collective self-determination has an external and an internal dimension. The *external* dimension finds expression in international law, where it used to be viewed as applying only to specific territories—initially, the defeated European powers and, later, overseas trust territories and colonies—and was also understood primarily as a right of secession. Over time it has come to be understood to apply to all peoples who seek independent political control over significant aspects of their common life.[4] In its external dimension, collective self-determination requires that those outside the collective refrain from interfering with the collective's decisions. The US Supreme Court emphasized this external dimension when it established the plenary power doctrine in US immigration jurisprudence (discussed in chapter 2); it defended a virtually absolute right to exclude foreigners as an essential feature of state sovereignty. Yet there is another dimension to collective self-determination. In its *internal* dimension, collective self-determination is the idea of popular sovereignty—that the people are the ultimate source of political authority. The people must authorize the binding collective decisions that the government makes in their name and to which they are subject. It is this internal dimension of collective self-determination that the US Supreme Court failed to take seriously in attributing sovereignty to the state rather than to the people themselves. Putting the internal and external dimensions together, collective self-determination can be understood as the right of a people to significant independent control over their collective life without external interference.

Second, consideration of the role of collective self-determination in domestic and international discourse helps to clarify its distinctive *value*. Colonized peoples have appealed to the idea of self-determination in mobilizing against colonial governments. Even proponents of humanitarian intervention by one state in the affairs of another in cases of genocide and other mass atrocities have held that occupiers have an obligation to restore the country to independence after the emergency has passed and a decent political order has been established. The claim of self-determination in these cases, by colonized and by occupied peoples, is a claim about who has authority to rule. The claim of self-determination says the legitimacy of political rule depends on authorization by the people. Failure to respect the claim of self-determination renders the colonizing or occupying government illegitimate. In other words, collective self-determination is a necessary condition of legitimate political authority. To be legitimate, political institutions must reflect the will of the people governed by those institutions. The people must be authors of those institutions in some meaningful way.

The distinctive value of collective self-determination becomes clearer when it is contrasted with the value of justice. Collective self-determination and justice are distinct components of legitimacy. Many liberal theorists approach the question of the legitimacy of states in terms of justice: the focus has been on the quality of state institutions and whether they provide certain rights and substantive goods, regardless of whether anyone has authorized those institutions.[5] The provision of basic rights and other substantive goods is a necessary condition of legitimate political authority, but it is not sufficient. People have an interest not just in receiving goods but also in shaping the institutions under which they live. Justice-based theories of legitimacy have tended to miss the distinctive value of collective self-determination.[6] A theory of immigration must be attentive to both claims of justice and claims of collective self-determination.

Third, collective self-determination is an important normative requirement, but it is *less demanding than democracy.*[7] Democracy requires equal rights of participation in collective decision-making by all those subject to those decisions. By contrast, collective self-determination requires that binding collective decisions result from and be accountable to a political process that represents the diverse interests of those who are subject to the decisions. It can be satisfied by a democratic form of government, but it can also be satisfied by nondemocratic forms of decision-making that offer opportunities for the people to hold government officials accountable that are more minimal than full democracy. Collective self-determination requires at least the following kinds of institutional mechanisms: First, there must be protections for basic rights and liberties, including the right to bodily integrity, subsistence, and freedom of speech and association.[8] Second, there must be institutional mechanisms of accountability, including the right to dissent from and appeal collective decisions. Third, government must provide public rationales for its decisions in terms of a conception of the common good of the society. I will say more about the distinction between democratic and nondemocratic forms of self-determination later in the chapter.

The final feature of collective self-determination I'd like to emphasize is that it is an irreducibly *collective right* but that its value derives from its importance for *individuals.* Value collectivists hold that collective entities like the nation have moral value that is not reducible to their value for individual members.[9] By contrast, value individualists hold that only individuals have ultimate moral value.[10] For value individualists, the task of justifying any set of collective institutions or activities must be pursued with reference to the interests of individuals. Individuals have a basic interest in self-determination. Individual self-determination is a valuable kind of freedom: the basic idea is that we should be able to direct our lives to a significant degree according to our own considered judgments. The idea of individual self-determination grounds basic liberties, including freedom of conscience, speech, association, and privacy. It also grounds a right to participate in the process of making the rules that govern our collective existence. This is the idea of collective self-determination.

Although its justification rests on its importance for individuals, the right to collective self-determination is an irreducibly collective right.[11] The value of collective self-determination rests not on the interests of individuals qua individuals but on individuals qua members of a collective. The interest of no single member of the group in the good of collective self-determination is sufficient by itself to justify holding another person to be subject to a duty.[12] The interest in question is the collective interest of all members. Collective self-determination enables, through its exercise, a distinctive kind of freedom, what Rousseau calls "moral liberty" and what we can call political freedom: "obedience to the law one has prescribed for oneself."[13] Collective self-determination is a form of political freedom that is only possible through membership in a collective. So, if a demagogue were to seize power without the support of the people, he would not take something away from individuals qua individuals; instead, he takes something from the group as a whole, the right to collective self-determination.[14]

The Agent of Collective Self-Determination

Nationalists view the agent of self-determination as a cultural group. Some Lockeans conceive of the agent as the joint property owners of state institutions. The freedom of association argument views the agent as individual associates, like individual parties to a marriage or members of a golf club. By contrast, I believe we should view the agent of collective self-determination as "a people." Peoplehood is a valuable form of group membership and a source of associative obligations: members of a people have special obligations to one another in virtue of their relationship to one another.[15]

What are peoples and how are they constituted? The idea is invoked in democratic theory and practice to refer to the agent in whose name political power is exercised. We can identify prominent invocations of peoplehood in political documents around the world. The US Constitution opens with the words "We the People of the United States." The French Declaration of the Rights of Man and Citizen begins, "The representatives of the French people [*Les Représentants du Peuple Français*]." The 1949 Basic Law of the Federal Republic of Germany presents itself as adopted by the "German people [*Deutsche Volk*]." The legitimacy of political rule is said to depend on authorization by the people.

Peoplehood is considered synonymous with the more familiar idea of the nation, but my account distinguishes them. The idea of peoplehood is more capacious and based on participation rather than cultural markers. To be a member of a nation, one must share the national identity. Conceptions of nationhood may also include a component of willing on the part of members of the nation, a "daily plebiscite," to use Ernest Renan's phrase.[16] But for nationalists, sharing the cultural attributes considered central to the national culture is necessary for membership in the nation. By contrast, what is essential about peoplehood is participation in efforts that aim at collective self-governance. To be sure, political and cultural motivations are often fused when subnational groups mobilize for some measure of collective autonomy.[17] By using the idea of peoplehood over nationhood, I mean to foreground political agency over cultural identity. Many nations count as peoples, but the category "peoples" is broader and includes groups whose members do not necessarily share a set of cultural attributes. On my account, Canada is a people that includes multiple nations and cultural communities, including Quebec, indigenous communities, and immigrants of diverse backgrounds.

How can peoples be individuated or distinguished from one another if not by shared cultural markers? The most prominent alternative to the nationalist view is what we might call the strong statist view, which says that the state creates a people by exercising its coercive power over individuals in the territory.[18] On this view, the state is prior to and necessary and sufficient for the creation of a people. By contrast, on the peoplehood view, a people comes into being by *participating* together in ways that express an aspiration to be authors, not merely subjects, of the rules governing collective life. A people can come about through participating in already established state institutions, and in this regard, a people is not actually prior to the state. But it is the fact of acting together in ways that aspire to self-rule, not the mere fact of subjection to state coercion, that brings a people into being. One implication is that a group of individuals who have not achieved statehood but who participate in ways that strive for collective self-determination may be considered a people. By contrast, on the strong statist account, where there is no viable state, there is no coherent collective to speak of.

There are three main conditions of peoplehood. First, "a people" is a group of individuals engaged in a common political project that *aims at collective self-rule*. A contrast with Rogers Smith's notion of peoplehood is instructive. He defines peoplehood very broadly as "any and all human associations, groups, and communities that are commonly understood to assert that their members owe them a measure of allegiance against the demands of other associations, communities, and groups." On Smith's view, what makes a group "a people" is the fact that the group advances claims to "impose binding obligations" and claims to "governing authority" over members.[19] Smith's definition includes not only sovereign states like the United States and China and federal political entities like Quebec but also religious associations like Jehovah's Witnesses, voluntary associations like the AFL-CIO, and international organizations like Oxfam.[20] Smith's account admits of degrees: some peoples assert strong claims to governing authority over members and allegiance over a wide range of issues, whereas other peoples assert more moderate claims of authority over a narrower range of issues. By contrast, my account defines political peoples more narrowly: groups that assert strong claims to final governing authority over all persons in a certain territory. Although religious associations and labor unions assert claims of allegiance over their members, such associations do not aspire to collective self-rule over all persons and land in a particular territory. So my conception of "peoples" includes Americans, Chinese, and indigenous communities but not religious and voluntary associations.[21]

Although the aspiration to collective self-determination is a necessary condition of peoplehood, it is not sufficient. A second condition of peoplehood is sharing a *history of political participation and contestation*.[22] There are many different forms of political engagement through which a people can emerge. It can take the form of participating in already established state institutions. Participation includes not just voting, giving money to campaigns, or running for office but a much broader range of activities, including attending local meetings, organizing and participating in protests, and paying taxes and complying with the law. Participation can also take the form of political mobilization by a group that aspires to statehood or sub-state arrangements through which they can exercise self-determination. Through these forms of participation, individuals come to identify with one another and forge a common political identity. Although members of a people are strangers to one another and may disagree on political issues, they constitute a political community by virtue of a common history of participating together in shared institutions.

This participatory dimension of peoplehood distinguishes peoplehood from citizenship understood as legal status. My account of peoplehood is not necessarily restricted to those who possess the legal status of citizenship.[23] Noncitizen residents can become members of a people by virtue of participating in shared institutions. They do not have the right to vote in most jurisdictions, but they still participate in collective life in myriad ways, from engagement with civic and community organizations, participating in protests and marches, and contributing to their schools, neighborhoods, and communities.[24] This participatory dimension has been invoked to advance claims for full inclusion not only by immigrants who lack the legal status of citizenship but also by African Americans denied equal rights of citizenship.[25] As I argue in chapter 10, all persons present in the territory of a state for a period of time have a strong moral claim to be included as full members in virtue of their participation in shared institutions.

A third condition of peoplehood is that it has the *capacity* to establish and maintain political institutions. By capacity, I mean the ability to exercise self-determination and maintain effective forms of governance. A group of people may lack the resources or the institutions to establish effective governance. As Moore has argued, this condition should not be understood as a blocking condition that excludes groups lacking the capacities from ever being considered as "a people."[26] Instead, the capacity condition should be understood as giving rise to duties of assistance on the part of third parties. This means that third parties may have duties to ensure that the group in question is provided with the means to exercise effective governance. If a group lacks capacity in terms of resources or institutions but meets the other conditions for peoplehood, then the appropriate response may be to assist them in overcoming their disadvantage if assistance can be provided without perpetrating injustice.

To sum up, we should think of the agent of collective of self-determination as peoples. Yet they exercise the right through political institutions. Since collective self-determination derives from its importance for individual self-determination, for political institutions to be self-determining, members of a people must *authorize* the state and its institutions. But when, if ever, is the state authorized by the people?

The most familiar answer is based on individual consent. A legitimate government is said to rest on the consent of the governed. Consent plays a crucial rule in Rousseau's justification of the social contract. As he puts it, "Civil association is the most voluntary act in the world. Since every man is born free and master of himself, no one can, under any pretext whatever, place another under subjection without his consent." Those who oppose the social contract at the time of its formation do not invalidate the contract, but they are prevented from being included in it. "Once the state is instituted, residency implies consent," declares Rousseau. "To inhabit the territory is to submit to sovereignty."[27] The familiar problem with consent is there are few, if any, governments that are constituted by the actual consent of all citizens. Indeed, only a small subset of citizens in a given country, such as immigrants who become naturalized citizens, have actively given their consent to the social compact. Most of the world's people—roughly 97 percent—live out their lives in the countries they happened to be born citizens of, and most have never given their consent to be governed by the political institutions of their countries.

To answer the question of when the state is authorized by the people, I propose something weaker than consent: the people authorize the state when they *support* it. In the ideal case, support takes the form of explicit consent. As in public naturalization ceremonies of new citizens, all would pledge their allegiance to cooperate as members of the political community. In actual cases, support can be more minimal than consent. Supporting is less explicit than approving, championing, or commending their government. Signs of support for government include voting, debating political and social issues with friends and neighbors, and attending local school board and city council meetings. Support occurs in more mundane ways: by observing traffic laws, responding to jury summonses, paying taxes, and respecting the legal rights of others.

One might object that these examples do not really constitute support for the state.[28] Observing traffic laws and paying taxes are activities that one might want to do independent of the existence of any government, and one might respond to jury summonses not to signal support but because the costs of noncompliance are very high. I want to make several points to counter skepticism about the possibility of broad support for government.

First, fundamental interests are served by cooperating through political institutions, and it is reasonable to hope that individuals recognize these interests. We have an interest in our physical security and in the resources necessary to meet our basic needs, and membership in a political community is vital to securing our basic needs and interests. Without political membership, we lack, in Arendt's words, the "right to have rights."[29]

Second, support for government does not presuppose perfect consensus or the absence of disagreement about the government's policies and actions. Residents can recognize their shared interests in political membership while also vociferously disagreeing about how to interpret the conditions that define their shared interests and how best to pursue those interests.[30] Support for government is consistent with considerable political disagreement.

Finally, in circumstances where the institutional conditions of self-determination are met, we can be reasonably confident that people support their government. Collective self-determination requires basic protections for the security and liberty of persons. It also requires that people have ways to form and express public opinion. To be self-determining, some mechanisms for expressing dissent and initiating reforms must be provided before we can say that the state is authorized by the people.[31] Where these institutional conditions are met, it is reasonable to think that people support the state.

Having set forth the main conditions defining peoplehood and its relationship to the state, I turn to consider how to connect peoples to particular territories.

Collective Self-Determination and Territorial Rights

To exercise self-determination on behalf of the people it represents, the state requires territorial rights, the right to make and enforce laws throughout the territory. We can think of territorial rights as a bundle of rights that includes (1) the right of territorial jurisdiction, (2) the right to control resources in the territory, and (3) the right to control the movement of people and goods across the territory's borders.[32] My focus is on the third right in the bundle. But before turning to analyze the connection between collective self-determination and immigration control, it is important to lay out the broader theory of territorial rights of which immigration control is a part.

Let me begin with a conceptual point. Rights over territory, resources, and the movement of people are often bundled together as "territorial rights," but they can be unbundled and held by different authorities. For example, prior to the recent European migration crisis, European Union member states had agreed to follow a policy of open borders for citizens of other EU member states while retaining control over land and the resources within their own territories. Similarly, states might delegate aspects of resource management within a territory to an international body with states retaining jurisdiction over territory. It is possible to imagine a world in which people enjoy freedom of movement across borders but states continue to control jurisdiction and resources.[33] Immigration control can indeed be unbundled from other aspects of territorial rights, but this does not undermine the conceptual point that immigration control is part of a bundle of territorial rights. For example, the fact that Germany had an open admissions policy for citizens of other EU member states under the Schengen Agreement did not render Germany's right to control immigration moot. Germany exercised its right to control immigration to permit an EU-wide open-borders policy, but the right to control immigration remains a part of the German state's bundle of territorial rights.

What are the conditions under which states have a rightful claim to territorial rights in the first place? There are several conditions. First, the state must maintain order and protect the human rights of inhabitants of the territory. This is the substantive goods or "justice" condition of legitimate political authority I discussed at the start of the chapter. States must provide some level of security and rights protection if they are to be regarded as legitimate. There is reasonable disagreement about where exactly the threshold should be set, which I cannot resolve here, but for my purposes, we can distinguish between cases where a well-functioning legal and political system allows most residents to pursue their lives without threat of violence and destitution and cases where that is not true.[34]

Second, the state must provide conditions for collective self-determination of the people who reside in the territory. The state must serve as the political embodiment of a people that seeks to rule itself. This condition might be met through democratic institutions that provide equal rights of participation in collective decision-making. It can also be met through nondemocratic institutions that secure basic protections for the security and liberty of persons and provide ways for people to form and express public opinion.

Third, the people who are represented by the state must have the right to occupy the territory in question. This condition connects a particular group of people to a particular geographical area. A state's claim of territorial rights over a certain area depends in part on a prior entitlement to the area it seeks to govern. It is not the state but the occupants of the territory who hold these prior entitlements: only if the individuals residing in a particular place have a rightful claim of occupancy does the state, which represents those individuals, have legitimate jurisdiction over it.

The right of occupancy is a pre-institutional claim of those who justly inhabit a place to reside there permanently; to make use of the area for valued social, cultural, and economic practices; and to be immune from expropriation or removal.[35] Occupancy rights are pre-institutional in the sense that they are moral rights that could exist prior to a legal system or social practice. What grounds a pre-institutional right of occupancy is the importance of stable residence for the pursuit of our life projects. As Hobbes argued, a person entering the social contract retains some rights, including "to his own body (for example) the right of defending, whereof he could not transfer; to the use of fire, water, free air, and *place to live in*, and to all things necessary for life."[36] Walzer cites this passage from Hobbes to argue that the state's claim to territorial jurisdiction derives ultimately from an individual's right to place. What the state owes to "its inhabitants" is "the place where they and their families have lived and made a life. The attachments and expectations they have formed argue against a forced transfer to another country."[37] The basic idea here is that people have a right to occupy a particular place because occupancy in a particular place is a necessary condition for personal well-being. We form relationships and develop and pursue our life plans on the assumption of stable residency in a particular place.[38] Our goals and relationships require us to form expectations about our continued access to that place.

The most straightforward case of legitimate occupancy involves a group of people who settle on uninhabited land and reside on it continuously. This scenario is reflected in the familiar narrative that the United States is a country of immigrants. But if we look to history, we find, alongside voluntary migration, colonialism, slavery, war, conquest, and the mingling of peoples over time. This history generates more questions than answers about who is entitled to establish jurisdiction in any particular geographic area. For example, much   of what is today regarded as US territory was annexed against the will of its original inhabitants, who were forcibly expelled or forcibly incorporated into the territory. What are the implications for the occupancy claims of those residing on US territory today and for the territorial rights claims of the United States?

These are hard and important questions that I cannot fully answer here, but it is important to sketch the outline of a basic response.[39] In short, I do not think the legitimate occupancy condition unravels the case for the territorial rights of states if serious efforts are made to remedy the harms caused by historical injustice. Where the agents and victims of the unjust appropriation are still alive, the agent that was causally responsible for the injustice bears a responsibility to remedy the injustice. The appropriate remedy may take the form of acknowledging the wrongdoing, returning land, or other forms of compensation. What about cases where the perpetrators and victims of the injustice are long gone, as in the conquest and expropriation of Native American land by white settlers and US government officials? As a collective agent that has persisted through time, the US government must bear responsibility for remedying the ongoing harms suffered by Native American descendants. Why?

One approach, which we might call the *strict liability model*, rests on establishing causal connections between perpetrators and victims and holding the perpetrators responsible for remedying the injustice. This approach runs into the practical difficulties of determining causal responsibility, which become harder the farther back in time we go. Such difficulties have led some theorists to abandon principles of rectification of injustice, regarding them as "superseded" by present-day concerns of distributive justice.[40] In my view, political communities committed to justice and democracy must acknowledge and respond to historical injustices to foster the inclusion of those disadvantaged by the effects of those injustices. Individuals who have directly benefited from the injustices (e.g., descendants of white settlers) may bear a special remedial responsibility, but in light of the practical and moral difficulties of precisely linking existing structural inequalities with specific acts of injustice perpetrated by many different individual and group actors, I believe a more promising approach is to view remedial responsibility for addressing structural inequality as falling on the political community as a whole.[41]

Remedies may take symbolic and material forms, including apologies, return of stolen property, monetary compensation, and legal and constitutional provisions recognizing the self-government rights and land use rights of Native American communities. With respect to Native communities, at the very least, the US government's "trust responsibility" toward tribal communities must be reconceptualized from one of paternalistic protection toward one of strong federal support for the resurgence of tribal self-governance. As American Indian law scholar Kevin Washburn puts it, the federal trust responsibility might be understood "as 'rent' due Indian tribes for the United States 'occupying' Indian lands in North America." This responsibility requires the federal government to adopt a norm of noninterference with respect to internal tribal matters and to engage in consultation with tribes when making policy with tribal implications.[42]

Consideration of such remedial measures is a necessary step to addressing the concerns about unjust occupancy. The exact form of remedy depends on various factors, including what those harmed by the injustices want and how granting the remedy would affect the state's obligations toward all members of the political community. For example, returning all unjustly appropriated land may not be possible given the difficulties of verifying and adjudicating multiple competing claims made on a piece of land by the descendants of the victims of the unjust original acquisition and subsequent unjust transfers of

the land. Under certain circumstances, remedying historical injustice may take
the form of special migration policies targeted at certain groups. In chapter 7,
I consider reparative arguments in discussing obligations to refugees and
asylum seekers whose plight was caused by the military and colonial policies
of the world's most powerful states; a similar logic might be applied to postco-
lonial migrants. There are no easy answers, but the difficult questions the legitimate occupancy condition raises can be addressed through serious efforts
to remedy historical injustices.

   To sum up, where a people has the right to occupy an area, a state that
represents the people and protects their human rights is entitled to rights of
territorial jurisdiction, including the right to control immigration.

Collective Self-Determination and Immigration Control

I have argued that immigration control is part of a bundle of territorial rights
a people require to be self-determining, but why should we regard immigration control as fundamental to collective self-determination? I offer two main
arguments.

   The first is concerned with the effects of immigration on the pursuit of
particular goods valued by members of the political community. Attention to
the effects of immigration reflects the realistic part of my realistically utopian
approach to immigration: we must consider the real-world impact of immigration on the receiving countries.[43] In considering the effects of immigration,
some focus on the *economic* impact of immigration, such as the fiscal costs
and benefits of immigration and the effects of immigration on the wages and
working conditions of domestic workers. Others worry about the *political* impact of immigration, including the effects of immigration on social trust and
public support for social welfare programs. Still others are concerned about the
cultural impact of immigration on the host society. For example, the Quebecois
prioritize French speakers in making immigrant admissions decisions. Native
American peoples are recognized as having legal rights to control tribal
membership rules to protect the cultural and political integrity of Native
communities.[44] Control over migration and membership is fundamental to
collective self-determination because the entry of newcomers will affect the
collective life of the political community. We need empirical analysis of the nature and extent of the effects of immigration if they are to serve as the basis of
policy recommendations. I engage with existing empirical studies in chapter 9.

A second reason immigration control is essential to collective self-determination is based on deontic grounds, grounds that begin with fundamental rights rather than with particular goods. Which rights are at stake when it comes to immigration? Both Wellman and Blake offer deontic arguments for the state's right to control immigration, but their arguments do not capture the collective right that is at stake. Wellman appeals to the individual right of freedom of association, arguing by analogy: just as individuals can refuse to marry or admit new members to a golf club, individual citizens can choose to exclude foreigners as they wish. Wellman's argument misses the collective dimension of the right of collective self-determination. Blake commits a similar mistake. He grounds the state's right to control immigration on the individual right to avoid unwanted obligations: "The would-be immigrant who wants to cross into a given jurisdiction acts to impose a set of obligations upon that jurisdiction's current residents. That obligation limits the freedom of those residents by placing them under standing obligations to act in particular ways in defense of that migrant's rights."[45] To illustrate, he repurposes Judith Thomson's well-known example of the violinist. Imagine a violinist attached to an individual who is obligated to share his bloodstream with the violinist and who is doing a fine job meeting the violinist's needs, but the violinist would rather be attached to you instead. The violinist, Blake argues, does not have a right to place you under an obligation to provide her with goods to which she is morally entitled. The violinist and the immigrant commit the same wrong: they impose an obligation on those who have no independent obligation to accept being so obliged.[46] Prospective immigrants must provide some reason why the residents of the host state have an obligation to become obligated to them. In the absence of such a reason, the state has the right to use coercion to prevent the would-be immigrants from entering the jurisdiction of the state.[47]

What is missing from Blake's account is the irreducibly collective dimension of collective self-determination. It is not simply the freedom of individuals to avoid unwanted obligations that is at stake but also the political community's right of collective self-determination. Immigration does not affect just one individual, as in the violinist example, but the whole collective. It is not simply that obligations to immigrants fall on all members of the collective rather than one individual. When would-be immigrants enter or remain in a country without authorization, they sidestep the political process by which members of the political community can define who the collective self is. This contravenes the right of collective self-determination itself.[48]

Democratic Self-Determination and Immigration Control

I have focused on the value of collective self-determination to defend the state's right to control immigration. I now want to consider *democratic* self-determination. A people can be self-determining through a range of institutional arrangements, democratic and nondemocratic.[49] A people has the right to establish democratic institutions, but this does not mean that they must do so. If the world's most powerful states forcibly impose democracy on a nondemocratic country, they violate the right of self-determination of the people of that country. The value of collective self-determination itself offers a reason to resist the imposition of democracy on nondemocratic countries.

Before considering the relationship between democratic self-determination and immigration control, it is important to make clear what I mean by *democracy*. One prominent conception regards democracy as a fair procedure for aggregating people's interests. On this aggregative conception, democracy requires *equal consideration of the interests* of every individual in the collective decision procedure.[50] By contrast, on a deliberative conception, democracy is understood as *"reasoning together as equals* on matters of common concern."[51] Yet another conception regards democracy as a majoritarian process that gives *equal respect* to participants by respecting their differences of opinion about justice and the common good and giving equal weight to each person's views in the process of collective decision-making.[52] All these conceptions of democracy—indeed, any conception that calls itself democratic—takes equality to be fundamental. In contrast to collective self-determination, which requires that members of the collective have some say in collective decision-making, democratic self-determination requires that members of the collective have an *equal* say in the making of the laws to which they are subject.

Take any of these conceptions of democracy and consider the relationship between *democratic* self-determination and immigration control. First, immigration affects the conditions of democracy. Democratic participation does not happen in a vacuum but in relation to a rich network of institutions. Trust plays an indispensable role here. As Charles Tilly has argued, trust "consists of placing valued outcomes at risk of others' malfeasance, mistakes, or failures." Trust is more likely among a group of people who come together repeatedly within a stable infrastructure of institutions and who share a sense of trust rooted in a shared political culture. The more individuals integrate their trust networks into political institutions, the greater the stake they have in the successful functioning of those institutions. As Tilly puts it, individuals "acquire an unbreakable interest in the performance of government. The political stakes matter."[53] A shared political culture, arising out of interaction in common political institutions, is crucial for fostering trust and solidarity, which in turn enables and reinforces democratic participation.

 Social scientists have found that trust is more likely among people who share a common identity. The existence of racial and ethnic diversity, generated in part by immigration, is said to reduce social trust and solidarity, which in turn may undermine public support for redistributive policies and the deliberative character of democratic politics.[54] If these empirical findings are correct, then we need to have a debate about the tensions and trade-offs between immigration, on the one hand, and economic redistribution and deliberative politics, on the other. Yet, others have questioned the link between national solidarity and support for redistributive policies. Will Kymlicka and Keith Banting have cast doubt on the generalizability of the empirical evidence of the conflict between diversity and trust, which is largely drawn from either research on Africa, where the weakness of state institutions has meant limited usable traditions and weak institutional capacity for dealing with diversity, or on the United States, where racial inequality has been shaped by centuries of slavery and segregation. Where many minority groups are newcomers and where state institutions are strong, the impact of increasing diversity may be quite different.[55] David Miller and Sundas Ali's review of empirical work on the relationship between a shared national identity and support for redistributive policies finds variation across democratic societies and is rather inconclusive about the necessity of national solidarity for the pursuit of social justice.[56] Barbara Arneil has argued that it is not the fact of diversity per se that leads to changes in trust and civic engagement but the *politics* of diversity—that is, how different groups respond to and challenge the norms governing their society and how governments respond.[57] The implication, then, is not necessarily to reduce diversity by reducing immigration but to determine ways of fostering the integration of newcomers, as well as generating trust and solidarity. So, considerations about the impact of immigration on trust, democratic politics, and welfare-state policies do not necessarily support the case for decreasing levels of immigration, but they do show the need to be attentive to the empirical relationship between immigration and the conditions of democracy.

A second way of thinking about the relationship between immigration and democratic self-determination has less to do with the effects of immigration on the demos than with the structure of the right of democratic self-determination. The right to control immigration derives from the right of the demos to rule itself. The aspiration in democratic societies is that all members have an equal right to participate in shaping collective life. Deciding whom to admit into the territory and into political membership is a critical part of the task of defining who the collective is. It is up to members of the democratic political community to debate, contest, and pressure their representatives on the particulars of the immigration policies they would like to see enacted. Abrogating this right of the demos fails to take democratic self-determination seriously.

To say that members of a demos have the right to shape immigration policy is not to say that they can enact any immigration restrictions they please. This right over immigration is a qualified, not an absolute, right. In democratic societies, democratic values and principles should inform and guide public deliberation about immigration policy. It is not just humanitarianism but also democratic values that support taking in refugees who are fleeing persecution and violence in their home countries. Democratic values also support the reunification of families who have been separated by territorial borders and constrain the kinds of immigration restrictions that can be imposed. Categorical exclusions based on race, national origin, or religion are impermissible because they violate democratic norms. I develop these implications in Part III of the book.

If we take the principle of collective self-determination seriously, we can see that the power over immigration is a legitimate power of the people. In democratic societies, members of the people have an equal right to participate in collective decision-making. It is the people themselves who must deliberate and make judgments that authorize policymaking about immigration.

Objections

To develop my argument further, I want to consider two objections. The first has to do with the scope of state coercion and its implications for immigration control. The second has to do with the relationship between self-determination and immigration control.

One objection to my collective self-determination argument as applied to democratic societies comes from strong cosmopolitans concerned with the coercive nature of border controls. When a state enforces immigration restrictions, it subjects virtually everyone in the world to coercion, not just those who are actively trying to enter, but everyone else because they would face the threat of state coercion if they were to try to enter. Arash Abizadeh has argued that states that take democratic legitimacy seriously must justify border controls to everyone who is subject to them. In his view, "a state's regime of border control could only acquire legitimacy if there were cosmopolitan democratic institutions in which borders received actual justifications addressed to both citizens and foreigners."[58] Two assumptions are critical to Abizadeh's argument. First, the justification of coercion must take the form of equally enfranchising all those subject to coercion in a cosmopolitan scheme of democratic institutions, and second, a state's regime of border control coerces everyone in the world.

Regarding the first premise, we can ask whether coercion always requires democratic justification. In the case of foreigners subject to a state's border controls, one might argue that foreigners are entitled to some say but not necessarily an equal say in the collective decision-making that determines immigration policy. As David Miller has argued, those liable to be coerced by a foreign government might voice their concerns through representatives who appear before the legislature of the coercer state before the decision is made.[59] Bilateral treaties and international law can also play a role in constraining states from pursuing coercive policies against other states and their citizens. International law already covers military aggression and refugee law and could be expanded to include transnational economic relations. But Abizadeh might respond, such attempts to grant some, not equal, voice to subjected foreigners fail to take seriously the normative requirements of the coercion principle: state coercion must be democratically justified not just to citizens but all persons over whom it is exercised.

Another response to Abizadeh focuses on his second premise that a state's regime of border control coerces everyone in the world. We can point to disanalogies between territorial insiders and territorial outsiders. One might argue that foreigners are not coerced at all. According to Miller, foreigners are subject to "prevention," not coercion. When someone is prevented from immigrating to the United States, some important options are removed from the person's set of options, but she still has many other options available. On Miller's account, prevention generally requires "much less justification" than coercion. How much justification is required will depend on the value to the agent of the action that is being prevented. In the case of refugees, justifying prevention comes closer to justifying coercion, but where people are not at risk of serious harm, the person who is prevented from migrating is, Miller says, "not being forced to do anything else in particular."[60]

I think a better way of capturing the disanalogy between territorial insiders and outsiders is to view coercion as a matter of degree. Different degrees of coercion require different justifications. The foreigner who wishes to migrate is subject to the immigration power of the state she wishes to enter, but she is not subject to the entire legal system of that state. By contrast, every dimension of a territorial insider's life choices is structured by the laws of the state in which she resides, from the criminal laws to health, education, and tax policies. In virtue of such profound and pervasive coercion, territorial insiders are clearly owed a democratic form of justification, but it is less clear that all territorial outsiders are. They are owed some justification for the policies to which they are subject, but the justification need not take the form of equal enfranchisement in the demos.

There is one more reply we can make to Abizadeh's radically inclusionary argument. Rather than focus on the nature and scope of coercion, we should ask whether subjection to coercion is the proper basis for inclusion in the demos as equal members. As Abizadeh interprets the principle of democratic legitimacy, it must be justifiable to all those who are subject to a state's *coercive power*, but another way to think about the problem of constituting the demos to whom justification is owed is in terms of *legitimate authority*. Democratic legitimacy, as Joshua Cohen puts it, "arises from the discussions and decisions of members, as made within and expressed through social and political institutions designed to acknowledge their collective authority." We can recognize that democracy comes in many forms but also that "more determinate conceptions of it depend on an account of membership in the people, and correspondingly, what it takes for a decision to be *collective*—made by citizens 'as a body.' "[61] The demos is not an aggregation of individuals coerced by the same power; as I have argued, it is a collective body—a people—that is constituted by a history of participating together in ways that express an aspiration to be authors of the rules governing their collective life. So, while many territorial outsiders may be subject to the coercive power of the US government, most cannot claim to share in this history of aspiring to collective self-rule. By contrast, noncitizens who are already present in the territory and participate in collective life do share in this history, as I discuss in chapter 10.

I now turn to consider a second objection, which questions the relationship between collective self-determination and immigration control. A key premise of my argument is that self-determination entails a kind of self-direction of a collective "self." There is a strong and weak version of this argument. The strong version says that one must have full control over the character of her own "self" to be self-determining. The strong view is too demanding to be plausible since both individual and collective agents are, in part, the product of unchosen forces. The weaker version of the argument holds a subtler view of the kind of control we need to have to be self-determining: one must have the ability to act freely based on one's own judgments and desires. What makes a judgment one's own? According to prominent accounts of autonomy, a judgment or desire counts as one's own when the agent endorses it from the perspective of a higher-order attitude that reflects her practical judgment, her ability to weigh and engage with reasons.[62] There is also a critical reasoning component to self-determination: a self-determining agent must be able to reflect on her desires and values and modify or even reject them if she chooses.

What do these reflections on individual agency and self-determination suggest for collective self-determination and immigration control? For immigration to be in tension with collective self-determination, Bas van der Vossen has argued, two conditions must obtain. First, the entry of immigrants must be such as to "bring about a change in *the values of the community as a whole*"; but most forms of immigration do not have this result. The entry of new people into the political community typically does not change communal values; the values and ideas of the new arrivals do not become prominent parts of the state's public deliberations, at least in the short term. Second, when immigration does so change the group's values, the change must come about "in a way that *bypasses* the group's normal processes of deliberation and decision making."[63] So, if the political community is still able to evaluate the newly introduced values through its normal decision-making processes and to choose whether or not to endorse or oppose them, then immigration can change the community's values and character without violating its right to self-determination.

This objection has some force against the nationalist argument for immigration control, which is focused on the *effects* of immigration on the political community. Nationalists are concerned that immigration will interfere with the political community's ability to shape the community's national character. They might contest van der Vossen's first condition, arguing that most forms of regular immigration do impact the character of a political community, especially in the long run. For example, the immigration reform in 1965 marked a turning point in US immigration policy, allowing immigration from Latin America, Asia, and Africa and changing the racial and ethnic composition of the United States. Some proponents of the nationalist view, including Walzer and Miller, would not find the law objectionable simply because it changed the character of American society. They would be concerned about abrogation of the second condition outlined by van der Vossen: that immigration changes the character of society in a way that bypasses the normal processes of collective decision-making. Most forms of immigration seem consistent with a political community continuing to control its character and values; the main exception is if there is a large group of "like-minded people" who move in with the aim of bypassing the existing collective's ability to shape its character.

I think van der Vossen's argument misunderstands the connection between collective self-determination and immigration control. The connection does not depend solely on the particular effects of immigration (i.e., changing the cultural character or the values of a political community in such a way that the political community can no longer exercise self-determination over its future character). Political communities have a right to control immigration because it is a component of collective self-determination, regardless of the particular effects of immigration. Part of what it means for a political community to be self-determining is that it controls whom to admit as new members.

Consider the following example: imagine that a large group of Americans move to Cuba with the intent of settling there permanently and without going through any process by which Cubans could reflect and decide on whether to allow their presence in the country. Let's further stipulate that the Americans do not move there with the intention of bypassing the collective ability of Cubans to shape and evaluate their character and future course and that their presence does not radically alter the character and values of Cuban society because these American ex-pats speak Spanish and are eager to integrate into Cuban society. Has the Cubans' right to collective self-determination been undermined? I think so. This is because the Americans bypassed any process through which their entry and settlement could be authorized by the Cuban people.

Conclusion

If there is any compelling argument for the state's right to control immigration, it rests, I believe, on the right of collective self-determination, a right that flows from the legitimate power of peoples to govern themselves. On my account, the collective is not a nation, the joint-owners of state institutions, or the members of a voluntary association but "a people" engaged in the shared political project of collective self-governance. The right to control immigration is part of the bundle of territorial rights necessary for peoples to be self-determining.

My self-determination argument is not an argument for "closed borders" over "open borders." It speaks to the question of *who* has the right to control immigration, not how open or closed borders should be. Against strong cosmopolitans, I have argued that states have a pro tanto right to control immigration. Against absolutist views of state sovereignty, I have argued that this right is qualified by humanitarian and democratic values. This chapter concludes Part I of the book, which has explored the perspective of political communities. I turn now to Part II, which explores the perspective of prospective migrants.

PART II

Why Not Open Borders?

If people wish to move across borders in search of a better life, why shouldn't they be able to? The dominant position among philosophers and political theorists writing about immigration is that there should be open borders. The following two chapters critically examine the case for open borders. Chapter 5 considers the global distributive justice argument for open borders, and chapter 6 examines rights-based arguments for international freedom of movement.

5

Does Justice Require Open Borders?

UNTIL THE 1980S political theorists and philosophers had been mostly silent on the issue of immigration. They took for granted that their theories applied in the context of the nation-state. To take one prominent example, Rawls says his theory of justice is "for the basic structure of society conceived for the time being as a closed system isolated from other societies."[1] Rawls was not alone in assuming that the legitimacy of state borders and the obligations of distributive justice were based on political membership. Political theorists and philosophers have increasingly turned their attention to immigration over the last several decades. It is not an exaggeration to say that the open borders position has emerged as the dominant normative position.[2]

The case for open borders begins with the premise that all human beings are morally equal and pursues one of two main lines of argument: equality arguments about the demands of global distributive justice and freedom-based arguments about the right to free movement. This chapter focuses on the distributive justice argument. The next chapter examines freedom-based arguments. This chapter begins by laying out the global distributive justice argument for open borders. I argue that it rests on two faulty assumptions: (1) that global distributive justice requires global equality of opportunity, and (2) that global distributive justice requires open borders. I cast doubt on the coherence and desirability of a global equality of opportunity principle and argue that objections to global inequality are better captured by concerns about historical injustice, domination, procedural unfairness, and global poverty. Yet an open borders policy is unlikely to provide an adequate remedy to these concerns.

In showing how the leading arguments for open borders fall short, my aim is not to argue for a policy of closed borders. What is required is neither closed nor open borders but controlled borders and open doors. Considerations of global inequality support some degree of openness toward immigration, but this does not establish a right to entirely uncontrolled immigration.

The Global Distributive Justice Argument for Open Borders

The distributive justice argument for open borders is part of a broader conception of global distributive justice that expands the scope of obligations of justice beyond citizens of one state to include all of humanity. Carens begins with the premise that all human beings are morally equal and interprets it as requiring equality of opportunity:

> [L]iberal egalitarians are committed to equal opportunity. Access to social positions should be determined by an individual's actual talents and capacities, not limited on the basis of arbitrary native characteristics (such as class, race, or sex) . . . [L]iberal egalitarians want to keep actual economic, social and political inequalities as small as possible, partly as a means of realizing equal freedom and equal opportunity and partly as a desirable end in itself.[3]

Ensuring equality of opportunity for fellow compatriots is not enough; what is required is *global* equality of opportunity. Open borders, Carens argues, are "essential for equality of opportunity" because they allow individuals to access opportunities.[4] There is evidence that migrants from developing countries have the most to gain by migrating. On average, migrants from countries that are low on the Human Development Index have seen a fifteenfold increase in income, a doubling in education enrollment rates, and a 160-fold reduction in child mortality when they have moved to higher-HDI countries.[5] This evidence supports Carens's claim that open borders "would clearly contribute to global equality of opportunity." On his vision of global justice, there would be relative equality among states: "[A] just world would be one with roughly the same level of economic development and basic freedoms protected in each state, but with the right to move freely across state borders. That is a plausible, though of course contestable, picture of a just world from a democratic perspective."[6]

Carens is not alone in viewing global distributive justice in terms of global equality of opportunity. Ayelet Shachar's critique of birthright citizenship relies on a similar view: "In an unequal world like our own, birthright citizenship does more than demarcate a form of belonging. It also distributes voice and opportunity in a vastly unequal manner."[7] Simon Caney and Darrel Moellendorf also take the position that global justice ought to be understood as guaranteeing equality of opportunity, regardless of which society one is born into.[8]

It is important to get clear what is meant by equality of opportunity in these arguments. I focus on Rawls's principle of fair equality of opportunity because of its influence on subsequent discussions:

> [T]hose who are at the *same level of talent and ability*, and have the *same willingness* to use them, should have the *same prospects of success* regardless of their initial place in the social system, that is, irrespective of the income class into which they were born. In all sectors of society there should be roughly equal prospects of culture and achievement for everyone similarly motivated and endowed.[9]

Notice that the equal opportunity principle applies only to people who have the same level of ability and the same willingness to use it. If you and I are competing for a spot on the basketball team and you get the spot, I cannot claim that I've been denied equal opportunity unless you and I have similar levels of ability and similar motivation to use our ability. In other words, equality of opportunity is aimed at ensuring a level playing field for people who are already similarly talented and similarly motivated.

Recall that Rawls restricts the scope of his principles of justice, including equality of opportunity, to one society, which he assumes is "a closed system isolated from other societies."[10] By contrast, Carens and Moellendorf expand the scope of Rawls's principle of equality of opportunity to the entire world. The global principle of equal opportunity holds that *all human beings* who have the same level of ability and the same willingness to use it should have the same prospects of benefit, defined in terms of well-being, income, standard of living, or some other metric. As Moellendorf puts it, "[I]f [global] equality of opportunity were realized, a child growing up in rural Mozambique would be statistically as likely as the child of a senior executive at a Swiss bank to reach the position of the latter's parent."[11] He suggests that global equality of opportunity requires that everyone in the world have the *same* opportunity sets. The implication for immigration is that there should be open borders and open admissions into citizenship to provide the same opportunity sets for everyone.

One problem with the global equality of opportunity principle is that it presupposes a universal metric for measuring opportunities, ignoring cultural differences between societies in how different opportunities are valued. Perhaps it is more plausible to say that global equality of opportunity requires that people have *equivalent*, not the same, opportunity sets. So the child from rural Mozambique should have an equal chance to attain a senior executive post in a bank somewhere, not necessarily in Switzerland, with the same salary and benefits as a similarly talented and motivated child of a Swiss banker. In order to decide whether the two opportunity sets are equivalent, however, we still need a universal metric or standard of equality that applies globally.[12] We might be able to reach some agreement on certain items that should be included in the global list of equal opportunities, but given the culturally pluralistic understandings of what counts as opportunities, we may run into difficulties in reaching agreement on a globally shared meaning. How can we judge whether a child in Mozambique has better or worse educational opportunities than a child in Switzerland? We can certainly find metrics for making comparisons (literacy, numeracy, etc.), but we encounter another difficulty: how to decide whether it is appropriate to merge specific metrics into more general ones. For example, we might say that people in one country have better educational opportunities but that people in another country have better cultural or leisure opportunities. The valuation of all metrics into more general metrics will vary from society to society, based in part on the community's shared values. The fact of pluralism between societies about what constitutes the relevant metric for a global equality of opportunity principle poses serious, though perhaps not insurmountable, challenges.

A second, more serious problem with the global equality of opportunity principle is that it gives little weight to relationships and group memberships as a source of obligations. For proponents of global equal opportunity, what matters is whether one is a human being, not whether we stand in particular relationships or institutional contexts with others. By contrast, a relational approach to equality holds that distinctive obligations arise out of the particular relationships and group memberships that we have with others. This is the idea of associative obligations that I discussed in chapter 1. If equality and justice are fundamentally relational ideals, then our particular relationships and institutional contexts should matter for the types of distributive obligations we have. When it comes to principles of egalitarian distributive justice, it is reasonable to think that such principles are relevant in certain relational contexts—for example, as a way of ensuring that people are not subordinated or marginalized within relationships or institutional contexts of which they are a part.[13] As I argue in chapter 4, membership in a political community is a distinctive relationship, based not only on shared subjection but also on a shared project of collective self-governance, which generates special obligations. Political membership grounds a claim to a more extensive set of rights and obligations than the global obligations we have to all human beings.

This relational approach applies to the equality of opportunity principle. For example, when we claim that equality of opportunity in education has been denied, we assume that there is a government or some set of institutions that can make and enforce policies that outlaw discrimination in school admissions and ensure that academic standards are applied uniformly across different schools. The problem with the global equal opportunity principle is that there is no global agent responsible for ensuring global equality of opportunity in education. Proponents of open borders might argue that the absence of global governance structures does not undermine the claim that children in Mozambique are entitled to equality of opportunity in education on a level playing field with children in the United States and that leveling the playing field requires allowing children to go to where the opportunities are. But this response misses the relational point that claims of equal opportunity only apply to a group of people governed by shared institutions that have the power and authority to ensure equal opportunity. We lack such institutions at the global level. We need to look to other principles to capture injustices at the global level.

What Is Objectionable about Inequality and Its Relationship to Injustice

Now, one might reject the relational view that we have special obligations by virtue of our particular relationships and memberships and instead endorse the claim made by proponents of global equality of opportunity: because the distribution of citizenship is morally arbitrary, and being born a citizen of a wealthy country is hugely unfair given the enormous inequalities of wealth and opportunity that exist between countries, people should be permitted to migrate to where the opportunities are. This section is intended to speak to nonrelational egalitarians and to relational egalitarians by considering different kinds of inequality and whether they constitute injustice. I consider a diversity of reasons for objecting to inequality and then examine the implications for the global distributive justice argument for open borders.[14] My aim is to cast doubt on the claim that combatting unjust forms of global inequality requires open borders. What follows is by no means intended as an

exhaustive list; I focus on what I take to be some leading reasons for objecting
to inequality.

Historical Injustice

One circumstance in which we might think global inequalities are unjust is
where one country's wealth or poverty is the direct result of conquest, theft, or
exploitation by another country. Whether past injustices should be rectified
or whether they might be "superseded" are hard questions. Some argue that
past injustices per se do not make an existing order unjust; we need to show
how past injustices have contributed to injustice that persists into the present
day. It is difficult to determine causal responsibility for persisting injustices,
and connecting causal responsibility with moral responsibility for remedying
ongoing injustices is also difficult.[15] If we can determine who bears remedial
responsibility for the injustice, for our task at hand—considering whether
global justice requires open borders—we need to ask, Is the appropriate response to historical injustice the provision of global equality of opportunity
via open borders or some more narrowly tailored response that more directly
addresses the historical injustice and its persisting effects?

Considerations of historical injustice do not offer a clear-cut case for open
borders. In the context of immigration, rectification arguments have been
made on behalf of particular groups of people who have suffered injustices,
not on behalf of everyone who wants to migrate. For example, Walzer argues
that the US government had an obligation to admit Vietnamese refugees considering US intervention and war in Vietnam.[16] A similar argument might
be made in response to colonial occupation and subjugation: former colonial powers have an obligation to admit colonial subjects to compensate for
the injustices of colonialism. Along these lines, Rogers Smith has argued
that modern constitutional democracies are morally obligated to extend the
option of full membership to "all those whose identities have been substantially constituted through such regimes' coercive policies."[17] Such backward-
looking remedial arguments offer more compelling responses to what is owed
to those harmed by historical injustice than a general policy of open borders,
which applies to everyone in the world.

Domination

Another reason why inequality might be objectionable is that it gives some
people an unacceptable degree of power over the lives of others. Economic

power is an obvious example. Those who have vastly greater resources not only have more materially comfortable lives; they also get to determine what gets produced, how resources get distributed, and so on. The economically powerful have greater control over government and the media, which reinforces their dominant position in the economy. When it comes to relations between countries, when rich countries or powerful corporations interact with much poorer countries, the former set the terms of interaction in their favor. For example, wealthy countries use their power to establish terms of trade, lending, and conventions about the permissible use of military force in ways that favor their interests at the expense of those of developing countries. Thomas Pogge has argued that wealthy countries have shored up their power by creating and imposing unjust international resource and borrowing privileges upon the global poor.[18] As with historical injustice, the underlying concern here is not with ensuring equality of opportunity for everyone across the globe but with the violation of the rights of the poor.

What does the domination objection to inequality imply for immigration? A policy of open borders is neither necessary nor sufficient to reduce inequalities of power between countries. Open borders may improve the economic position of those migrants who move from poor to rich countries, but such migration is unlikely to reduce intercountry inequalities of power in any serious way and may even contribute to worsening intercountry inequalities via brain drain, which I discuss later in the chapter. There is a mismatch in the unit of analysis here: if a country as a collective entity is dominated, how is that domination addressed by the migration of individual citizens of that country to other countries? A more radical argument about power would be to call into question the legitimacy of the entire system of states on the grounds that the global order premised on the state system harms much of the world's population in the sense of thwarting their interests,[19] but we would have no need to debate open borders in a world without states.

Furthermore, open borders may exacerbate global economic inequalities, reinforcing domination of already vulnerable individuals. The implicit sociology underlying the open borders position is a benign liberal cosmopolitan scenario: in a world of open borders, it would be people from poor countries migrating to wealthier countries. But a neoliberal scenario seems more likely: wealthy individuals moving across borders in search of beautiful natural landscapes, attractive cultural opportunities, and even better economic opportunities than what they already enjoy. After all, the wealthy have resources that facilitate migration and settlement in other countries, including in poorer countries with attractive landscapes. They can buy up property and take control of economic and political life in those areas. If this were to happen—and proponents of open borders haven't given us reason to think it wouldn't—open borders would reinforce rather than ameliorate the economic vulnerability of people in poor countries.

Procedural Unfairness

Another reason we might be concerned about inequality is that it undermines the fairness of basic social and political institutions. To take a familiar example, great inequality in family income and wealth contributes to inequality in people's prospects of success in the marketplace. The basic idea is that procedural fairness requires equality of starting places. This is weakly egalitarian because even after equal starting positions are provided, large inequalities could result and they would not be objectionable so long as they did not impair a fair process.

Consider another familiar example: how economic inequality threatens the fairness of the political process. Critics of the US Supreme Court decision striking down restrictions on political speech by corporations and unions argue that the fairness of the political process has been undermined.[20] Regulating the role of money in politics by placing limits on campaign contributions and through the public financing of political campaigns and election expenditures are, in Rawls's words, "essential to maintain the fair value of the political liberties."[21] The argument here is for ensuring equality of starting places via public financing of political campaigns and restrictions on campaign contributions.

What are the implications of the procedural fairness objection to inequality for immigration? Opening borders is not likely to lead to greater procedural fairness in interactions between countries. In the domestic context, one way to try to prevent inequalities of income and wealth from creating unfairness is through regulatory measures, such as employment contracts, inheritance taxes, and campaign finance restrictions. In the international realm, we can insist on the duty of fair dealing among countries, including nonexploitation; the duty to curb the capacity of one country's citizens or corporations to harm or exploit citizens of other states; and doing one's fair share to address common global problems. Since such regulatory measures are unlikely to be enacted on a global scale anytime soon, another strategy would be one in which richer countries compete with one another, thereby checking each other's power vis-à-vis third parties. Neither strategy depends on opening borders.

Unequal Benefit

There may be circumstances in which justice requires not only equality of starting places but also equality of outcomes. As Scanlon puts it, "[I]f members of a group have equal claims to a certain benefit, then a distributive procedure that is supposed to be responsive to these claims will be fair only if it yields equal shares."[22] The egalitarian thrust of this claim rests on the antecedent being true—that members of certain groups do have prima facie equal claims to the benefits produced. For example, we could say that partners in a business venture have equal claims to the benefits produced by their venture. One might also say that a society is a cooperative scheme for mutual benefit in which members have equal claims to the benefits of social cooperation. The basic idea is that if each member has the same claim to be given a certain kind of benefit, then, absent special justification, each should receive this benefit. Yet, as Scanlon suggests, the idea seems false since every member of a group may be in extreme need, but it does not follow that I must benefit all of them equally or that I need a strong reason to benefit some more than others. To make the claim for equal benefit plausible, we need to add something about the stringency of the claims in question—that is, that some individual or institutional agent is obligated to respond to *all* of the claims equally.

What are the implications for immigration? Strong cosmopolitans like Carens seem to hold highly stringent assumptions about both the content and scope of the claim for equal benefit. They assume that respecting the moral equality of all human beings requires providing everyone with a full range of benefits, including opportunities for education and jobs, and we must provide strong reasons to benefit some more than others.

In response, three points are worth emphasizing. First, an open borders policy is a limited, perhaps even counterproductive, means to pursuing a global principle of equal benefit insofar as the individuals most likely to take advantage of an open borders policy are the members of poorer societies who are relatively advantaged.

Second, the principles of equality of opportunity and equal benefit presuppose participation in a shared scheme of social cooperation. For example, in thinking about the distribution of education or jobs, whether the principle of equality of opportunity or equal benefit applies depends in part on there being competition: when people compete for certain goods, the fairness of the competition and its outcomes will depend on the relative positions from which the competitors began. Scanlon suggests the differences in the quality of education between two localities in the United States, as opposed to between the United States and Mozambique, are more objectionable on egalitarian grounds because there is no competition between students in the United States and students in Mozambique. The argument for preserving equal starting places or equal benefits holds only where there is competition of this kind.

Third, the membership-based approach I am developing in this book is less stringent. As I discuss in chapter 1, we have global obligations, but we also have special obligations to members of our own political community. To value one's membership in a political community just is to see one's political membership as giving reasons to do things on behalf of members. At the same time, valuing political membership need not entail ignoring the suffering of people in other countries. We must balance special obligations of political membership with global obligations to those beyond our borders. I will say more about what this requires in terms of immigration later in the chapter.

Unequal Status

Another objection to inequality centers on inequalities of social status that lead some statuses to be viewed as superior and others as inferior. Political and economic inequalities are often associated with status inequalities in a society, which, in Rawls's words, "may arouse widespread attitudes of deference and servility on one side and a will to dominate and arrogance on the other." Because status is a "positional good," if I seek a higher status for myself, I support a scheme that entails others having a lower status. When it comes to income and wealth, the well-being enjoyed by some may set the standard for society such that those who are much worse off feel inferiority and shame. Rawls points to "fixed status ascribed by birth, or by gender or race" as "particularly odious."[23] Strong cosmopolitans might extend the critique across state borders, arguing that economic inequality on a global scale generates similarly objectionable inequalities of status. For example, in critiquing citizenship as the "modern equivalent of feudal privilege," Carens argues that citizenship is a morally unjustifiable status ascribed by birth.[24]

It is important to emphasize that Scanlon's and Rawls's discussions are focused on the ideal of equal status within one society—in particular, a democratic society in which members of the society regard one another as equals. The idea of status as a "positional good" presupposes a set of shared understandings about social status and its relationship to political and economic inequalities. Even if we could agree that there is a globally shared understanding of social status such that some are clearly on top and others are at the bottom, it is not clear that open borders would alleviate global inequalities of status. In a world of open borders, migrants may move from poorer countries to wealthier countries, but their movement would be unlikely to disrupt the existing global hierarchy of social status. Indeed, open borders may exacerbate inequalities of status insofar as the more privileged members of poorer countries migrate to wealthier countries.

Insufficiency

Perhaps the strongest objection to inequality arises from the concern to alleviate human suffering and deprivation. Consider the following facts about global poverty:

1.1 billion people lack access to safe drinking water;[25]

795 million people (about one in nine people in the world) suffer from chronic undernourishment;[26]

2.4 billion people lack access to improved sanitation (flush toilets or latrines with a slab), and 950 million people practice open defecation for lack of other options;[27]

1.6 billion people lack adequate shelter.[28]

These facts describe extreme deprivation and provoke a sense of moral urgency, but our motivation to respond is not rooted in opposition to inequality per se. The reason for acting toward greater equality seems to be, in Scanlon's words, "a function of the urgency of the claims of those who are worse off, not the magnitude of the gap which separates them from their more fortunate neighbors."[29] In other words, the central concern is to improve the situation of the world's worst off above some threshold, not to reduce inequality per se. Along these lines, Harry Frankfurt has argued for replacing the concern for equality with a principle of sufficiency: "What is important from the moral point of view is not that everyone should have *the same* but that each should have *enough*. If everyone had enough, it would be of no moral consequence whether some had more than others."[30] On this view, the existence of economic inequality is not in itself objectionable. There is no intrinsic importance to narrowing or eliminating the *gap* between rich and poor, domestically or globally. There may be circumstances in which, even if everyone had enough, some having more than others is objectionable, but the objection is grounded in reasons having to do with historical injustice, domination, and fairness.

My aim is not to argue for the sufficiency principle as the best account of our domestic or global distributive obligations. Instead, my point is that the concern for sufficiency captures the core concern of the global distributive justice argument for open borders: to raise all human beings above some basic level of well-being. What animates Carens's case for open borders is a concern for the world's most disadvantaged:

> The exclusion of *so many poor and desperate people* seems hard to justify from a perspective that takes seriously the claims of all individuals as free and equal moral persons.[31]

Concern for the world's most disadvantaged is reflected in his choice of examples in his earliest essay on open borders:

> To Haitians in small, leaky boats confronted by armed Coast Guard cutters, to Salvadorans dying from heat and lack of air after being smuggled into the Arizona desert, to Guatemalans crawling through rat-infested sewer pipes from Mexico to California—to these people the borders, guards and guns are all too apparent. What justifies the use of force against such people?[32]

In his most recent work, Carens focuses on the poor in reiterating his defense of open borders:

> [A]rguing for open borders draws attention to the fact that at least some of the people who are poor remain poor because we will not let them in . . . Opening borders might not be the best way to address these problems, but the open borders argument takes away any justification for complacency and inaction.[33]

As these examples suggest, it is concern for the world's poorest that underlies the global distributive justice argument for open borders. If that is the true concern, then what global justice requires is not a general principle of global equality of opportunity or a general policy of open borders but the wealthiest countries opening their borders to the world's poorest people. I turn now to assessing this claim.

The Limits of Open Borders as a Response to Global Poverty

You might agree that not all global inequalities per se constitute injustice yet nonetheless argue that a policy of open borders is required to alleviate global poverty. Compared with the most advantaged human beings, the level of opportunity enjoyed by the world's least advantaged is far below what justice would allow. So, a global sufficientarian might argue:

1. Global distributive justice requires that the opportunity-level of the least advantaged be raised considerably so that it reaches an adequacy threshold.
2. There is no reasonable prospect for raising the level sufficiently unless a regime of open borders is established.

As I argued earlier, open borders are neither necessary nor sufficient for meeting a strict equality of opportunity principle applied globally. I believe the same is true of meeting the opportunity threshold applied globally. I offer both normative and empirical arguments to cast doubt on the notion that open borders will alleviate global poverty.

First, proponents of open borders assume that open borders will reduce global poverty in part by permitting the poor to migrate to wealthier countries, but empirical studies suggest that it is not the poorest but those who have some financial means and access to human and social capital who are more likely to migrate. As the economists Devesh Kapur and John McHale put it, "Indeed the greater the economic travails of the country, the greater the likelihood that those trying to [migrate] will be more educated and skilled."[34] The poorest citizens lack the knowledge, skills, and resources necessary to undertake the risks of migrating. Migration is, of course, regulated by the immigration laws of receiving countries, so current flows should not be taken as definitive of who is likely to migrate if borders were opened. But we have good reasons to think that those most likely to migrate would not be the world's poorest people but those who are already more advantaged in terms of skills and resources.

Consider the following points of evidence. The first has to do with very low rates of migration from the poorest countries. Even though people from the poorest countries have the most to gain from moving, they are the least mobile. For example, only 3 percent of Africans live in a country other than the one they were born in and less than 1 percent of Africans live in Europe. If we correlate emigration rates with levels of development, the relationship resembles a "hump" whereby emigration rates are lower in poor and rich countries than they are among countries with moderate levels of development. The median emigration rate in countries with low levels of human development is only about one-third of the rate out of countries with high levels of human development.[35] Household-level studies also suggest that poverty is a serious constraint to emigration. A study of Mexican households found that the probability of migration increased with higher income levels for household incomes lower than $15,000 per year.[36] After assessing such studies, the 2009 UN Development Report concludes that "the potential of mobility to improve the well-being of disadvantaged groups is limited, because these groups are often least likely to move."[37]

Second, we also need to consider the impact of migration on those who stay behind. The emigration of large groups of skilled individuals is not likely to improve, and may worsen, the position of those who are left behind. Emigrants do send remittances back home, but because the emigrants are typically not from the poorest class, the money they send goes to the more privileged in the poor countries that receive the remittances. Some of these funds may trickle down to assist the poorest members of the sending countries, but the remittances may also reinforce existing inequalities within the sending countries. Remittances aside, those who are left behind would suffer from the departure of their more educated compatriots who possess the skills necessary to demand and build better institutions in their home country. This is the concern that has come to be called the brain-drain problem. Although the negative effects vary by country and by sector, emigration, especially of more productive members of society, is likely to hurt the institutional development of developing countries.[38]

Third, the simple fact of moving to a wealthy country does not ensure that one will get a job. As Rainer Bauböck has argued, the most likely effect is a reduction in wage differentials between sending and receiving countries, but this is an average effect and the side effects of deregulating labor markets may well lead to even greater inequality and no net reduction of poverty worldwide.[39]

Finally, we see how truly limited a policy of open borders targeted at the world's poorest would be when we consider the sheer number of people who are in desperate need. There are 795 million people, about one in nine people, in the world who suffer from chronic undernourishment. Even if hundreds of thousands of them were able to migrate to wealthy countries, millions more would be left in need. The sheer scale of migration that would be necessary to alleviate global poverty through migration gives us reasons to doubt the feasibility of an open borders policy as a primary answer to global poverty. These empirical claims about feasibility do not block the normative claim that we *should* accept a policy of open borders as one tool for alleviating global poverty. But on the realistically utopian approach developed in this book, such empirical considerations should be brought to bear in reflecting on how to pursue the goal of alleviating global poverty.

Carens himself seems to acknowledge the limits of an open borders policy when he says, "Opening borders might not be the best way to address these problems, but the open borders argument takes away any justification for complacency and inaction."[40] Building on Carens's concession about the limits of an open borders *policy*, I think we should re-channel the normative force of the open borders *argument* by linking it directly to another tool in the broader debate about global distributive justice: development assistance. If alleviating global poverty really is the animating concern behind the open borders argument, it is both more desirable and feasible to turn to development assistance aimed at addressing global poverty rather than opening borders to everyone. Remedying certain forms of injustice will sometimes require targeted admissions policies, as in the case of countries that have contributed to the creation of refugee crises.[41] Otherwise, the global redistribution of resources is a more effective and desirable alternative to open borders. Development assistance can take many forms, including not only money transfers but also assistance in building institutions. Money transfers cannot happen without a reliable way of distributing funds to individuals who may not have bank accounts they can access and an environment in which individuals can spend money. What is needed are institutional improvements in building up infrastructure in banking, medicine, and education.[42]

In sum, immigration policy is just one tool—and not the best tool—for discharging our global obligations. The central focus of a theory of global distributive justice should be not on moving people from poorer to richer countries but on improving conditions and opportunities in poorer countries. The global distributive justice argument for open borders points to an important qualification of the right of states to restrict immigration: wealthy states cannot exclude the world's poorest people if they do not do their part to alleviate global poverty by providing development assistance and through other measures aimed at ensuring a minimally adequate standard of living for all.

Conclusion

This chapter has offered a critique of the claim that global justice requires open borders by challenging two key assumptions: (1) that global distributive justice requires global equality of opportunity and (2) that global distributive justice requires open borders. If one accepts that equality and justice are fundamentally relational ideals, then our particular relationships and institutional contexts should matter for the types of distributive obligations we have. This does not mean that we have no global obligations. Some circumstances of global inequality constitute injustice, and in those circumstances, we have an obligation to remedy the injustice. Yet even in cases where inequality constitutes injustice, an open borders policy is unlikely to provide an adequate remedy. In cases of historical injustice, the proper response is not a general policy of open borders but a targeted admissions policy for those who have suffered injustice. An open borders policy is also limited as a response to concerns about domination, procedural unfairness, and global poverty.

Alleviating global poverty is the major animating concern of the global distributive-justice argument for open borders, but it is typically not the world's poorest who migrate, and the departure of a country's more-skilled members tends to deepen, not mitigate, global inequality. Development assistance is a better way of meeting our obligations to the global poor. Next, I consider freedom-based arguments for open borders.

6

Is There a Right to Free Movement across Borders?

RESIDENTS OF OHIO enjoy the right to move to California if they wish. Residents of Ontario or Oaxaca may want to move to California for the same reason. Why shouldn't they be able to? In arguing for freedom of international movement as a basic right, some appeal to international human rights documents.[1] Article 13.1 of the Universal Declaration of Human Rights states, "Everyone has the right to freedom of movement and residence within the borders of each state." Article 12 of the International Covenant on Civil and Political Rights also says: "Everyone lawfully within the territory of a State shall, within that territory, have the right to liberty of movement and freedom to choose his residence"; "Everyone shall be free to leave any country, including his own"; and "No one shall be arbitrarily deprived of the right to enter his own country." But these international human rights documents restrict the scope of free movement. They refer to the right of free movement of those lawfully *within* a country, the right to *leave* any country, and the right to *enter one's own* country. There is no general right of international freedom of movement under current international law. What about as a matter of morality?

This chapter examines several freedom-based arguments in support of a general moral right to freedom of international movement. The first claims freedom of movement is a fundamental human right in itself. The second adopts a "cantilever" strategy, arguing that freedom of international movement is a logical extension of existing fundamental rights, including the right of domestic free movement and the right to exit one's country. The third argument, developed by libertarians, is that international free movement is necessary to respect individual freedom of association and contract. This chapter shows how these arguments fall short of justifying a general right to free movement across borders.

A Human Right to Migration

The most direct argument for a general right of migration rests on the premise that freedom of movement is a fundamental right in itself. As Darrel Moellendorf argues, "Restrictive immigration policies appear to be a blatant violation of the right to freedom of movement."[2] Joseph Carens holds that freedom of movement is "a basic human right from a liberal egalitarian perspective"; thus, "the presumption is for free migration and anyone who would defend restrictions faces a heavy burden of proof."[3] Kieran Oberman also argues that people have "a human right to immigrate to other states." The claim here is not only for a right to travel to another country for a temporary period of time but a right "to enter and reside in foreign states for as long as they like."[4] In arguing that we have a human right to immigrate, proponents are really making two claims: first, that people have an interest in immigration that is fundamental to their well-being, and second, that this interest is of sufficient weight to ground a duty on others to respect her right to immigrate.[5]

To assess whether we have a human right to immigrate, we need a theory of human rights that tells us what the purpose and grounds of human rights are. Theories of human rights tend to be grounded on some account of basic human needs or fundamental human interests. The content of human rights is far from settled, but most accounts include a list of basic rights encompassing core human needs necessary for a decent human life. The basic rights included in the key human rights conventions in international law are

> the right to life, the right to security of the person, and the right against torture;
> the right against enslavement;
> the right to resources for subsistence;
> the rights of due process and equality before the law;
> the right to freedom from religious persecution and against at least the more systematic forms of religious discrimination;
> the right to freedom of expression;
> the right to association; and
> the right against persecution and against at least the more systematic forms of discrimination on grounds of ethnicity, race, gender, and sexual orientation.[6]

The direct argument for a human right to immigrate depends on showing that immigration is necessary for people to live decent lives. There are nomadic peoples whose way of life may require movement across borders, such as gypsies, Roma, and nomadic peoples of Mongolia, but these ways of life are quite specific and do not apply to most of humanity. A direct argument for a human right to immigrate must be grounded in generalizable human interests. Oberman argues that we have a general interest in having access to "the full range of existing life options." By "life options" he means "options that give our lives meaning and purpose: friends, family, civic associations, expressive opportunities, religions, jobs, and marriage partners."[7] Options include not only what we have already chosen (attachments) but also options we haven't chosen but which we may wish to pursue in the future (possibilities). Possibilities include forming new relationships, joining new associations, and learning about and converting to new religions.[8] To access the full range of life options, people must have the right to migrate to countries of their choosing.

It is important to note that the basic human interest at stake in Oberman's argument is not freedom of movement itself but our interest in forming and pursuing particular relationships and goals. It is undeniable that people must be able to move freely in physical space to fulfill this basic interest, but how extensive must the scope of free movement be? On the one hand, confining a person to her house or her neighborhood would be objectionable. She would not be able to exercise her basic freedoms, including the freedom to associate with family and friends and the freedom to engage in religious worship. Restricting a person's freedom of movement in such a way would deny her the chance to live a decent life. On the other hand, the right of free movement cannot be unlimited. Some limits on free movement are justifiable. For example, my right of free movement does not permit me to interfere with your body unless you give me permission. I cannot walk upon your property without your consent except in special circumstances. I cannot move about the public highway in any way I please. These constraints are not merely matters of efficiency or convenience; they are principled constraints, constraints we have good reasons for accepting, including respecting the liberty of others. What about freedom of movement across borders?

A conception of human rights should reflect general interests that people have, but when it comes to determining the specific form these interests should take, it should take account of what is feasible. Under conditions of moderate scarcity, saying everyone should have access to a full range of options seems radically utopian.[9] This concern with feasibility has led David Miller to argue for what we might call an adequacy account of free movement: what people need is adequate, not unlimited, freedom of movement to protect the basic interests that the right to free movement is intended to protect.[10] Having access to an adequate range of options is necessary for personal autonomy. Personal autonomy also requires that we possess the mental capacities to create and pursue life plans and be free from subjection to the will of another through coercion.[11] What constitutes an adequate range of options is famously difficult to specify, but a good place to start is an account of basic human interests of the sort reflected in the list above.

There are cases in which international migration is necessary for individuals to have their basic interests met, but in many cases, respecting people's freedom to move about *within* their country seems sufficient to protect their basic interests. If one has the right to security, subsistence, and freedom of religion and expression within one's country, international freedom of movement is not required to vindicate these basic interests. There are circumstances in which international migration *is* morally required to meet people's basic interests. The paradigmatic cases involve those fleeing persecution and violence. In such cases, international migration is necessary to secure basic interests, but the right to migrate in such cases derives not from a human right to immigrate. Rather, it is a *remedial right* that is justified by the fact that the person's basic interests cannot be met in the country where she resides because of state persecution or the state's failure to secure an individual's freedom from persecution by third parties.

While the adequacy account is attractive in certain respects, it runs into a serious problem: it restricts not only international migration but also domestic migration. Say a resident of Ohio wants to move to California; but if she has access to an adequate range of options in Ohio, she would not be permitted to migrate across the country.[12] While our interest in having an adequate range of options provides some justification for the right to domestic migration, which many take to be a fundamental right, it does not show why that right should extend across the entire territory of the country. This suggests the need to look elsewhere for the grounds of domestic free movement.

Proponents of the human right to immigrate point to another problem with the adequacy view: it misses the fundamental interest at stake for migrants. As Carens puts it, people have a "vital interest in being able to go where you want to go and do what you want to do, so long as you do not violate anyone else's rights." The vital interest he refers to is "freedom itself."[13] But the appeal to freedom *as such* doesn't get us very far. One person's right to freedom as such comes into conflict with everyone else's freedom as such.

A regime of property rights infringes on your freedom as such by preventing you from entering my house uninvited. Sexual harassment law infringes on your freedom as such by regulating your conduct toward your colleagues in the workplace. A plausible theory of rights must be more precise, developing a set of rights that are broadly consistent with one another such that we don't include rights whose exercise would interfere with other rights we regard as fundamental. Freedom of movement is instrumentally valuable: we must move to pursue relationships, engage in religious worship, and pursue educational and job opportunities. Most of the time, domestic freedom of movement is sufficient to exercise these basic freedoms.

This reply will not satisfy those who think freedom of movement is not merely instrumentally valuable but also intrinsically valuable as a constituent of what is good in itself. This intrinsic view is echoed in the 2009 UN Human Development Report's definition of freedom of movement: "people's ability to choose the place they call home is a dimension of human freedom that we refer to as *human mobility.*" It is "a dimension of freedom that is part of development—with intrinsic as well as potential instrumental value."[14] Even if we grant the view that freedom of movement has intrinsic value, we would still have to show that the interest in free movement is of sufficient weight to hold others under a duty. To establish that others have a duty to respect my right of free movement, we must compare the strength of the interests protected under the proposed right against the strength of countervailing interests. Whether a right generates a duty depends not only on the basis of that right but also on the absence of conflicting considerations.

In the case of immigration, there are countervailing considerations that support principled constraints on my right of freedom of movement, including your right to bodily integrity and your property rights. Another countervailing consideration is a political community's right of self-determination. To return to the 2009 UN Human Development Report on migration, its authors do not advocate "wholesale liberalization of international mobility" because they "recognize that people at destination places have a right to shape their societies, and that borders are one way in which people delimit the sphere of their obligations to those whom they see as members of their community."[15] As I argue in chapter 4, the right of collective self-determination is an important countervailing consideration that justifies limits on freedom of movement.

To return to an earlier example, imagine there were open borders between Cuba and the United States with the attendant openness to American economic might.[16] If American billionaires decided that Cuba's natural beauty could be used for unrestricted tourism and started buying up land in Cuba, there is very little, according to Carens or Oberman, that would allow them to be excluded. Given a world characterized by global inequalities of the kinds discussed in chapter 5, unrestricted migration would involve not only the world's less advantaged moving to rich countries but the world's most privileged moving to poor countries. There is the real possibility that unrestricted migration would undermine the ability of members of less-advantaged states from exercising collective self-determination, thereby exacerbating political injustice. If there is a right to migrate, it is contextual and depends on its effects not only on migrants but also on sending and receiving countries.

Let me now turn to the "cantilever" arguments for the moral right of freedom of international movement. These arguments begin with rights we regard as fundamental and argue that international free movement is a logical extension of these rights. There are two consistency claims. The first rests on an analogy between domestic and international free movement. The second rests on an analogy between exit and entry.

From Domestic to International Freedom of Movement?

Some proponents of open borders analogize domestic migration and international migration, arguing that the reasons that support domestic freedom of movement also support international freedom of movement. Carens has argued that "treating the freedom to move across state borders as a human right is a logical extension of the well-established democratic practice of treating freedom of movement within state borders as a human right."[17] To pursue our life plans and relationships, we need the freedom to migrate not only domestically but internationally:

> Every reason why one might want to move within a state may also be a reason for moving between states. One might want a job; one might fall in love with someone from another country; one might belong to a religion that has few adherents in one's native state and many in another; one might wish to pursue cultural opportunities that are only available in another land. The radical disjuncture that treats freedom of movement within the state as a human right while granting states discretionary control over freedom of movement across state borders makes no moral sense. We should extend the existing human right of

free movement. We should recognize the freedom to migrate, to travel, and to reside wherever one chooses, as a human right.[18]

The cantilever argument rests on the claim that the very same values underlying the right to domestic free movement also support the right to international free movement. What are the grounds of the right to domestic free movement and can they be extended to international free movement?

I begin by looking to the law as courts have taken up the question of domestic migration. In 1849, the US Supreme Court declared the right to domestic migration to be a basic right of political membership.

> For all the great purposes for which the Federal government was formed, we are one people, with one common country. We are all citizens of the United States; and, as members of the same community, must have the right to pass and repass through every part of it without interruption, as freely as in our own States.[19]

The court has never questioned the assumption that the right to domestic migration is constitutionally protected, but it has not settled on a clear basis for the right. Writing over one hundred years later, the court said:

> Although the Articles of Confederation provided that 'the people of each State shall have free ingress and regress to and from any other State,' that right finds no explicit mention in the Constitution. The reason, it has been suggested, is that a right so elementary was conceived from the beginning to be a necessary concomitant of the stronger Union the Constitution created. In any event, freedom to travel throughout the United States has long been recognized as a basic right under the Constitution.[20]

The court suggests that the strength of the country depends on the ability of its citizens to travel freely. It also says that the right to domestic free movement has become a part of the nation's tradition. While the argument from tradition and precedent is good enough for the court, it is unconvincing as a normative justification since it assumes that the founders were correct in their assessment of the relevant values and costs associated with the right to domestic migration.

So why should we regard the right to domestic free movement as a basic right of membership? While the court has not explicitly located the right in

any specific value, the court has implicitly emphasized certain values as underlying the right to domestic migration. The first is the value of personal autonomy. In the *Slaughter-House Cases*, the Court declared, "The right to move
with freedom, to choose his highway, and to be exempt from impositions,
belongs to the citizen."[21] In a 1969 case, Justice Stewart proclaimed the right
to domestic migration as "assertable against private interference as well as
governmental action . . . a virtually unconditional personal right, guaranteed
by the Constitution to us all."[22]

There are two distinct components of autonomy at stake. The first has
to do with the necessity of domestic migration to access an adequate range
of options. As discussed above, the force of the personal autonomy interest
depends on the circumstances of the individual seeking to migrate. If someone
living in Ohio has access to an adequate range of options, then his personal
autonomy interest does not justify his claim to migrate to California. The
same logic applies to the context of international migration. A citizen of Syria
might have a strong personal autonomy interest in migrating, but a citizen
of Canada might not. Carens concedes as much in making his case for open
borders: "The argument is strongest . . . when applied to the migration of
people from third world countries to those of the first world."[23] This is because the argument about personal autonomy is strongest for people whose
life choices are extremely limited to begin with. The adequate options component of personal autonomy is thus a limited basis for justifying the right to
domestic migration, as well as to international migration.

Another component of personal autonomy is freedom from coercion.
The court speaks of being "exempt from impositions" and "a virtually unconditional right" against "private interference as well as governmental action."
Liberal democratic governments are justified in coercing their citizens in certain ways. For example, I am justifiably subject to the traffic laws that forbid
me to drive through a red light because, although the law infringes on my
freedom, it provides significant benefits to others. But if California were
to put armed guards at its borders to prevent Nevadans from entering, we
should object unless California could demonstrate a compelling justification for doing so. When governments have imposed restrictions on domestic
free movement, they have done so to target particular groups for exclusion
and discrimination. Historical examples abound: the Soviet Union's forced
resettlement policies of the 1930s and 1940s, Jewish ghettos created by the
Third Reich during World War II, the apartheid regime in South Africa, and
restrictions on the movement of poor people by state governments in the
United States. The right to domestic free movement serves as an important

check on state domination of vulnerable minorities within the political community. The right to domestic migration is grounded in a concern to protect citizens against abuses of government power. Carens seeks to extend this concern about potential abuse of the government's coercive power to international migration. As he puts it,

> Perhaps borders and guards can be justified as a way of keeping out criminals, subversives, or armed invaders. But most of those trying to get in are not like that. They are ordinary, peaceful people, seeking only the opportunity to build decent, secure lives for themselves and their families. On what moral grounds can these sorts of people be kept out? What gives anyone the right to point guns at them?[24]

Carens is right that justification is owed to those subject to coercive border policies. National governments have reasons for restricting migration, grounded in the value of collective self-determination (see chapter 4), which are much stronger than the reasons that California has for restricting migration from Nevada. What are these reasons?

This takes us to another value underlying the right to domestic migration in US law, the value of social cohesion. In the *Slaughterhouse Cases*, the US Supreme Court stated, "The States in their closest connection with the members of the State, have been placed under the oversight and restraining and enforcing hand of Congress. The purpose is manifest, to establish through the whole jurisdiction of the United States ONE PEOPLE."[25] In a more recent case, *Saenz v. Roe*, the court says, "The Fourteenth Amendment, like the Constitution itself, was, as Justice Cardozo put it, 'framed upon the theory that the peoples of the several states must sink or swim together, and that in the long run prosperity and salvation are in union and not division.'"[26] The claim about cohesion is that a country is stronger and more prosperous when its citizens feel they are part of a common cause and regard themselves as one people. The right to domestic migration is important, even for those who already have access to an adequate range of options, because the country is stronger and more cohesive when citizens enjoy freedom of movement within the country. The value of social cohesion is central to Walzer's argument for state authority over immigration:

> Admission and exclusion are at the core of communal independence. They suggest the deepest meaning of self-determination. Without them, there could not be communities of character, historically

stable, ongoing associations of men and women with some special commitment to one another and some special sense of their common life.[27]

When the Supreme Court wrote in the *Slaughterhouse Cases* about the value of establishing a nation with "ONE PEOPLE,"[28] the values of self-determination and social cohesion were likely at the forefront of the justices' minds. Although allowing citizens to travel freely within their country fosters cohesion, Walzer suggests that opening borders to the entire world would diminish cohesion.

Carens has a reply to Walzer's concern about the challenges immigrants pose to social cohesion. Carens argues that cohesion is not threatened by international migration because the cohesion of more local communities has not been threatened by permitting domestic free movement.[29] For example, there is freedom of movement between Georgia and New York, and yet they have maintained distinctive communities of character, so why should we think social cohesion in the United States would be threatened by an influx of immigrants from around the world?

It is true that states and localities within the United States have maintained distinctive cultures in spite of widespread movement, but Carens's argument is too quick to assume that the differences between countries are essentially the same as differences between states and localities in the United States. The latter are bound together by a shared set of political and legal institutions that shape the cultural character of the country. If someone from Georgia moves to New York, she will already share with her new co-residents a common language and cultural idioms and practices, such as celebrating many of the same national holidays and watching the same TV shows and sporting events. By contrast, the cultural distance will be much greater for international migrants to the United States, whether they are from Norway or Ethiopia, because they do not have the experience of living under common political institutions and sharing cultural idioms and practices. The nature and degree of cultural differences are empirical questions that require further study, but even if Carens is right that international migrants do not pose greater challenges to social cohesion than domestic migrants do, he still has not succeeded in equating international migration with domestic migration with respect to social cohesion. The right to domestic migration is justified in large part because of its positive effects on social cohesion. Carens has not shown that international migration contributes to social cohesion in the way that domestic migration does. Thus, his cantilever argument, whether based on extending the value of social cohesion or personal autonomy, falls short of justifying a right to international freedom of movement.

Does the Right of Exit Entail the Right of Entry?

The second argument in the cantilever strategy begins with the premise that people have a moral right to *exit* their countries and extends the same logic to justify the right to *enter* another country. Article 13.2 of the Universal Declaration of Human Rights states, "Everyone has the right to leave any country, including his own, and to return to his country." Article 12 of the International Covenant on Civil and Political Rights upholds a similar right. Both international documents declare a right of *emigration* but are silent on the question of *immigration*. Theorists have argued that if we accept that individuals have a right to *exit* their native country, we must also accept that they have an unrestricted right to *enter* another country. The philosopher Phillip Cole has framed the argument in terms of the "symmetry" between exit and entry:

> [O]ne cannot consistently assert that there is a fundamental human right to emigration but no such right to immigration; the liberal asymmetry position is not merely ethically, but also conceptually, in- coherent . . . [I]f it can be shown that the state *does* have the right to control immigration, it must follow that it also has the right to control emigration: the two stand and fall together.[30]

To assess whether freedom of exit and freedom of entry stand or fall together, let us look more closely at the different normative positions on exit and entry. Cole has outlined three positions:

1. illiberal symmetry, where the state has discretionary control over both im- migration and emigration;
2. liberal asymmetry, where the state has discretionary control over the im- migration of noncitizens only; and
3. liberal symmetry, where there is no state control over migration in either direction.[31]

Contra Cole, I think the liberal asymmetry position can be defended. There is a structural difference between exit and entry. Exit restrictions involve not only interfering with voluntary acquisition of new forms of personal relationships

↑ but what about your brain drain argument?

as entry restrictions do. As Michael Blake has argued, exit restrictions also co-erce people into maintaining an unwanted form of political relationship.[32] If someone no longer wishes to be a member, then the state cannot force her to remain. Even if my basic interests are met in the state of which I'm a member, being forced to remain in a political relationship that I want to leave behind violates something morally important. Preventing an individual from exiting the country for the sake of the good of other members of the society fails to adequately respect, in Rawls's words, the separateness of persons. On this view, the right of exit is a strong right, stronger than a right of entry.

Although the right of exit is strong, it is not unconstrained. To be clear, I am not talking about the blanket restrictions on exit imposed by the Democratic People's Republic of Korea, Iran, or Myanmar. In liberal dem-ocratic states, we can think of circumstances in which it may be justifiable to restrict the exit of persons, such as those who are "genuinely in possession of state secrets" or who are "criminals seeking to escape their just reward."[33] It may also be justifiable to restrict emigration for a limited period of time in order to minimize brain drain from developing countries. The departure of educated and skilled citizens to the developed world can have negative consequences on developing countries. The economists Devesh Kapur and John McHale provide evidence that the emigration of skilled citizens hurts those who are left behind in origin countries. The loss of skilled workers can result in financial loss, such as loss of tax revenue and the loss of investments made by developing countries in their training; the loss of skills and services in healthcare, education, and other sectors; and the loss of those who are best positioned to demand and build institutions that are crucial for promoting development.[34] Yet, as Michael Clemens has cautioned, the conditions under which the emigration of skilled workers results in a net depletion of the stock of skilled workers in the origin country is not well-established in the economics literature. The nature and extent of "negative externalities" of emigration depend critically on which mechanisms are used to explain human-capital externalities, whether it is knowledge spillovers, research and development, physical health, political leadership, fertility, and capital accu-mulation.[35] The brain drain thesis also rests on empirical assumptions that we do not know will be true in the long run, such as whether skilled workers will continue to be productive if they remain in their home countries and whether skilled workers depart for good rather than build bridges between the sending and destination countries.

Let's assume, for the sake of argument, that emigration does result in a substantial loss of skilled workers in poor countries, at least in the short-term.

What is the right thing to do in response? One of the best-known proposals is Jagdish Bhagwati and William Dellalfar's call for a Pigovian tax on skilled migrants to compensate countries of origin.[36] Others have argued that wealthy countries receiving skilled migrants should be required to pay a tax to help compensate for the losses to the sending countries, which could help fund essential institutional capacity-building.[37] Temporary restrictions on freedom of exit may also be justifiable. As Gillian Brock has argued, prospective migrants themselves should bear some responsibility for remedying the losses caused by their departure. For example, those who have received government funding of tertiary education should be subject to a short period of compulsory service or required to pay back the costs of their education as a condition of exiting their native countries. The principle at work here is reciprocity or fair play. If one's home country has collectively contributed scarce resources toward one's education and training, the beneficiary incurs some obligations to his country, and the country is entitled to claim some compensation from the beneficiary.[38]

Where does this leave us in responding to Cole's argument that the right of exit stands or falls with the right of entry? The right of exit does not entail an unrestricted right to enter any country of one's choice.[39] There are many rights whose exercise depends on finding cooperative partners with whom to exercise the right. Consider the case of marriage. The right to marry is a right that allows people to marry partners of their choice, but it is not a right to have a partner provided for you. Similarly, the right of exit is a right held by an individual, which grounds a duty on the individual's state of residence not to prevent her from leaving, but the right of exit does not entail a duty on another particular state to let that person in. Of course, if no state is willing to admit the person, then the right of exit cannot be exercised. If states are willing to consider entry applications from people who want to migrate, and if those people get offers from at least one of those states, then the right of exit can meaningfully be exercised. Where a person's basic interests are not protected by the states where they reside, as in the case of refugees, then states with integrative capabilities have an obligation to take in their fair share of refugees, as I argue in chapter 7. In the case of those whose human rights are being met in their home countries, their right of exit must be weighed against the right of states to restrict entry. If states have a pro tanto right to control immigration, as I argued in chapter 4, the liberal asymmetry position is not incoherent but defensible. We need to look to the state's reasons for restricting entry and weigh them against the reasons underlying the migrant's claim for entry.

An Instrumental Argument from Freedom
of Association and Contract

I turn now to consider a third argument for the right of free movement, based on the value of individual freedom of association and contract. This freedom-based argument has been advanced by libertarian thinkers. In commemorating the Fourth of July in 1984, the *Wall Street Journal's* editorial page called for a constitutional amendment for open borders: "Our greatest heresy is that we believe in people as the great resource of our land . . . so long as we keep our economy free, more people means more growth, the more the merrier." In 2001 the paper ran a piece entitled, "Open NAFTA Borders? Why Not?" hailing open borders as being in keeping with a free market mentalité:

> The proportion of immigrants with postgraduate education is three times the native rate. New immigrants are no longer eligible for welfare, removing that bugaboo . . . The opportunity north of the border is inevitably a huge magnet for the poor but ambitious. There is no realistic way to stop the resulting flow of people.[40]

Before getting to the philosophical arguments, it is important to identify the empirical assumptions underlying the libertarian case for open borders. One key assumption is that complete or even partial elimination of migration barriers would bring vast economic gains, especially for individual migrants and the firms that employ them.

The economist Michael Clemens provides a striking metaphor: policies restricting emigration are tantamount to leaving trillion-dollar bills on the sidewalk. Imagine the world is divided into two regions: a rich region, where one billion people earn $30,000 per year, and a "poor" region, where six billion earn $5,000 per year. In a world without border restrictions, people would move from low-wage to high-wage regions out of a desire to improve their economic well-being. Suppose emigrants from the poor region have lower productivity, so each gains just 60 percent of the simple earnings gap upon emigrating ($15,000). This marginal gain shrinks as emigration proceeds, so suppose the average gain is $7,500 per year. If half the population of the poor region migrates, migrants would gain $23 trillion, 38 percent of global GDP. For nonmigrants, the outcome would have complicated effects: average wages would rise in the poor region and fall in the rich region, while returns to capital would rise in the rich region and fall in the poor region. Clemens concludes we can plausibly expect overall gains of from 20 percent to 60 percent of global GDP.[41]

There are some difficulties with this economic story. First, to realize the predicted global economic gains, billions of workers would have to move from poor to rich countries. Logistically, the sheer number of migrants may make it impossible to achieve the economic gains in a realistic time frame. For example, if the entire developed world were permitted to migrate at triple the current rate in the United States, it would take five hundred years for all the migrants to move.[42] Second, if large numbers of migrants were able to move, the gains from open borders depends on how destination countries react to the influx of migrants. Migrants are not only workers but people with social, cultural, and political identities and practices.[43] As Clemens acknowledges, the large influx of low-skilled migrants would put downward pressure on the wages of low-skilled native workers, which pits concerns about distributive justice against global efficiency gains. Immigrants shape not only the economic but also the social, cultural, and political life of destination countries. So, while the libertarian argument rests on the optimistic scenario of huge global efficiency gains, the real-world effects of opening borders are more complicated.

Let's turn now to the philosophical argument. Drawing on Locke, contemporary libertarian philosophers take individuals as having natural rights to acquire and use property. Individual property holders are viewed as forming a social contract for the purpose of protecting their persons and their property. The libertarian state is a voluntary association among consenting property owners. Although neither Locke nor Nozick wrote directly about migration, one can see how a libertarian might interpret the right of freedom of association as including the freedom to invite foreigners onto one's property for some mutually agreed upon enterprise. On such a view, the state would not be justified in restricting immigration.[44] If the owners of large American farms want to employ workers from Mexico, the US government would have no right to prohibit such a contract. So long as migrant workers do not violate the security and property rights of others, a Nozickean minimal state could not prevent such migration. That would violate individual rights of freedom of association and contract.

On the libertarian account, the only way for citizens and noncitizens alike to be excluded from the state's territory would be for individual property owners to come together and voluntarily agree to restrict entry and membership to particular individuals. Hillel Steiner has developed this line of thinking. He provides the example of his parents' summer cottage community outside Toronto. The community of fifty families voluntarily banded together for the sake of maintaining common amenities, such as the roads, the beach, and the day-camp facilities. The group also had the collective power to restrict the admission of new members and to restrict leaving the community by levying what amounted to a tax on it.

From the standpoint of libertarians, the cottage community's restriction on *emigration* is justified insofar as such an exit clause was part of the contract to which cottage owners voluntarily agreed at the time of purchase. On the question of *immigration*, libertarians seem divided. Some argue for a simple "first come, first served" rule by which individuals who appropriate an unowned thing come to be the rightful owners of that thing. Others follow Locke's own qualifications on the original acquisition of property: any original title must be consistent with treating individuals as "all equal and independent."[45] What, then, does the Lockean principle of equal freedom require?

Locke himself suggests the proviso that original acquisition must leave "enough and as good" for others. Because God gave the earth "to mankind in common," all the world's natural resources belong to all persons equally.[46] One way of interpreting the Lockean proviso is the nineteenth-century American political economist Henry George's "single tax" proposal. Like Locke, George believed that everything found in nature, including land, belongs equally to all humanity. George's economic philosophy, known as "Georgism," holds that because every human being is entitled to an equal portion of the value of natural resources in the world, those who are fortunate enough to be property owners have a corresponding obligation to pay a tax to eliminate poverty and reduce social inequality.[47] Although George himself was silent on the issue, Steiner reminds us that the underlying Lockean principle about everyone's entitlement to the earth's resources is *global* in scope.

As a matter of nonideal theory, taking the world as it is, Steiner suggests that libertarians should strongly oppose legislated restrictions on international migration since such restrictions are taken to defend neither contractual agreements nor property rights. The role of the libertarian minimal state should be limited to enforcing "individuals' moral rights which consist exclusively of property and contractual rights." Thus, "migration restrictions aimed at protecting the *value* of property rights—let alone broader cultural values are entirely beyond its rightful authority."[48]

As a matter of ideal theory (i.e., in a world in which all current land titles were justly acquired or transferred), Steiner argues that the state also lacks the right to prohibit the movement of people across borders: "If I am willing to lease, sell, or give away space to other persons and am under no contractual obligation to refrain from doing so, the state has no authority to establish whether they are insiders or outsiders before permitting me to do so." For libertarians, such as Steiner, "the territorial claims of nations are justified by and derived from the territorial claims of individuals." Steiner construes Locke's principle more narrowly than does Locke himself, who endorsed the practice of "commonwealths not permitting any part of their dominions to be dismembered, nor to be enjoyed by any but those of their community."[49] By contrast, Steiner argues that Locke's prohibition on secession "flies in the face of basic Lockean—and libertarian—property right principles."[50] The only legitimate restrictions on transnational migration would be the enforcement of trespass laws and the detention of those who violated fundamental rights.

Despite Steiner's best efforts at appropriating Locke for libertarian purposes, his libertarian argument fails to justify open borders for several reasons. First, the political community is not merely an aggregation of summer cottage associations or business associations.[51] The cottage "community" that Steiner analogizes to the state already operates *within* the jurisdiction of the state. When American farm owners contract with foreign workers, their contracts presuppose the broader context of the political community, including both the system of laws within which their contracts are made and enforced and the provision of public roads by which the worker travels to his employer. When a foreign worker sets foot on his American employer's property, he not only enters a parcel of private property; he also enters the territorial space of the political community. In other words, the libertarian case for open borders fails to differentiate between the private property rights of individuals and the jurisdictional rights of states.

Second, the scope of freedom of movement need not be unlimited to respect the right of freedom of association. In many cases, ensuring domestic freedom of movement is sufficient for the vindication of basic human interests, including the interest in freedom of association. This is not to suggest that levels of immigration should not be much higher than they currently are in liberal democratic societies, but rather that government restriction of American employers' access to foreign labor does not necessarily constitute a violation of their interest in freedom of association and contract if there are domestic laborers who are able and willing to perform the job.

Finally, it is interesting to note that the value of freedom of association has cut both ways in the immigration debate. It has been marshaled in favor of open borders (Steiner) and in favor of the state's right to exclude (Wellman). Appealing to the value of freedom of association by itself leaves undetermined whether the right of association of those who want to exclude trumps, or is trumped by, the right of association of those who want to admit new migrants. This suggests that appealing to freedom of association alone cannot help us resolve questions about the scope of freedom of movement.

Conclusion

This chapter has considered several freedom-based arguments for a general right of international migration: the direct argument for the human right to immigrate, the cantilever arguments based on analogies between domestic and international migration and between exit and entry, and an instrumental argument based on freedom of association and contract. I have argued that none of these arguments succeeds in establishing a general right of international migration.

One may not be convinced by my critique, but even proponents of a general right of international migration recognize that it is a defeasible right that must be weighed against countervailing considerations. The arguments for the "human right to migration" are indifferent to the reasons people have for wanting to migrate; everyone who wants to migrate for any reason at all is able to migrate. By contrast, I think a compelling normative theory of migration should be able to distinguish and prioritize among different reasons for migration. In Part III, I examine different reasons prospective migrants have for wanting to migrate and consider how they might be weighed against the reasons political communities have for restricting immigration.

PART III

Implications

The preceding chapters have explored the perspective of political communities (Part I) and the perspective of migrants (Part II) and offered an intermediate position between closed borders and open borders. States have the right to control immigration, but this right is not absolute. It is qualified by obligations to respect the basic rights of prospective migrants. What is required is not closed borders or open borders but controlled borders and open doors. The question then becomes, to whom should the country's doors be open? Part III is addressed to members of democratic societies as they think about what kinds of immigration policies to pursue. They must weigh what is at stake for prospective migrants against what is at stake for the political communities they seek to enter.

There are circumstances in which states are morally required to admit prospective migrants. Chapter 7 examines the claims of refugees and other necessitous migrants. Chapter 8 explores family-based immigration claims. I argue that both types of claims constitute what we might call *obligatory admissions*, cases where the decision to admit a prospective migrant is morally required. By contrast, cases where the decision to admit a prospective migrant is not morally required are what we might call *discretionary admissions*.[1] I discuss discretionary admissions in chapter 9.

I adopt the distinction between obligatory and discretionary admissions over the more commonly used distinction between "refugees" and "economic migrants," which I believe is limited for two reasons. First, not all those who face serious threats to their human rights meet the international legal definition of a refugee. There is a good case to be made for regarding other groups of forced migrants as part of obligatory admissions. Second, those migrants who are not driven by necessity do not always move purely or primarily for "economic" reasons. According to neoclassical economic theories, migrants are rational economic actors who move from low-wage countries to high-wage countries to maximize lifetime earnings. While some migrants do move to take advantage of wage gaps, it is important to acknowledge the structural conditions that shape the contexts within which people make migration decisions.[2] One important structural factor is the scope and structure of global markets.[3] Motivated by a desire for greater profits, owners and managers of large firms in wealthy countries enter poor countries in search of land, raw materials, labor, and markets. This process of market expansion and penetration results in disruptions and dislocations that drive migration. In addition to these "push" factors, there are also "pull" factors, including the permanent demand for unskilled labor that is built into the economic structures of developed countries.[4] Once international migration is initiated and migrants gain access to social networks and institutions in the receiving countries, migrant networks become a source of social capital for people back home. Migration becomes "cumulative" as each act of migration changes the social context within which subsequent migration decisions are made, which in turn increases the likelihood of additional migration.[5]

The upshot is that we should think of the circumstances under which people migrate as a matter of degree. On one end of the spectrum are people forced to flee by persecution and violence. On the other end are truly voluntary migrants whose human rights are not threatened but who move in search of better opportunities. Many migrants fall somewhere in between, and there is reasonable disagreement about where to draw the line, but I believe it is important to maintain some distinction between those who have fundamental interests that can only be met through migration and those who do not. Doing away with the distinction altogether would leave us without any way to prioritize truly necessitous migrants. According to proponents of open borders, everyone has the right to migrate to the countries of their choice. By contrast, on the realistically utopian theory developed in this book, what is morally required is not a general right of free movement across the globe for anyone who wishes to move but an approach that privileges those whose human rights are at stake. The following chapters examine obligatory and discretionary admissions in greater depth.

7

Refugees and Other Necessitous Migrants

THE DUTY TO protect refugees and other forcibly displaced migrants is one of the moral constraints on the state's right to control immigration. Writing in the wake of World War II, Hannah Arendt described the condition of refugees and stateless people as involving not only "the loss of their homes [which] meant the loss of the entire social texture into which they were born and in which they established for themselves a distinct place in the world." Their "fundamental deprivation of human rights" is the loss of "a right to have rights . . . and a right to belong to some organized community."[1] The duty to protect refugees can often only plausibly be met by taking them in because their need is not only for safety, food, and shelter but political membership itself.

The challenges of forced displacement are greater than ever. There are 65.6 million forcibly displaced people worldwide, including 22.5 million refugees, 40.3 million internally displaced people, and 2.8 million asylum seekers.[2] Yet, the dominant approach adopted by most developed states in the global North is one of deterrence and exclusion: interception on the high seas, erection of walls and fences, sanctions on airline carriers, bilateral and regional agreements to prevent onward movement of migrants and refugees, and expedited removal procedures.[3] Few of these developed states have directly challenged international refugee law or taken steps to withdraw from the 1951 Refugee Convention or other human rights instruments protecting refugees. They recognize that international refugee law serves as an important tool to ensure the continued commitment of the less-developed states that host the vast majority of the world's refugees.

Many believe that states have an obligation to assist refugees, but the nature and extent of this obligation requires elaboration. What are the grounds of the obligation toward refugees? Who should be regarded as a refugee? What does the duty to assist refugees entail, and how should this duty be shared among states? And what are the limits on the duty to refugees?

The International Refugee Protection System

Before considering how states should respond to the claims of refugees, it is important to begin by examining how things work now. The current international refugee protection system was established with the Office of the United Nations High Commissioner for Refugees (UNHCR) in 1950 and the adoption in 1951 of the United Nations Convention Relating to the Status of Refugees (the 1951 Refugee Convention). The system was designed to respond to the displacement of people because of the Second World War and was limited in scope to persons fleeing events occurring in Europe before 1951. The 1967 Protocol removed these limitations, giving the convention universal coverage. It has since been supplemented by refugee protection regimes in several regions and the development of international human rights law.

The convention sets forth basic minimum standards for the treatment of refugees, including the right to access courts, to work and establish businesses, to elementary education, to public assistance on the same terms as nationals, and to choose their place of residence within the territory of signatory states.[4] The convention also says that signatory states shall not impose penalties on refugees "on account of their illegal entry or presence . . . provided they present themselves without delay to the authorities and show good cause for their illegal entry or presence" (art. 31), nor shall contracting states return (*refouler*) a refugee to the territories "where his life or freedom would be threatened" unless there are "reasonable grounds" for regarding the refugee as "a danger to the security of the country" (art. 33).

The UNHCR is charged with leading and coordinating international action to protect refugees. The convention calls on signatory states to cooperate with the UNHCR to carry out the provisions of the convention. One hundred and forty-eight countries have signed onto the Refugee Convention, but it is increasingly marginal to how refugee protection happens around the world. Describing a refugee protection system under stress, a UNHCR report states, "The host countries, countries of origin and donor countries seem less able to work together to find solutions, with host countries resisting local integration and other countries offering too few resettlement places."[5]

The Grounds of the Duty to Refugees

Why do states have a duty to assist refugees? I want to consider three distinct reasons that generate an obligation on the part of states to assist refugees. I will discuss what refugees are owed later in the chapter.

The first is what we might call *causal responsibility* for turning people into refugees. The primary agents in forcing people to flee are sometimes the refugees' home states and, of course, they are not going to give assistance to those they have turned into refugees. This suggests that causal responsibility is, at most, a partial element of a broader account of the responsibility to assist refugees. We might call the duty to assist refugees a *remedial responsibility* on the part of other states to step in when the refugee's home state is unable or unwilling to secure her basic rights. The home state's failure may be the result of its weakness and incapacity or be because it is persecuting its population rather than protecting it. The question then becomes how remedial responsibility is to be distributed among states. In cases where other states have played a causal role in turning people into refugees, they bear remedial responsibility to assist refugees to repair the harm they have caused.[6] For example, Americans have special obligations to those who were turned into refugees by US intervention in Vietnam and the wars in Iraq and Afghanistan. Writing in the 1980s, Walzer makes such a reparative argument about the obligations of Americans toward Vietnamese refugees: "The injury we have done them makes for an affinity between us: thus Vietnamese refugees had, in a moral sense, been effectively Americanized even before they arrived on these shores."[7] Notice that Walzer emphasizes not only the harm caused by American actions but also the effect on the identities of Vietnamese refugees. This move broadens the actions for which reparation is owed to include not only serious physical and material harm to people's lives but also to coercively shaping their identities.[8] The extent of the causal connection is difficult to determine with any precision, but when significant causal connection can be established, remedial responsibility follows. The case of Afghan and Iraqi interpreters is perhaps even clearer. They have served alongside American troops and are at risk of serious harm as a result; the US government therefore bears a special remedial responsibility to assist them. On the reparative argument, the obligation to assist refugees is particular: it is an obligation on particular states to assist particular groups of refugees by virtue of a prior relationship.

A second source of the duty to assist refugees is universal in scope: *humanitarian concern*. What distinguishes refugees from other migrants is their pressing need for protection against serious harm. This is akin to a duty of rescue in emergencies: when someone faces the threat of death or serious harm, we have a duty to rescue them.[9] Refugees need rescue from persecution by their home states or the failure of their home states to protect them from persecution and violence by third parties. This duty may be rooted in a variety of religious and secular worldviews that support a duty to help those in dire need. Liberal democratic values are one source of support for the humanitarian duty to refugees. When critics of Donald Trump's travel ban called it "un-American," they were referring not only to the religious discrimination it implied but also to the closing of the door to all refugees.[10] The claim here is that refusing admission to those fleeing persecution and violence is a failure of humanitarianism and a betrayal of the American ideals that support humanitarian ideals. The democratic values of religious liberty, equality, and respect for pluralism make us allies of those who are persecuted because of their religious, political, and other affiliations. According to these humanitarian grounds, what links particular actors to a harm that demands remedy is not causal responsibility but having the capacity to assist, either in terms of the institutional capabilities or the resources needed for providing a remedy.[11]

A third ground of the duty to assist refugees are the *legitimacy conditions of the modern state system*. The world is divided up among sovereign states, which are regarded as possessing rights of territorial jurisdiction. What, if anything, legitimates this system? One answer proceeds from a global original position in which a representative person must choose fair principles that will regulate the international system.[12] This person would recognize the importance of membership in a self-determining political community, but she would also regard the protection of her human rights as important. She would see that an international system in which states have an absolute right of self-determination and territorial control, including the right to exclude all refugees, would not secure human rights. Instead, she would opt for a system in which each state bears the primary responsibility for protecting the human rights of its members, but if it fails to do so, the responsibility falls on other states to step in. Even if we reject such reasoning from a global original position, we can still say that the legitimacy of the state system depends on states accepting collective responsibility for assisting those individuals made vulnerable by the failures of their own state. Many states have agreed to participate in the international refugee-protection system, and this agreement is the source of their obligation. But even states that have not signed onto the Refugee Convention bear collective responsibility for refugees because they participate in and benefit from the state system. It is only in a world carved into states that people can become refugees. When people are forcibly displaced from their homeland, there is nowhere else on earth they can go but to another state. The legitimacy of the state system depends on states sharing responsibility to assist those who have been forcibly displaced from their home states.

Each of these grounds is by itself sufficient to generate a prima facie duty to assist refugees. As a matter of moral psychology and politics, the reparative argument may wield more influence than humanitarianism or the legitimate state-system rationale. For example, the high levels of support in Western European states for Kosovar refugees, compared to non-European refugees, can partly be explained by the sense of responsibility for their plight.[13] Similarly, Afghan and Iraqi translators have been singled out as a group whom the US government has a special responsibility to take in.[14]

Now that we have a sense of the grounds of the duty to refugees, we need to consider who counts as a refugee.

Who Is a Refugee?

A theory of our obligations to refugees requires a conception of who refugees are. A good place to begin our inquiry is the definition in international law. According to the 1951 Refugee Convention, a refugee is defined as someone who

> owing to well-founded fear of being persecuted for reasons of race, religion, nationality, membership of a particular social group or political opinion, is outside the country of his nationality and is unable, or owing to such fear, is unwilling to avail himself of the protection of that country; or who, not having a nationality and being outside the country of his former habitual residence as a result of such events, is unable or, owing to such fear, is unwilling to return to it.[15]

The convention definition centers on those who are persecuted in virtue of group membership. It does not include individuals who are forced to migrate for other reasons, such as famine or natural disasters. It also does not include those who remain inside their country of origin. On the other hand, the convention definition has been interpreted fairly broadly to include cases not only where the state is the agent of persecution but also where the state fails to protect individuals from persecution by non-state actors. It also has been interpreted as applying to persons fleeing persecution on the basis of gender and sexual orientation, as well as race, religion, and nationality.[16]

A number of scholars have argued for a much broader definition of refugees. Most notably, Andrew Shacknove has argued that persecution is a sufficient, not necessary, condition for severing the relationship between an individual and her state. Persecution accounts for circumstances where state protection is absent because the state is tyrannical, but it says nothing about other circumstances where state protection is absent. Refugees are "in essence, persons whose basic needs are unprotected by their country of origin, who have no remaining recourse other than to seek international restitution of their needs, and who are so situated that international restitution is possible."[17] On Shacknove's account, those suffering from severe economic deprivation and natural disasters should also count as refugees if they are unprotected by their country of origin and if they have no other recourse than to seek international protection. In addition, one need not have crossed a state border into another country to qualify as a refugee. What matters morally is the urgency of a person's needs, not the cause of her dire situation or whether she is outside the borders of her country of origin. One upshot of Shacknove's definition is that it would add 40.8 million internally displaced persons and 10 million stateless people to the 21.3 million people the UNHCR has already certified as refugees.[18]

Several reasons speak in favor of a broader definition of "refugee" based on the urgency of a person's needs, regardless of the cause of her dire situation or whether she has managed to get out of her country of origin. As Matthew Gibney has argued, first, refugees who meet the Convention definition of persecution are not necessarily more endangered than other groups of forced migrants, such as those fleeing civil war and natural disasters.[19] Second, the harms faced by Convention refugees are not more socially consequential than those faced by other forced migrants. The fact of persecution based on race, religion, and other social identities may be an additional reason for bringing those responsible to justice, but it is not in itself a reason for prioritizing the needs of victims of persecution over those of other forced migrants. Think of the sick and injured awaiting treatment in a hospital: those with the most urgent needs are treated first, regardless of the cause of their injuries. Third, the needs of refugees and other forced migrants may not be significantly different. Defenders of the narrower convention definition have argued that there is a morally significant difference between refugees and forced migrants: Convention refugees need substitute membership in a new state because they were persecuted by their home states, whereas forced migrants need, at best, temporary protection before returning home. But the generalized violence and impoverishment that generate forced migration stem in part from poor governance, and if poor governance is likely to be long lasting, so are the outcomes that flow from it. We should not exaggerate the difference between convention refugees and other forced migrants because convention refugees are often eager to return home if conditions change, and the generalized violence experienced by other forced migrants may make it impossible for them to return home.

I agree that those forcibly displaced by war, natural disasters, and famine have urgent needs that must be met, but the broader definition of refugees proposed by Shacknove suffers from at least two problems. First, it includes people in dire need who remain inside their countries of origin. For his account to be of practical use, he needs to provide an account of humanitarian intervention that shows when it is permissible for states to intervene in the affairs of another state to provide the entitlements refugees are owed. This raises a whole host of challenges that he does not address. A second problem has to do with the importance of a contextual approach to justice. Principles of humanitarian assistance and justice are general principles that require us to assist those who cannot meet their basic needs, but how we specify the content of the duties to different people in dire need will depend on their particular situations. There is a tendency among moral and political theorists writing about refugees to separate the question "who is a refugee?" from the question "what do we owe refugees?" As Shacknove puts it, "A conception of refugeehood is prior to a theory and policy of entitlements."[20] If one adopts this approach, there is no reason to distinguish between those in dire need because of persecution and those in dire need because of war, natural disasters, or extreme poverty. There is also no reason to distinguish between those who have crossed state borders and those who remain inside their countries of origin. Yet, as Matthew Lister has argued, if we are looking to develop a normative theory that provides practical guidance, then we need to address the questions "who is a refugee?" and "what do we owe refugees?" together, working back and forth between the two.[21]

What is normatively significant about refugees is not simply that their basic needs are not being met. Rather, it is that their basic needs can only be met by allowing them to enter a safe country and not returning them to the country where they will face danger. Refugees are defined by their need for membership itself, which can only be granted by taking them in. There is a contingent but strong relationship between persecution and refugee status: those persecuted in their countries of origin, by state or nonstate actors, face a serious threat that is likely to be indefinite, making asylum necessary.[22] By contrast, asylum is not the only or best remedy for those suffering from severe poverty.[23] The same goes for those suffering from natural disasters and environmental problems. If the environmental problem is temporary, as is often the case with hurricanes, earthquakes, or floods, it is reasonable to expect people to return home after the danger has passed, assuming that assistance in rebuilding communities is given.[24] Those displaced by environmental problems may be entitled to refugee status if the displacement is indefinite and makes settlement in another country necessary, such as in the case of low-lying islands faced with rising sea levels. Recognizing "climate change refugees" is in keeping with the rationale of the Convention definition, broadly understood.[25] As I noted earlier, the Convention definition has been interpreted broadly to include cases of persecution by both nonstate and state actors and asylum claims based on not only race and religion but also gender and sexuality. Shacknove's definition of "refugee" is more radically inclusionary, encompassing all people forcibly displaced by war, natural disasters, and poverty.

Instead of stretching the legal definition of "refugee" to include all forced migrants, we should instead extend international protection to other groups of forced migrants, who, together with refugees, constitute a broader category of *necessitous migrants*.[26] The appropriate form of assistance will depend on the particular situation of necessitous migrants. Sometimes the only remedy is to grant them asylum; in other cases, necessitous migrants may be able to receive emergency assistance in their home countries and eventually return to their homes. If we look to international practice, we can see that international assistance has already been extended to a wider circle of people beyond the Convention definition. The UNHCR mandate now effectively covers all persons who flee violence and conflict, whether remaining inside or moving outside their countries of origin.[27] People displaced by natural disasters, such as earthquakes in Haiti, floods in Pakistan, tsunamis in the Philippines and Indonesia, and the drought afflicting the horn of Africa, have been the focus of international concern and have received large amounts of foreign assistance. Regional and global institutions seek to predict natural disasters and to support programs to mitigate their harm and prevent displacement, and concerns about displacement have made their way into global efforts to reduce climate change. Rather than shoehorn all forced migrants into the category of refugee, states and international organizations should provide assistance tailored to meet their particular needs.[28]

What Is Owed to Refugees and How Should the Duty Be Distributed among States?

The primary duty for meeting a person's basic needs falls on her own state, but when her state fails to do so, other states must step in and bear the responsibility. But what must states do to assist refugees and how should the duty be distributed among states?

The ultimate goal of refugee protection is to find durable solutions to refugee problems, which meet the needs of refugees by allowing them to acquire or reacquire the full protection of a state. The immediate needs of refugees are for safety and the protection of their basic human rights, but in the long run, refugees who cannot safely return to their countries of origin within a reasonable period need to acquire membership in a new political community. Consider the three main solutions outlined by the UNHCR.[29]

The first is for refugees to return home, what the UNHCR calls *voluntary repatriation*. The Refugee Convention's cessation clause makes clear that states are not required to admit refugees permanently; they are required to protect refugees for the duration of the risk in their home country. The 1990s were dubbed the decade of repatriation, but the overall numbers of refugees repatriating voluntarily declined sharply in the first decade of the 21st century. In 2014, only 126,800 refugees returned to their countries of origin, making for the lowest level of refugee returns since 1983. In 2015, the number of refugees returning to their countries of origin increased to 201,400.[30] For many refugees, repatriation is not possible because of continuing conflict and violence or threat of violence in their countries of origin. In 2015, around 41 percent of refugees under UNHCR's mandate were in a "protracted situation" in which 25,000 or more refugees from the same nationality have been in exile for five or more years in a given asylum country. Most of these protracted refugee situations have lasted for more than twenty years.[31] There is a limit to how long refugees can be kept in a temporary status; as time passes, their claim for membership in a new state increases.

A second solution identified by the UNHCR is *local integration* in the countries where refugees have sought safety. The vast majority of refugees end up in a neighboring country because it is the first place they can get to. The states that have signed onto the Refugee Convention have a duty of nonrefoulement: they should not return refugees to a place where they would face persecution and violence. By arriving in the territory of a state, migrants make themselves vulnerable to that state and have a particular claim against that state. Asking neighboring countries to shoulder the responsibility of

providing temporary shelter may make sense in terms of meeting the immediate needs of refugees and facilitating repatriation.

The problem, however, is that these neighboring states tend to be relatively poorer. 86 percent of the world's refugees are currently hosted by developing countries.[32] More than half of all refugees today are from three
countries: Syria, Afghanistan, and Somalia. The top host countries are
Turkey (2.5 million refugees), Pakistan (1.6 million), Lebanon (1.1 million),
Iran (979,400), Ethiopia (736,100) and Jordan (664,100).[33] These host
states have set up refugee camps or sought to restrict the mobility and work
opportunities of refugees rather than facilitate their integration. Part of the
reason is that refugee camps are a concrete, one-size-fits-all answer that can
be set up and financed by the UNHCR and its humanitarian partners, which
means that the costs of assisting refugees do not have to be born entirely by the
host society. Keeping refugees in camps also appeals to richer states seeking
to avoid their duty to assist refugees.[34] Another reason for favoring camps
over local integration are the costs of integrating large numbers of refugees
for host societies. These neighboring states have not been able to deter the arrival of refugees, but by restricting their mobility, states send the message that
refugees are not welcome in the long-term.

Richer states have tended to favor a humanitarian aid approach focused
on providing material assistance to refugees over an approach that aims at
fostering the self-sufficiency of refugees. This humanitarian aid approach,
when pursued over a long period of time, becomes an end in itself, crowding
out funding for programs dedicated to ensuring that the rights guaranteed by
the Refugee Convention, other than the right of nonrefoulement, such as the
right to education, work, and establish businesses, are respected. A humanitarian aid approach serves the interests of states. The states refugees have fled
are not at risk of intervention from other states; states hosting refugees do so
largely on the international community's funding and face little pressure to integrate the refugees living in their territories; and richer states that are farther
away can provide humanitarian assistance without committing much in the
way of taking in refugees. Thus the de facto rule determining where refugees
end up has traditionally been *geographic proximity*. Because the first countries refugees are able to get to are, overwhelmingly, developing countries, the
principle of nonrefoulement has resulted in a system of refugee protection
that reinforces existing inequalities between richer and poorer countries.

This leads us to consider a third solution: relocating refugees from the
neighboring country in which they have found safety to a third country
for permanent residence, a solution that is known as *resettlement*. Whereas

can't force them to return

nonrefoulement is recognized as an obligation in international law, there is no generally recognized obligation to take in refugees for resettlement. In 2015, the UNHCR submitted 134,000 refugees to states for resettlement, and states ended up admitting 107,100 refugees.[35] This is only .66 percent of the 16.1 million refugees currently under the UNHCR's mandate. So there is an enormous disparity in how the responsibility to assist refugees is currently distributed among states: the vast majority of refugees currently reside in developing countries while developed countries have taken in only a tiny fraction of refugees. What might a fairer distribution of responsibility be based on?

One essential component of a fair scheme of responsibility sharing with respect to resettlement is the capacity of states, what Matthew Gibney has called their *integrative capabilities*.[36] Relevant capabilities include the size of the state's territory, its population size and density, gross domestic product, and unemployment rates. Taking such factors into account reflects the idea that wealthier countries are generally better able to bear the costs of providing for refugees, and that countries with more territory and lower population density are more likely to be able to absorb the arrival of newcomers.

What about levels of nativism and xenophobia among the population? Should such factors count in defining a state's integrative capabilities to take in refugees? Gibney rejects such factors on the grounds they "are almost impossible to measure with any degree of objectivity (a fatal hazard since we want a universal standard for states)."[37] In my view, the better argument with respect to democratic states is that such nativist attitudes are not a legitimate reason for refusing to take in refugees because they violate the democratic value of equal respect. Such attitudes say more about the willingness, not the capacity, of states to take in refugees. The appropriate response to such unwillingness is public debate and persuasion to counter nativism, not acquiescence to such attitudes. Countries like the United States, Canada, and Australia that have a long history of admitting refugees and immigrants are better equipped to deal with the challenges of diversity than countries like Japan and South Korea that have historically been less open to migrants and refugees. More insular countries may indeed have a harder time integrating newcomers, but it would be wrong to use a country's history of insularity as a justification for its refusing to take in any refugees at all.

What if a country's reason for prioritizing a particular group for resettlement is not prejudice but *cultural affinity*? Given the large number of refugees who are seeking to be resettled, is it permissible to engage in cultural or religious selection of refugees? Walzer argues it is when the numbers of refugees are large and "we are forced to choose among the victims, we will

look, rightfully, for some more direct connection with our own way of life."
He says, for example, that it was right for the United States and Britain to
take in thousands of people fleeing Hungary after the failed revolution of
1956, given the dynamics of the Cold War and both countries' expressions
of sympathy with the East European "freedom fighters."[38] During the Cold
War, US asylum policy prioritized those fleeing communism, perhaps the
starkest example being the welcome it extended to Cubans in contrast to
Haitians.[39] Should democratic countries give priority to those with cultural
affinities?

Cultural selection is a legitimate exercise of the state's pro tanto right to
control immigration, as I argue in chapter 9, but not when it is a cover for
discriminating against disfavored groups. For example, the United States
regarded all but a handful of Haitians arriving in the 1970s as "economic
migrants" and denied them any meaningful opportunity to present their
asylum claims. The primary reason was the close political relationship between the US government and the Duvalier regime, which shared its anti-
Communist objectives. In a case blocking the deportation of Haitians, Judge
James Lawrence King also pointed to a racial double standard in US asylum
policy:

> The plaintiffs are part of the first substantial flight of black refugees
> from a repressive regime to this country. All the plaintiffs are black.
> Prior to the most recent Cuban exodus all of the Cubans who sought
> political asylum . . . were granted asylum routinely. None of the over
> 4,000 Haitians processed during the INS program at issue in the law-
> suit were granted asylum. No greater disparity can be imagined.[40]

Another example is Trump's call for giving preferential treatment to Christian
refugees from majority-Muslim countries because of a cultural affinity with
a vision of America as a Christian nation. But the preference for Christians
seems to be a thinly veiled attempt to ban Muslims, something Trump prom-
ised to do during his presidential campaign, which several courts held was
behind his executive order banning travel from predominantly Muslim countries.[41] Even where a preference for one group is not motivated by animus
against another group, it is hard to justify selecting on the basis of religious
or cultural affinity in the case of refugees given the urgency of their needs
and unless there are other countries who will take in the disfavored groups.
The United States could only prioritize Christian refugees if there are indeed
other countries that are willing to take in Muslim refugees at comparably

higher numbers to make up for the United States taking in lower numbers of Muslim refugees, but this assumption seems unlikely to be met.

Another principle that should be factored into determining a fair distribution of the responsibility to take in refugees is *causal responsibility* for turning people into refugees—that is, the idea that an agent who has caused a particular outcome bears a duty to remedy that outcome. We might adopt a principle of proportionality in assigning remedial responsibility: the greater the agent's role in causing the harm, the greater the remedial responsibility. Causal responsibility for refugee crises is often the result of military involvement, such as the NATO bombings impacting Kosovar Albanians, US encouragement of Kurdish rebellions during the Gulf War, and US and Australian actions in Indo-China during the 1960s and 1970s.[42] Another example is US involvement in the civil wars in Central America. In 2014, President Obama declared the "surge" of Central American children crossing the US border to be a humanitarian crisis; but the causes of the displacement had been developing over a much longer period, as intense drug wars, gang violence, and failing infrastructure turned Honduras, El Salvador, and Guatemala, known as the Northern Triangle, into the "murder capitals" of the world. The current violence in these three countries stems in part from the civil wars in the region in the 1970s and 1980s, which were funded by the United States and resulted in the prevalence of arms in the region.[43] The US government bears some causal responsibility for creating the conditions that have forced unaccompanied minors to flee, and it has the integrative capabilities to take them in, but the Obama administration chose to treat the "surge" as an enforcement problem rather than a refugee crisis, placing these children on a "rocket docket" limiting meaningful due process and access to competent counsel. Meanwhile, immigration judges moved in the opposite direction as the Obama administration, granting asylum to thousands of women and children who had fled gang violence in Honduras, El Salvador, and Guatemala.[44]

To sum up, a fair distribution of the responsibility to take in refugees is one based on integrative capabilities and causal responsibility, not solely or primarily on geographic proximity. Wealthier countries with stronger integrative capabilities should bear more responsibility than poorer countries with weaker integrative capabilities. Causal responsibility for creating refugee crises should also play a part in the process of assigning refugees to specific countries.

The foregoing discussion is admittedly utopian. States have shown little political will to do more than the bare minimum to assist refugees, and they are unlikely to agree on the criteria for determining a "fair share" of refugees to take in. Currently, the UNHCR is the international agency that registers refugees and presents them to states for resettlement consideration, but this process is entirely dependent on the good will of states. Participation in the international system is viewed as discretionary, not obligatory, and resettlement takes place on a small scale, and states tend to select the "best and brightest" refugees.[45] But these difficulties do not obviate the duty of states to do their fair share to assist refugees, including taking them in.

Just as nonrefoulement has come to be regarded as a duty with a binding character, resettlement should also be regarded as a binding duty. States have a duty to cooperate in an international refugee-protection system, and this involves working with international organizations like the UNHCR to determine a fair allocation of financial contributions to be made and refugees to be taken in. It would be a huge step forward for states to recognize that they have a duty to resettle refugees and to engage in debates about the relevance of different criteria for determining a fair distribution. Some principled determination of what constitutes "fair shares" must be pursued in advance of any particular refugee movement, but this must also be open to revision as new conflicts and crises arise. In mass-flight situations, with large unorganized arrivals, as European countries have recently seen, a fair burden-sharing scheme must include not only taking in a fair share of "overseas" refugees awaiting permanent resettlement but also asylum-seekers who have already set foot in the countries in which they are seeking asylum.

States could assume a range of protection roles in fulfilling their responsibility-sharing quotas (e.g., protection for the duration of risk, permanent integration, resettlement), but all states would be required to make financial contributions and take in refugees, with no trade-offs between the two.[46] While the number of refugees is at a historic high, the 21.3 million refugees still constitute less than 0.3 percent of the world's population. The UNHCR's budget for 2016 is substantially lower than the amount American consumers spend annually on Halloween costumes, decorations, and candy.[47] The "crisis" of refugees is less a crisis in terms of numbers and protection capacity and more a failure among states to meet their moral responsibilities.

While I have offered normative arguments for why developed countries should do more to assist refugees, there are also systemic pressures for them to do more. There is a real risk that the states hosting most of the world's refugees will stop cooperating in the international refugee protection regime without greater assistance from developed countries. The perception that wealthy countries in the global North can play by different rules risks prompting the major refugee-hosting states such as Turkey, Lebanon, and Jordan to pursue restrictive policies of their own. In addition, the deterrence approach taken by many wealthy countries sometimes proves ineffective. Rather than wait for international assistance that may not be forthcoming, many people fleeing persecution and violence have taken matters into their own hands, undertaking perilous journeys to Europe and North America. Over one million people arrived by sea in Europe in 2015, more than a fourfold increase over the previous year's 216,000 arrivals.[48] Although specific deterrence measures may be successful in stemming particular migration paths in the short term, sophisticated smuggling operations and the rerouting of migration flows toward alternative routes can significantly undermine border control efforts.[49] Migrants have shown extraordinary determination and resilience in the face of restrictive border policies, revealing the limits of state capacity to keep migrants out. States have not only an obligation to do their fair share to assist refugees; it is also in their self-interest to cooperate in the international refugee-protection system.

The Role of Refugees' Preferences

Imagine that there is an international refugee responsibility-sharing regime in place, with widespread agreement on the definition of who counts as a refugee, what is owed to refugees, and how to distribute that responsibility fairly among states. The next step would be to resettle refugees across states in a way that reflects the predetermined fair shares. What role, if any, should refugees' preferences for particular countries play in their resettlement?

The current UNHCR framework does not take refugee preferences into account. Some scholars argue this is as it should be. Refugees have a moral right to state protection in a safe country, not a right to gain asylum in the country of their choice. David Owen argues that "a refugee's right to sanctuary . . . does not entail a right to residence in a state of their choice, rather it simply designates a right in some state which is not their own." Similarly, Joseph Carens has argued that "refugees have a moral right to a safe place to live, but they do not have a moral entitlement to choose where that will be."[50] But why shouldn't refugees' preferences play a role in their resettlement? Some refugees express their preference by undertaking dangerous journeys to reach the countries of their choice, even after they have reached safe countries. They strive to reach countries where their families and ethnic kin are already settled and where they believe labor markets will be most receptive to their skills. Other refugees wish to remain close to their native countries, partly out

of a desire to return home when conditions are safe and partly because they
have linguistic and cultural affinities with neighboring countries.

One problem with privileging refugee's preferences for where they are
resettled is that it risks undermining the fair distribution of refugees across
states since some states are more popular destinations than others. Think of
the Syrian refugees risking their lives to get to Germany and unaccompanied
minors from Central America traveling through Mexico to get to the United
States. One way to address the distributive concern would be to compensate
the states that take in more refugees beyond their fair share. Compensation
could take the form of direct payments to more popular destination states
or payments to support the work of the UNHCR that would reduce the
amount the popular destination states must contribute. Paying states for
taking in more refugees may sound like a market in trading refugee protection quotas in which less-popular destination countries pay more popular
destination countries to take in refugees. But the idea here is not a market
scheme like the one proposed by Peter Schuck in which countries that are unable or unwilling to assume their share of the responsibility to take in refugees
trade that responsibility to another country in exchange for money.[51] Instead,
states would still be required to take in their fair share of refugees, but the
more popular destination states that accept additional refugees would be
compensated by less-popular destination states. Another contrast with the
market in refugee quotas is this: it is the preferences of refugees themselves,
not the preferences of states, which push against the fair distribution of
quotas. There would likely be tensions between aiming at fairness in responsibility sharing among states and respecting the agency and legitimate interests
of refugees. The tension may be diminished if, instead of granting refugees
their first choice, they were offered a limited range of different asylum countries that take their preferences into account.

There are no easy answers here. My point is that the interests of refugees
themselves should play some role in the deliberations of the responsibility-
sharing regime that determines where they are to be resettled but in a way that
does not undermine the basic fairness in the distribution of responsibility
among states. The role of refugees' preferences is especially important in the
case of those who seek to be reunited with family members already residing
in particular host states and in reparative asylum cases in which refugees seek
admission to a particular country in virtue of a prior relationship.[52] Other
preferences, such as going to a country with labor markets most receptive to
one's skills or with more generous social welfare provisions, seem less weighty
than the family reunification and reparative claims.

Limits of Our Obligations to Refugees

Are there limits to our obligations to refugees? The Refugee Convention outlines specific limits on the responsibility of states to assist refugees. States may expel refugees "on grounds of national security or public order," but such a decision must be reached "in accordance with due process of law" (art. 32). The duty of nonrefoulement is overridden when there are "reasonable grounds" to regard a refugee as "a danger to the security of the country" (art. 33). Other than these specific provisions, the Convention does not outline any general limits on the obligation of states to protect refugees. Is there an upper bound to how many refugees states must take in?

David Miller has argued that the obligation to admit refugees is limited by considerations of cost. "A state that has set an overall immigration target, on grounds that are publicly justifiable, can also take steps to ensure that the number of refugees it admits does not exceed that target." He acknowledges that this may lead to "a tragic conflict of values: on the one side, people who are liable to be severely harmed as a result of the persecution they are undergoing; on the other, bounded political communities that are able to sustain democracy and achieve a modicum of social justice but need closure to do this." Faced with such a conflict, he concludes, "it is better to say honestly that not everyone can be rescued."[53]

I agree that states should give priority to securing the basic rights of its own members over the basic rights of outsiders.[54] There are limits to the duty of rescue: we are required to assist only if we can do so without incurring serious risk of harm to ourselves. But I disagree with where Miller seems to set the upper bound on the costs that wealthy democratic countries should bear. We need to weigh what is at stake for the receiving countries against what is at stake for refugees in need of resettlement. States have the right to control their own borders, but this right is qualified by a duty to assist refugees. Miller suggests that states can set a cap on refugees wherever they please, regardless of their integrative capabilities to take in refugees and without consideration of the worldwide need for resettlement. It is hard to see why the urgent interests of refugees should not take priority when the interests at stake for the receiving countries is much less vital. The costs to host societies would need to be much more serious—for example, genuine threats to public order or serious erosion of social welfare provision—to justify turning refugees away. Determining where to draw this line is fraught with difficulty, but virtually no wealthy democratic state can reasonably maintain it has taken in so many refugees that it has reached the upper limit.[55]

Some Implications

I want to consider the implications of the foregoing discussion for one pressing contemporary refugee crisis. The UN estimates that over ten million Syrians have been displaced by the civil war since it began in 2011. Many have been internally displaced within Syria, and others have fled to neighboring countries, where they are eking out an existence. Those in refugee camps are dependent on humanitarian assistance and food aid, and have limited or no opportunities for education or work. There are roughly 5.6 million registered Syrian refugees, making up 25 percent of the 22.5 million registered refugees worldwide.[56] As of April 2017, the UNHCR had submitted a total of 211,446 Syrian refugees for resettlement, with the largest numbers submitted to Canada, Germany, and the United States[57]

Over a million Syrians have taken matters into their own hands, attempting the perilous journey by land and sea to reach Europe. As of October 2017, 996,204 Syrians had applied for asylum in thirty-seven European countries, and 64 percent of those applications were made to Germany and Sweden.[58] The pattern of asylum applications has not fallen equally across European countries, pointing again to the need for regional and international cooperation to assist refugees. The European Union should support a more equitable resettlement program among member states by creating incentives for compliance, such as joint skills training and employment-generation projects. Creating a new system for managing this reality requires cooperation with the UNHCR and political will among EU member states, which has been lacking.

Some take the view that the migration crisis in Europe is largely Europe's responsibility, but distant wealthy countries such as the United States also have a remedial responsibility in virtue of their integrative capabilities. The US overseas refugee program has admitted around 70,000 persons per year for the last several years.[59] In response to the Syrian refugee crisis, President Obama negotiated with Congress to increase the overseas refugee resettlement quota from 70,000 to 110,000. By contrast, President Trump has cut the total number of refugees to be admitted down to 45,000, the lowest that any US president has sought since Congress delegated the power to set the quota for annual refugee admissions to the president.[60] Meanwhile, Canada has admitted the largest number of refugees in nearly four decades, resettling nearly 30,000 refugees in 2016 and a total of 40,081 Syrian refugees from November 2015 to January 2017.[61] The United States is moving in the wrong direction. These necessitous migrants need a new start in a new country and countries with integrative capabilities must do their part by taking them in.

Conclusion

There is no reformed refugee or migration system that can solve the humanitarian problems caused by war and pervasive conflict. Addressing the challenges of migration must be part of broader efforts to end the conflict, violence, and deprivation that fuel migration. Ending violence is a necessary, not sufficient, step for sustaining peace and security. Additional forms of assistance and support are needed: peace-building efforts to help restore the rule of law and development assistance, including creating infrastructure, delivering public services, and supporting economic reconstruction and community engagement. Establishing robust development programs rather than militarizing the borders should be an essential component of any migration-control program and should be presented as such to citizens of democratic societies. States have the right to control immigration, but this right is qualified by the obligation to assist refugees. This means states have a duty to co-operate in the international refugee-protection system and take in their fair share of refugees.

8

The Claims of Family

FAMILY-BASED IMMIGRATION MAKES up a large share of the regular admissions for permanent residence in many democratic countries. Family-based immigration represents just under 50 percent of total admissions in Germany and less than one-third in the United Kingdom. In France, Canada, and Australia, family-based immigration is around 65 percent.[1] In the United States, about 65 percent of all visas for permanent residence in 2015 were granted based on explicit family categories.[2]

Considering these large percentages, it is not surprising that family migration schemes have come under criticism for crowding out other kinds of migration. The economist George Borjas has argued the United States should move toward a skills-based points system like Canada's:

> By restricting the entry of persons who are "too old" or "too unskilled" or "doing the wrong kind of job," the point system attempts to match immigrant skills with labor market needs and reduces the fiscal burden that immigration would place on Canada's generous system of public assistance.[3]

Borjas is concerned not only with the fiscal costs that low-skilled immigrants place on the social welfare systems of host countries but also how the immigration of low-skilled workers impacts low-skilled workers who are already part of the labor market.[4] Based on similar concerns, political theorist Stephen Macedo has suggested reforms "limiting immigration based on family reunification (perhaps limiting that preference to spouses and minor children)" and prioritizing high-skilled migrants.[5] Lawmakers have indeed tried to restrict family-based immigration. The 2013 immigration reform bill proposed in the US Congress sought to create a points system prioritizing skills and education and reducing family visas to 50 percent of the total number of permanent residence visas. The bill also sought to eliminate the preference for siblings and adult children of citizens.[6]

Such moves to restrict family-based immigration beg some important normative questions. Why should states privilege family relationships in designing immigration policy? Is the family an appropriate basis on which to distribute rights and responsibilities, including admission and membership in a country? Which relationships have counted as family, and which relationships should count? The first section examines why family relationships are an appropriate basis for distributing visas. I argue that claims for family migration involve both human rights and membership-based claims that constitute obligatory admissions.[7] I then critically assess the traditional model of the family reflected in contemporary immigration law and argue for a more pluralistic conception of family. I contend that the reasons for privileging family relationships in immigration policy apply to nonfamilial relationships of care.

Justifying Family-based Immigration

In considering what might ground the state's obligation to keep families together in its immigration decisions, we need to keep in mind two distinct points of view: that of prospective migrants who wish to be with their families and that of citizens who want to sponsor their families. Arguments from both points of view rely on the premise that people have a basic interest in forming and maintaining family relations, which grounds a human right to family life, but the claims of prospective migrants rest entirely on an appeal to human rights, whereas the claims of citizens are claims of membership.

A basic human interest in family is recognized in international human rights documents. Articles 12 and 16 of the Universal Declaration of Human Rights declare "the right to marry and to found a family" and the right to be protected against "arbitrary interference" with one's family to be basic human rights. The declaration states the family is "the natural and fundamental group unit of society and is entitled to protection by society and the State." The same language appears in articles 17 and 23 of the International Covenant on Civil and Political Rights.[8] We need not accept the characterization of the family as "natural" to recognize that family relations are a fundamental component of human life.

What is the moral significance of family relations? Family relations are intimate relations of love, affection, and care. They involve not only material caregiving, such as the provision of food, clothing, and housing, but also attitudinal care, which involves an affective stance on the part of the care-giver who is personally attached to and seeks to promote the well-being of the cared for.[9] Young children depend on adult caregivers not only to provide for their material and psychological needs but also to foster their physical, emotional, and moral development. To meet these developmental interests, children need intimate caring relationships with particular people, be they parents, grandparents, or other guardians. Adults also depend on one another for material caregiving and attitudinal care, especially during times of illness, injury, and advanced age. Family relationships are "intimate" in two senses. First, they are intimate in form: they feature "strong and mutual familiarity, ordinarily grounded in regular, intensive, 'face to face' interaction." Second, they are intimate in purpose: their primary purpose is "the pursuit and enjoy-ment of intimacy-related goods," such as companionship, love, and mutual care.[10] What is significant about intimate family relationships is the provision of material caregiving and attitudinal care.[11]

These morally significant features of intimate family relations undergird the human right to family life. The implication for immigration policy is that states should admit families together, instead of separating them, when it offers admission to prospective migrants. What about families who are separated by state borders? Are states obligated to permit migration for the sake of family reunification?

One might ask why the fundamental interest in family life must be protected by admitting family members from abroad instead of asking the citizens to move abroad or, more harshly, by demanding that they establish new families, however painful that might be. Consider the example of an American citizen who marries a Mexican citizen. Why should the United States admit the Mexican spouse when the American citizen could move to Mexico or when each could find a new partner instead? The right to family is the right to be with particular people, so if the state were to insist that the couple find new partners, it would fail to acknowledge the significance of the right to family. Why is the state obligated to design its immigration policies to accommodate the locational preferences of individuals who wish to remain *and* have their family members from abroad join them where they currently reside?

The answer rests on another fundamental interest people have: the in-terest in continuing to live in a place where they have settled and developed attachments and expectations.[12] The American citizen can say that she has built a life in the United States and that she and her Mexican spouse have decided that living in the United States is best for them. It is the right to the particular place where one has built a life, combined with the right to family, that grounds the case for family-based immigration. Individuals should not be forced to choose between living with their families and living in the particular place they call home.

But what if the Mexican citizen has set down equally deep roots in Mexico? Why can't the United States insist that the couple reunite and live in Mexico? This is where the membership-based argument comes in. Political membership offers a distinct ground for the duty of states to permit family reunification through immigration. The right to sponsor one's family is a right of political membership. That we have distinctive rights and responsibilities in virtue of political membership is part of the ethic of membership developed in this book. This idea is reflected in the domestic law of Western states and by transnational legal bodies, such as the European Court of Human Rights, which has held that family reunification is about the right of insiders (citizens and permanent residents) to be joined by their migrant family members, and not the right of outsiders who want to be admitted.[13]

Matthew Lister has developed the most comprehensive membership-based argument for family immigration to date, based on the value of freedom of association.[14] Following Rawls, Lister characterizes the value of associational freedom in virtue of its role in nurturing the moral powers necessary for good citizenship. First, by interacting with others within a range of associations, we learn to moderate our desires and consider the good of others, thereby developing a sense of justice. Rawls himself highlights the crucial role of the family in "the raising and caring of children, ensuring their moral development and education into the wider culture."[15] Freedom of association is also critical to fostering our ability to form, revise, and pursue our own life plans. Lister advances these considerations to defend the right to form and maintain intimate relationships as "a subspecies of the general right to freedom of association."[16] He posits that the degree of intimacy of the association makes a normative difference: the more intimate the relationship, the less discretion the state has to limit it. So, his argument has greatest force with respect to "immediate family members," who include the adult partners and dependent children who constitute "the minimal core of the family."[17]

There are at least two problems with Lister's account. First, freedom of association is a value that has been used to argue for the state's right to *exclude* migrants. Lister's freedom-of-association argument that citizens can be joined by their noncitizen family members conflicts with the freedom-of-association argument that allows citizens to keep noncitizens out.[18] Why should a citizen's right to associate with her family trump the right of the political community to exclude nonmembers? Appealing to the value of free association itself does not help us resolve this conflict. Lister thus appeals to the idea of intimacy to explain why the claims of familial association should trump the claims of political association, but this points to a second problem. How should we understand intimacy? In terms of the size or purpose of the association or how well associates know one another? Lister does not provide criteria for defining intimate associations, appealing instead to our "common understanding of what is important about and to the family."[19] He suggests there is a universal overlapping consensus about the "core" of family as made up of two adult partners and their dependent children, but as I'll argue, there is no such consensus. Instead of identifying an overlapping consensus, Lister has defined the "core" of family in accordance with the dominant legal definition of family.

The Family in US Immigration Law

The marital nuclear family enjoys legal supremacy, but it is a mistake to regard this conception of family as fixed or settled. I focus on the United States to show how the law has privileged the marital nuclear family over other relationships, but such privileging is by no means unique to the United States

The federal government's power to regulate immigration over and above state governments was established in a series of cases in the late nineteenth century involving Asian migrants (see chapter 2). Even during the era of Chinese exclusion, some provision for family reunification with spouses and children was made for Chinese men who were merchants. Some Chinese merchants were permitted to be reunited with their spouses and children, partly because of the gendered privilege of a man's right to family unity and partly because the class status of Chinese merchants aligned with the class bias of the idealized American family.[20]

The 1924 National Origins Quota Act sought to maintain a white Anglo-Saxon America, capping immigrant admissions with "quotas" intended to reflect the existing US population. A committee jointly administered by the Departments of Labor, Commerce, and State was charged with apportioning quotas based on the number of inhabitants in the United States in 1920 who could trace their ancestry back to particular countries. It had the effect of almost doubling the UK quota and curtailing immigration from southern and eastern Europe. The law expressly excluded all Asian nationalities from admissions. But the law did contain a family-unity provision: spouses of US citizens who were racially eligible for citizenship did not count against the national origins quotas. Asian spouses and children of US citizens were barred from admission as non-quota immigrants.[21] Chinese exclusion and the bar on Chinese naturalization were repealed in 1943 as part of the American diplomatic alliance with China against Japan. Immigrants of Chinese descent were still limited to 105 a year, but an exception was made for spouses.[22]

It was the 1965 Immigration and Nationality Act that made family reunification the centerpiece of US immigration law. It removed the national origins quotas. Seventy-four percent of all visas in the preference system were reserved for family members of citizens and permanent residents. The 1965 Act also plucked the *parents* of US citizens from the preference system and redefined them as "immediate family" members, alongside spouses and children, all of whom were exempt from the quotas. The 1965 preference system established the following family preferences:[23]

Nonquota (no cap)	"Immediate family members" of US citizens
First preference	Unmarried sons and daughters of citizens (20%)
Second preference	Spouses, unmarried (minor and adult) sons and daughters of permanent residents (20%)
Third preference	Members of professions of exceptional ability in the arts and sciences and their spouses and children (10%)
Fourth preference	Married sons and daughters of citizens and their spouses and children (10%)
Fifth preference	Brothers and sisters of citizens and their spouses and children (24%)
Sixth preference	Skilled/unskilled workers in occupations in which labor is in short supply and their spouses and children (10%)
Seventh preference	Refugees (6%)

This preference system remains in place today. In 1990, to address serious backlogs that divided immigrants from their spouses and dependent children, Congress subdivided the second preference into two subcategories they labeled 2A and 2B:

2A preference   Spouses and (minor) children of permanent residents

2B preference   Unmarried (adult) sons and daughters of permanent
                       residents

Congress allocated a much greater percentage of admissions to the 2A preference, requiring that at least 77 percent of the second preference be set
aside for 2A applicants (referred to as the "2A floor") and 75 percent of the
2A floor be exempt from per country limits. Adult children in the 2B category cannot claim more than 23 percent of the admissions available under
the second preference. Any additional spots that happen to become available for family-sponsored immigration in a given year are granted to 2A
applicants.

In 1995, the Commission on Immigration Reform, created by the 1990
Immigration Act and chaired by former US Representative Barbara Jordan,
sought to privilege spouses and minor children even more. The commission
recommended the elimination of *all* family preferences except 2A in order
to create more openings for 2A applicants.[24] The commission also urged that
150,000 additional visas be made available annually on an interim basis until
the 2A backlog was addressed, which at the time was 1.2 million applicants. By
privileging 2A over other family preferences, the commission sought to prioritize the reunification of lawful resident *noncitizens* with their "nuclear family"
over the reunification of *citizens* with their nonnuclear family members (adult
sons and daughters or brothers and sisters). The commission's recommendation suggested that the citizenship status of the sponsor matters less than
reuniting residents with their "nuclear family." A diverse coalition made up
of ethnic advocacy and business organizations successfully mobilized against
the recommendations.

Current immigration law allows the following categories of family-based
immigration:

Nonquota   Immediate relatives of US citizens (no cap)

First preference   Unmarried sons and daughters of citizens[25] (23,400
                      admissions annually)

2A preference   Spouses or children of LPRs (lawful permanent
                      resident) (minimum of 114,200 admissions annually)

2B preference   Unmarried sons and daughters of LPRs (no more
                      than 23% of all 2nd pref. admissions)

Third preference   Married sons and daughters of citizens, their spouses
                      and children (23,400 admissions annually)
Fourth preference   Brothers and sisters of citizens (65,000 admissions
                      annually)[26]

If we look at the statistics for actual admissions for the most recent year available, we see that the family relationships given greatest priority are indeed spouses and children of US citizens and lawful permanent residents (LPRs). In 2015, the total number of people granted lawful permanent residence was 1,051,031. Table 8.1 shows the numbers and percentages for the different admissions categories in 2015.

Spouses and children of US citizens accounted for 31.3 percent of the total number of visas granted, and parents of US citizens made up 12.7 percent. Spouses and children of LPRs accounted for 10 percent of the total number of visas and half of all family-sponsored preferences. Combining the spouses and children of citizens and of LPRs, spouses and children made up 41.3 percent of all admissions in 2015. If we add up all immediate relatives of citizens and all family-sponsored preferences, they constitute almost 65 percent of all visas granted in 2015, compared to only 14 percent for employment-based preferences and 11 percent for refugees.

The percentage of family-based immigration is even higher than the 65 percent officially counted by government statistics. The government counts spouses and children accompanying or following to join a "principal" applicant admitted under an employment preference under the same employment preference.[27] In 2015, there were 75,423 spouses and children admitted under employment preferences, constituting 52 percent of all persons admitted under the employment preferences. If we include all immigrants who are admitted *on the basis of family ties* but officially categorized under "employment" or "refugee" admissions, the percentage of family-based immigration exceeds 75 percent.[28] In sum, family-based immigration makes up the lion's share of visa allocations in the United States, and the family form most privileged by immigration law is the marital nuclear family.

Changing Family Practices and the Limits of the Argument from Tradition

The traditional model of the marital nuclear family is the standard against which all other forms of intimacy and kinship are judged. One might argue

Table 8.1 Persons Granted Lawful Permanent Resident (LPR) Status
by Category of Admission for 2015*

Admissions category	No. of persons	Percentage of total admissions
Immediate relatives	465,068	44.2%
Spouses	265,367	25.2%
Children	66,740	6.3%
Parents	132,961	12.7%
Total family-sponsored preferences	213,910	20.3%
First family preference (unmarried sons/daughters of citizens)	24,533	2.3%
Second family preference (spouses, children, unmarried sons/daughters of LPRs)	104,892	10%
Third family preference (married sons/daughters of US citizens and their spouses and children)	24,271	2.3%
Fourth family preference (brothers/sisters of US citizens and their spouses and children)	60,214	5.7%
Immediate relatives plus all family-sponsored preferences	678,978	64.5%
Employment-based preferences	144,047	14%
Diversity lottery	47,934	4.5%
Refugees	118,431	11%
Asylees	33,564	3%
Total admissions for 2015 (including new arrivals and adjustment of status)	1,051,031	

*My calculation of percentages is based on data provided by Department of Homeland Security, *Yearbook of Immigration Statistics 2015*, table 6, https://www.dhs.gov/immigration-statistics/yearbook/2015.

this is as it should be: the law *should* privilege the socially dominant form of family. Call this the argument from tradition. According to this argument, the law should mirror and support the traditional family forms and practices that have persisted over time. Mark Krikorian, the executive director of the Center for Immigration Studies, makes such an argument:

Husband, wife, and young children constitute the family core, and these should be the only relationships that trigger immigrant admission.

Most of the other relationships—adult sons and daughters of citizens or permanent residents, parents and siblings of citizens—cover people who are adults, with their own lives, for whom the "family reunification" rationale for this element of immigration policy is a misnomer.[29]

The assumption is that the traditional "family core" consists of a husband, wife, and their young children, and therefore to regard one's adult children or siblings as part of one's "family" is a category mistake.

This narrow view of family is also reflected in the 2007 immigration bill introduced in the US Senate. The bill sought to increase visas for spouses and children of citizens and LPRs and eliminate visas for siblings and to shift toward more skills-based immigration. The Republican senator Jeff Sessions criticized broad definitions of family while also seeking to avoid the charge of being "anti-family":

> I reject the idea that a movement to a system such as Canada's or Australia's that is based on merit and skills for immigration is somehow, as I think Senator Reid said, an attack on the family . . . So how is this an attack on the family if we say: You can come, you can be a citizen, but right up front, you cannot bring your parents, adult children, and siblings, you don't have any special rights to do so, but they can apply if they qualify, just like everybody else, based on their own merit.[30]

By Sessions's logic, the family simply does not include parents, adult children, and siblings. Therefore, a bill to eliminate these categories in immigration law is not an attack on the family.

But this argument from tradition is undermined by changes in family practices over the last forty years. In the United States, the marital nuclear family has been declining since the 1970s. Consider the following highlights from US Census Bureau data about how American families have changed since 1970:

- Family households were down from 81 percent in 1970 to 66 percent in 2012. Nonfamily households (defined as someone living alone or a householder who shares the housing unit only with nonrelatives) represented one-third of all households.
- The share of households that were married couples with children declined from 40 percent in 1970 to 20 percent in 2012.
- "Other family" households (families whose householder was living with children or other relatives but had no spouse present) has increased from 11 percent in 1970 to 18 percent in 2012.

- Living alone has become more widespread. The proportion of one-person households increased from 17 percent in 1970 to 27 percent in 2012. In 2011, there were 32 million one-person households compared with 56 million married-couple households.[31]

The most noticeable trends are the decline of married-couple households with children and the increase of "other family" households. These "other families" include unmarried-parent couples, single mothers with children under age eighteen, single fathers with children under eighteen, and grandparents living with their grandchildren. Both the absolute number and relative size of all "other family" groups, except for unmarried mothers, have increased since 2007.[32] Married couples with children remain the most common type of family group regardless of race, but if you add up all the other-family households, the total is roughly equal to the number of married-couple-with-children households. Another striking trend is the increase in people living alone. The sociologist Eric Klinenberg calls these individuals, whether never married, divorced, or widowed, "singletons."[33]

Despite this changing social reality, US immigration law continues to rest largely on the traditional image of the marital nuclear family. Grandparents, aunts and uncles, cousins, and nieces and nephews generally lack rights of immigration, regardless of their emotional or financial relationship to the potential sponsor. The United States allows citizens to sponsor their parents but not their grandparents, and LPRs can sponsor spouses and children but not their parents. This legal privileging of marital nuclear families over multigenerational families disadvantages Latino and Asian American households more than other households.[34]

Marital nuclear families are also privileged in Europe. According to the 2003 European Union Family Reunion Directive, third-country national residents can apply to sponsor spouses and dependent children. Parents, grandparents, and adult children may be sponsored in six EU countries, but they face restrictions in other EU countries. For example, third-country nationals have no clear entitlement to sponsor their parents in Belgium, adult children in Latvia and Luxembourg, or either group in Austria, Bulgaria, Cyprus, France, Greece, and Malta.[35] The European Court of Human Rights has tended to define family narrowly as parents and their dependent children, depriving all other family members of protection from deportation under article 8 of the European Convention of Human Rights, which codifies the right of everyone to respect for private and family life.[36]

Which Relationships?

How should family be defined? Which relationships should be recognized as bases for legal protections and privileges? The law should move beyond the traditional model of family as based on marriage and blood ties to recognize a broader range of personal relationships.

Philosophers and political theorists have provided reasons why we should regard the family as essential for human well-being. In developing a theory of human capabilities, Martha Nussbaum includes "affiliation" on the list of basic human needs, pointing to "intimate family," as well as to social and civic affiliations.[37] But what is special about family as a form of affiliation? As I discussed earlier, the family has been critical to meeting basic human needs of love and care deriving from what legal scholar Martha Fineman calls our "inevitable dependencies," from infancy and early childhood through illness and disability to the fragility of advanced old age. These circumstances of dependency are undeniable facts of human existence. The philosopher Eva Kittay points to the fact that human dependency and interconnectedness are necessary for our survival to argue for a moral principle of care: "[I]n order to grow, flourish, and survive or endure illness, disability and frailty, each individual requires a caring relationship with significant others who hold that individual's well-being as a primary responsibility and a primary good."[38] It is important to stress that caring relationships consist not only of the giving and receiving of material care; they are also deep attachments to particular people based on love, affection, and emotional interdependence. The principle of care, together with the principle of doulia, which requires supporting those who do the work of caring, offer reasons to authorize the use of collective resources to support particular relationships of care and dependency.

If caretaking is what we value about family, then we should define the family in terms of this caretaking function, not simply by marriage or biological ties as has been the case. Over twenty years ago, Fineman called for ending marriage as a legal category and replacing what she called the "sexual family" with the "caretaking family" as the core of our ideal of family. On Fineman's approach, the protections historically extended to the "sexual dyad of Husband/Wife" would be replaced by protections to the "nurturing unit of caretaker and dependent" exemplified by the Mother/Child dyad.[39] Given the decline of the marital nuclear family, adopting an approach that includes a broader range of caretaking family relationships is prudent, as well as morally required.

What does this imply for immigration policy? At the very least, we should adopt a more pluralistic conception of family and extend legal recognition to a broader range of caregiving relationships. This approach continues to attach rights and responsibilities to family over nonfamily relationships because, as political theorist Iseult Honohan has argued, "the family, more than friends, remains as a locus of relatively permanent or durable relations of shared affection and support, of joint projects over time, characteristically relations of intergenerational care and concern across a lifetime."[40]

We can see a more pluralistic notion of family reflected in Canadian immigration law. Like the United States, the "family class" in Canadian law includes a spouse, fiancé(e), parent, and dependent child (defined as under twenty-two years old and unmarried) or a child whom the sponsor intends to adopt. Unlike in the United States, a Canadian citizen or permanent resident may also sponsor:

- an unmarried common-law or conjugal partner (including same-sex partners);
- a grandparent;
- an uncle or aunt;
- a nephew or niece;
- *another relative of any age or relationship* if none of the other listed relatives could be sponsored and the applicant has no other relatives who are Canadian citizens, permanent residents, or registered Indians under the Indian Act;
- accompanying relatives of the above (for example, spouse, partner, and dependent children).[41]

Canadian law goes beyond the marital family by permitting unmarried partners, grandparents, and other extended relatives to be sponsored by citizens. In doing so, Canadian law reflects the judgment articulated by the Canadian Immigration Legislative Review Advisory Group's framework for immigration: "Individuals best understand where their emotional priorities lie, and consequently what constitutes their family."[42]

A more pluralistic definition of family is also reflected in the work the UNHCR does with refugee families. The UNHCR has advocated for shifting away from predetermined legal conceptions of the family toward a broader definition of family in assessing the reunification claims of refugee families. Because refugees typically depend on extended family members, the UNHCR contends that "economic and emotional relationships between refugee family members be given equal weight and importance in the criteria for reunification as relationships based on blood lineage or legally sanctioned unions."[43]

Beyond broadening the definition of family, a more radical approach would involve *disestablishing the family* altogether. If the reason for privileging marital family relationships is on account of the caregiving function, we should stop privileging family per se and recognize all relationships that serve the same function, including nonfamilial ones. On this more radical approach, family relationships based on biology or marriage alone would no longer serve as a basis for allocating public benefits and burdens. Analogizing with church-state relations, the legal scholars Alice Ristroph and Melissa Murray have argued that the state has "established" the family in the state's preferred image of the heterosexual marital family. It has regulated families qua families in ways that encourage monogamy, procreation, industriousness, and financial self-sufficiency of the family, which has gone hand in hand with fostering financial dependency within the family:

> In the traditional family recognized in early American law, men were disciplined by their obligations to support wives and children, women were disciplined by their caregiving obligations and their financial dependence on their husbands, and children were disciplined by their disciplined parents ... Even as American law has changed to recognize a broader array of familial relationships, these norms of order, discipline, and intrafamilial dependence have persisted.[44]

Ristroph and Murray argue for disestablishing the family for the same reasons marshaled in support of religious disestablishment: respecting the freedom of individuals to make the most important personal decisions themselves. We can see signs of "familial disestablishment" in the dismantling of adultery prohibitions, legitimacy classifications, and sodomy bans, all of which have loosened the grip of the marital family in American law.

In liberal democratic societies, we can point to two fundamental values that support recognizing a broader range of personal relationships beyond the traditional family. The first is personal autonomy, the freedom of individuals to make personal decisions for themselves. Forming and pursuing intimate relationships is one key way we exercise personal autonomy, and intimate relationships are also critical to fostering our sense of self-respect. In the United States, one way this freedom has been legally articulated is as a constitutional right to privacy, which has served as the basis for the right of married and unmarried couples to use contraception, the right of a woman to choose to have an abortion, and the right to engage in intimate conduct. As the court put it in *Lawrence v. Texas,* "Freedom extends beyond spatial bounds. Liberty presumes an autonomy of self that includes freedom of thought, belief, expression, and certain intimate conduct."[45]

The second value is equality. Since the immigration reform in 1965 that opened the United States to immigration from Asia, Latin America, and Africa, the population has become more culturally diverse. Cultural diversity includes differences in conceptions of family and other personal relationships. Some accommodation of cultural differences is required as a matter of equality and fairness.[46] Equality requires recognizing familial and nonfamilial relationships that fulfill the caretaking function.

It is not only immigrants who have caretaking relationships that fall outside dominant cultural understandings of family. Many people seek and receive care in relationships beyond the families they were born or adopted into. Offering a critique of the marital family in another context, political theorist Wendy Brown points to "webs of connection across households, often consisting of overlapping circles of friends" as the most important enduring associational and affective relationships for many people. This "loose extended tribe" might include "single parents, childless adults, married couples, homosexual parents, step-families, queer and straight loners, ex-lovers, selected neighbors, and grown children."[47] Indeed, an extended tribe of friends and neighbors may be more durable than many marriages and other couplings.

What might "disestablishing the family" look like in the context of immigration? We can see moves toward disestablishment in the report of the 1997 Canadian Immigration Legislative Review Advisory Group's report, *Not Just Numbers: A Canadian Framework for Future Immigration.* The report recommends recognizing a broader range of family relations along the lines of the pluralistic approach to family discussed above. The family class should be divided into three-tiers. The first would include spouses and dependent children, and the second would include fiancé(e)s, parents, and grandparents. It is the third tier that takes a step toward disestablishing the family. It would allow the citizen sponsor "to decide who is most important to them, and who is part of what they consider family in the broadest sense. *It could even include a best friend.*" Sponsors within the third tier would have to prove that the individual they are sponsoring is "known and emotionally important to them" and also assume "a long term enforceable sponsorship commitment."[48] A 2001 Canadian Law Commission report, *Beyond Conjugality,* endorses these recommendations as part of a broader re-evaluation of many areas of law governing personal relationships in order to establish "a system that allowed for self-selection beyond ties of blood and marriage" and "would significantly advance the value of choice or autonomy, at the same time as it would respect the diversity and equality of close personal relationships."[49] The report's most radical suggestion—that citizen sponsors be permitted to identify their most meaningful relationships themselves—was not adopted by the government.[50]

The prospects for disestablishing the family in US immigration law seem much dimmer. Efforts to recognize "marriage-like" relationships have failed. In 2000, Congress briefly entertained a more inclusive approach in considering a *functional* definition of "spouse" for immigration purposes. The proposed bill, the Permanent Partners Immigration Act, would have added the phrase "and permanent partners" after the word "spouse" in many sections of the Immigration and Nationality Act, and defined "permanent partner" as an individual "in a committed, intimate relationship" that both partners intended to be lifelong.[51] Congress ultimately rejected this more inclusive functional approach.

Even as the percentage of marital families has been declining, marital supremacy seems resurgent in American law. Although the 2015 US Supreme Court decision in *Obergefell v. Hodges* guaranteeing same-sex couples the right to marry was an important civil rights victory for LGBT equality, it has also reinforced marital supremacy over other personal relationships. The ruling invalidated state laws that prohibited the legal recognition of same-sex marriage and opened the door to national recognition of marriage rights for same-sex couples. The court held that these state laws "burdened the liberty of same-sex couples" and "abridged central precepts of equality."[52] In the immigration context, this means LGBT citizens and LPRs can now sponsor their foreign national spouses for immigration. Yet, as Melissa Murray has argued, "*Obergefell* builds the case for equal access to marriage on the premise that marriage is the most profound, dignified, and fundamental institution into which individuals may enter. Alternatives to marriage . . . are by comparison undignified, less profound, and less valuable."[53]

Considering the declining social significance of marriage and the increasing diversity of personal relationships, we need an approach that decenters marriage and blood ties and recognizes a more pluralistic range of family forms and personal relationships. In democratic societies in which the values of personal autonomy and equality are of fundamental importance, members should be able to decide for themselves who their most important affiliates are. The marital nuclear family is unlikely to be disestablished anytime soon, but the values of autonomy and equality require a more pluralistic approach in which unmarried partners, grandparents, other extended relatives, best friends, and anyone else in caregiving relationships should be eligible for reunification through migration.

Objections

I want to consider two objections to the more inclusive approach to family migration schemes I have just proposed. The first concerns administrative process and efficiency.[54] From the state's perspective, immigration officials would have to devote more time and resources to screening individuals and evaluating their relationships. A more formalistic approach that narrowly focuses on marriage or a parent-child relation simply requires showing a marriage certificate, a birth certificate, or adoption papers. The administrative ease of such an approach serves an important goal of immigration law: admitting people relatively quickly and without unnecessary delay. In contrast, a functional approach would require determining whether, for example, a grandparent-grandchild relationship was the functional equivalent of a parent-child relationship as commonly understood or really counted as a caring relationship. Legislators and higher-level agency officials would have to delegate this task to lower-level officials, who may lack the relevant background and training. Implementing a functional approach may open the door to the greater abuse of discretion on the part of officials. Indeed, interviews might entail intrusions into personal and family privacy.

This concern has come up in the context of transnational marriages. Under the reforms enacted by the 1986 Immigration Marriage Fraud Amendments, a citizen-sponsor and his or her spouse of less than two years have to show that their marriage was not entered into for the "wrong" reasons, that is, for the sole purpose of immigration.[55] Having to prove the validity of one's marriage can have the effect of incentivizing couples to misrepresent their relationships, especially in ways that suppress bad yet perfectly ordinary behavior common to many marriages. As Mary Anne Case has argued, such recognition imposes additional requirements on couples with worrying consequences for their privacy.[56]

In my view, concerns about administrative efficiency, abuse of discretion, and potential intrusions into privacy do not by themselves and without more empirical evidence constitute decisive reasons for excluding a more functional approach that recognizes caring relationships for immigration purposes. A functional approach is still the right thing to do for reasons I have already discussed. The proper response is to consider how to implement a functional approach in ways that guard against abuse of discretion. One way to begin to address this concern is to identify reasonable forms of evidence for caring relationships, such as documents showing a history of living together and financial interdependence.

Anticipating such objections, the Law Commission of Canada's report "Beyond Conjugality: Recognizing and Supporting Close Personal Adult Relationships" suggested certain constraints on the right to sponsor. Instead of restricting the types of relationships that qualify for immigration sponsorship, we might place limits on sponsors: (1) the number of persons an individual could sponsor over the course of a lifetime could be capped, (2) the individual being sponsored must be "known and emotionally important" to the sponsor, and (3) to address concerns about administrative ease and privacy, the duration of the relationship might serve as a proxy for the importance of the personal relationship (the commission suggested a "close personal relationship" of at least one year). The commission also stressed that current law already imposes financial requirements: sponsoring an immigrant already entails a "serious financial commitment," and this is true not only in Canada but also in the United States and in Western Europe.[57] Many sponsors might continue to prioritize spouses and dependent children, but they would also have the option of prioritizing parents, best friends, or other close personal affiliates on the condition that they assume a long-term sponsorship commitment.

A second objection to a functional approach is a concern about the extent of the power it gives to individual citizens or permanent residents to sponsor family or other intimates from abroad. The concern is partly about numbers: the sheer volume of immigrants who may seek to enter as a "functional equivalent" of a romantic partner or long-term care provider. The US government's adoption of a more formal, as opposed to functional, approach serves to limit the numbers of immigrants seeking to use the "immediate relative" or "family preference" categories. If we were to shift to a more functional approach, we might be faced with webs of care that, arguably, extend to entire communities of people. The worry here is that individual citizens or permanent residents would have the power to unilaterally determine membership decisions via family-based immigration.[58]

This worry can be addressed by establishing criteria based on the strength and duration of relationships and by placing limits on the number of people who can be sponsored this way. States have an obligation to keep families together in immigration policy, but states also have obligations to admit refugees (chapter 7) and the discretion to admit migrants with particular skills (chapter 9). How, then, should liberal democratic states balance family migration claims with the claims of refugees and the claims of skilled migrants? A just immigration policy cannot prioritize family immigration at the expense of all other forms of migration. It must weigh different claims for admission with an eye to what is at stake both for prospective migrants and for members of the sending and receiving countries. This chapter has argued that the claims of family migrants involve basic human rights and fall into the category of obligatory admissions. The upshot is that states cannot refuse claims for family reunification without showing there is some equally morally compelling interest that would be jeopardized by permitting family migration. I will return to the question of trade-offs and priorities among different claims for admission in the final chapter of the book.

Conclusion

There is a serious gap between immigration law's narrow definition of family and the social reality of the pluralistic family forms and personal relationships that sustain individuals today. An approach that goes beyond marriage and blood ties to recognize a broader range of caring relationships would help to narrow this gap. In deciding whom to sponsor for immigration, people may continue to prioritize spouses and minor children, but the law should recognize a broader range of intimate caregiving relationships such that individuals have the choice to decide for themselves which relationships are most important to them. Such an approach would come closer to respecting the freedom and equality of individuals to fashion their personal lives for themselves.

9

Discretionary Admissions

THIS CHAPTER EXPLORES *discretionary admissions*, where the decision to admit a prospective migrant is not morally required.[1] For example, consider the case of my own family. My parents immigrated to the United States from South Korea in 1980. They had a modest life serving a small church in a town south of Seoul. They wanted to migrate to the United States for better opportunities; they were not driven by fear of persecution or necessity nor did they have any family ties to the United States. I do not think my family's claim for admission to the United States was morally obligatory in the way that the admission of refugees and other necessitous migrants (chapter 7) and those with family connections (chapter 8) is. To say that the US government was not morally required to admit my family is not to say that it should not have admitted them. As I argued in chapter 4, states have a qualified right to control immigration without external interference, which gives them considerable discretion to set immigration policy. This right is qualified by an obligation to assist those outside their borders whose basic interests are threatened, as in the case of refugees. But when the basic interests of prospective migrants are not at stake, what kinds of reasons should inform public deliberation about whom to exclude and include?

I begin by considering temporary admissions programs, asking whether they are permissible or whether all migrants must be admitted on a permanent basis. I then assess different criteria for excluding and selecting migrants for admission. The criteria for exclusion include those based on race and ethnicity, national security concerns, public health issues, and economic impacts. The criteria for admission considered include family ties, cultural affinity, protection of vulnerable cultural groups, and economic skills and contribution.

Temporary versus Permanent Admissions

The admission of migrants on a temporary basis far outnumbers admission for permanent residence in many liberal democratic countries. For example, in 2015, a total of 1,051,031 people received permanent residence visas in the United States, including 144,796 through employment-based preference categories.[2] By contrast, the total number of temporary admissions in 2015 was over 181 million, including foreign students, diplomats, and tourists. I leave aside tourists, students, diplomats, and other short-term visitors and focus on migrants admitted to work for a temporary period. In 2015, there were 2,306,962 admissions for "temporary workers and trainees."[3] These include temporary workers in specialty occupations (H-1B), agricultural workers (H-2A), and nonagricultural workers in the landscaping, hospitality, and janitorial services (H-2B).

Temporary migrant labor schemes originated in the late nineteenth century, when state actors began to assert their authority to regulate immigration and to enact immigration restrictions. The first temporary-worker programs emerged in Prussia and South Africa in the context of state-building and developing industries in need of stable workforces. According to historian Cindy Hahamovitch, temporary labor schemes were the result of state-brokered compromises that allowed states to meet their domestic labor needs while also placating anti-immigrant movements. Labor organizations and labor parties organized in opposition to immigration out of concerns about its impact on the wages and working conditions of domestic labor. Nativists of all classes feared that immigrants would undermine the racialized visions of national identity they favored. Temporary labor schemes appeased trade unionists by promising to restrict migrant workers to the most dirty and dangerous jobs and to expel them during economic downturns, and they appeased nativists by restricting migrants from integrating into the general population. Employers got foreign workers who could be disciplined by the threat of deportation, and states were able to get labor needs met without the responsibility of having to integrate migrants or provide for their welfare. In this sense, temporary migrant workers were the "perfect immigrants."[4]

Temporary labor schemes have since proliferated around the world. To name just a few examples: farmworkers and high-tech workers in the United States, construction workers and domestic servants in the Middle East, and live-in caregivers in Canada. What these schemes have in common is the temporary nature of their labor contracts. Temporary migrant workers are also typically denied access to the political and social rights that citizens enjoy, including the right to vote, to receive social welfare benefits, and to sponsor family members for migration. They are also often tied to a particular sector of the labor market and prevented from changing employers.[5]

Should temporary labor programs be permitted in democratic countries, or should all migrant workers be admitted only on a permanent basis? In what has become a touchstone discussion of guest-worker programs, Walzer argues that if democratic societies want to bring in new workers, "they must be prepared to enlarge their own membership; if they are unwilling to accept new members, they must find ways within the limits of the domestic market to get socially necessary work done. And those are their only choices."[6] Walzer's argument against temporary migrant worker programs has two parts. The first highlights the vulnerability of temporary migrants to exploitation. The second focuses on the normative requirements of democratic political communities.

Consider first the argument about exploitation. Walzer suggests that temporary migrant workers are vulnerable to exploitation because they lack access to political membership. They may appear to have consented to temporary labor schemes, but we should not regard their consent as truly voluntary. Unless migrant workers have the option to become citizens, Walzer argues, "their other choices cannot be taken as so many signs of their acquiescence to the economy and law of the countries where they work."[7] Political rights are of particular importance:

> Participants in economy and law . . . ought to be able to regard themselves as potential or future participants in politics as well . . . [T]he processes of self-determination through which the democratic state shapes its internal life must be open, and equally open, to all those men and women who live within its territory, work within the local economy, and are subject to local law.[8]

Walzer focuses on two specific cases: metics in ancient Athens and the Gastarbeiter in postwar Germany. Both groups were recruited to work for indefinite periods of time and excluded from citizenship. Because contemporary guest workers, like the metics and Gastarbeiter, are disenfranchised in the countries where they labor, they are unable to participate in shaping the rules that govern them, rendering them vulnerable to abuse. Picking up on this concern about exploitation, Patti Lenard and Christine Straehle have argued that extending citizenship to temporary workers will give them "the authority they need to demand that their rights are respected by employers, since they no longer need to fear automatic deportation." Justice requires "the end of inviting in workers on a temporary basis."[9]

I share the concerns about exploitation of temporary migrant workers, but I think the recommendation to cease temporary migrant worker programs is too hasty. First, it is important to take the agency of migrants themselves seriously: some wish to settle permanently but others may genuinely want to work for a period and return home.[10] Temporary workers' goal of returning home is reflected in their higher rates of saving and remittance than those who have permanently settled.[11] To be sure, we cannot simply assume that participants in temporary labor schemes have freely consented to their labor contracts. We need to examine the circumstances and conditions under which they make the agreements. Do migrant workers have adequate options from which to choose? We might regard visiting foreign professors and other high-skilled workers as having freely consented to the terms of their short-term stay. But for many low-skilled workers, if their only options are economic destitution or accepting a temporary labor contract, then their situation looks more like indentured servitude than a voluntary agreement. The worry about whether labor contracts are truly voluntary is more likely to apply to poor, low-skilled workers than to high-skilled workers who have greater resources and options. Low-skilled workers are not in a position to bargain for more favorable terms. This concern has led critics of temporary labor schemes to argue that migrant workers should not be *required* to return home after they complete their contracts.[12] I agree that liberal democratic countries are morally required to avoid exploiting foreign workers, but simply ending temporary labor schemes is problematic from the perspective of the workers themselves for reasons having to do with a second problem with ending temporary labor schemes.

The second problem is that it may drastically curtail opportunities for impoverished foreign workers to improve their lives. If migrants could only be admitted on a permanent basis, wealthy countries may well decide to admit far fewer migrants. This would mean many potential migrants would never have the chance to gain legal admission in the first place. In 2015, the United States granted 1,051,031 permanent residence visas, and only 144,796 of them were for employment, compared with 2,306,962 temporary-worker visas. There would need to be a massive increase in employment-based permanent admissions to fill the jobs currently held by temporary workers. Many industries depend on temporary workers; they may well push for large increases in the number of employment-based permanent resident visas if temporary programs are no longer available. But the decision is not just up to employers; it is one that must be made through the democratic process. It would be reasonable, as Walzer argues, for citizens to argue against hiring foreign workers and instead press employers to recruit more domestic workers by offering higher wages and better working conditions. This may be a good outcome from the point of view of domestic workers, but it would come at the price of fewer foreign workers having access to work opportunities.

Third, there is more room for debate about the source of exploitation of temporary migrant workers than Walzer suggests. Is it the lack of access to permanent residence and citizenship or the lack of a robust set of rights that make temporary migrants vulnerable to exploitation? After all, domestic workers are also vulnerable to exploitation. Indeed, one might argue all workers in the global economy are vulnerable to exploitation by virtue of having to sell their labor for wages to survive.[13] Temporary labor programs benefit employers at the expense of temporary foreign workers *and* domestic workers, who are often pitted against each other. In other words, the exploitation of workers is endemic to the structure of the global economy, and the goal should be to press for measures that reduce the exploitation of all workers. One crucial difference between domestic and foreign workers is that domestic workers have much stronger rights protections and they are not subject to deportation if they lose their jobs.

Putting the power to deport workers in the hands of employers is a key source of temporary workers' vulnerability.[14] In the United States, the government created and managed the emergency farmworker programs during World War II, but it dropped out as the official manager in 1947, permitting employers to import and deport temporary workers. Today, temporary-worker programs in the United States continue to bind workers to particular employers, making workers' ability to obtain and retain a visa dependent on remaining in the good graces of their employers.[15] The United Kingdom was one of the few countries that provided foreign domestic workers with a "mobile" work visa that allowed them to easily change employers. The British government established this unique domestic worker visa status in 1997 in response to high levels of documented abuse of migrant domestic workers by their employers. In 2011, the government eliminated the open work permit and prohibited migrant domestic workers from changing employers. According to data collected by Kalayaan, an organization that advocates on behalf of migrant domestic workers' rights in the United Kingdom, prior to 2012, the British government had a good record of protecting migrant domestic workers against the exploitation that was prevalent in private households, but since 2012, "it is clear that abuse has increased profoundly." All workers surveyed reported being paid less than £100 per week, as opposed to 60 percent of those on the earlier visa, and 62 percent were paid no salary at all, compared with 14 percent prior to 2012.[16]

Another key source of migrant workers' vulnerability is the lack of workplace protections. For example, in the United States H-2A and H-2B workers have no right to go to federal court to enforce their contract rights and are not entitled to representation by the small number of federally funded lawyers who have knowledge of these temporary worker programs. A few prominent exploitation cases have been pursued with the Department of Labor, but they have not resulted in significant changes to the structure of temporary-worker programs. By contrast, in Israel, where there is a strong tradition of labor rights and a large network of public-interest labor lawyers, temporary foreign workers have successfully mobilized to win greater rights protections. In particular, through several cases brought before the Israeli Supreme Court, the policy of granting residence permits to foreign workers on the condition that they remain working for a specific employer (the tied-worker visa) was struck down and the government was ordered to monitor employers' recruitment practices. In its ruling, , the court held that the tied-worker visa "violates the dignity and liberty of foreign workers" and was "disproportionate" in the sense that "the sweeping violation of the rights of foreign workers is not proportionate in any degree to the benefit that is derived from the restrictive employment arrangement."[17] Although migrants have weaker access to citizenship in Israel than in the United States or Canada, they enjoy stronger labor rights and access to labor-enforcement mechanisms in Israel.[18]

These considerations lead me to a different conclusion from Walzer's. Temporary-worker programs are permissible so long as a robust set of rights protections are put in place. According to Hahamovitch, one of the few times in the history of guest-worker programs when foreign workers were treated as "guests" rather than deportable workers was during World War II. When the United States signed its first formal labor agreement with Mexico in 1942, allowing for temporary migration of an unspecified number of Mexicans to work on American farms, they agreed to an "unprecedented" list of conditions designed to protect Mexican workers. A few months later, British colonial officials made similar arrangements with the United States for British West Indian workers. Mexican and Caribbean contract workers were guaranteed a minimum wage, or the prevailing wages if it was higher; work or wages for at least three-quarters of the term specified in their contracts; housing that met certain minimum standards; and free transportation to and from the United States. Unlike earlier guest-worker programs, the agreements made US officials responsible for the care of Mexican and West Indian workers. US officials not only helped recruit, screen, and transport foreign workers on navy ships and chartered planes but also housed them in federal labor camps, fed them, and provided medical care when they were sick or injured. When these protections failed to eliminate the abuse of workers, Mexico sent "consuls" and the British West Indies sent colonial officials to serve as "liaisons," who were authorized to intervene when workers complained of mistreatment and to deny abusive employers access to workers.[19]

This historical example points to some key components of a fair temporary migrant program. First, temporary migrant workers should have the ability to change jobs without fear of being deported, and they must be given a reasonable amount of time to find another job. Second, they must have a robust set of rights. This includes civil rights, such as rights to personal security, freedom of expression, and freedom of association. It should include workplace protections and labor rights, including health and safety standards, the right to collective bargaining, and access to legal remedies for wage theft and other abuses. It should also include certain social rights, including rights to housing and medical care. Temporary migrant workers should be exempt from having to pay into long-term social insurance and pension schemes if they cannot expect to benefit from them.[20] Temporary migrant workers would not have access to citizenship and the political rights typically attached to citizenship status, but they would be exempt from the obligations of citizenship, including serving in the military and on juries. Finally, these rights cannot be merely "on the books"; there must be enforcement mechanisms, so that migrant workers can in fact exercise them. Employers and the governments of receiving countries owe such rights protections to temporary migrant workers as a matter of fairness, not charity or mercy. The employers and citizens of the receiving countries benefit from the labor of temporary migrant workers, and in return, they must meet their end of a fair agreement: providing them with fair wages and decent working and living conditions during their stay.

I turn now to consider Walzer's second argument against temporary-worker programs: that democracy cannot tolerate "permanent alienage— either for particular individuals or for a class of changing individuals." This is partly because of the concerns about exploitation, but it is also because "[m]en and women are either subject to the state's authority, or they are not; and if they are subject, they must be given a say, and ultimately an equal say, in what that authority does."[21] Walzer makes a simple, powerful argument against treating any group as "second-class" citizens. All who are subject to the state's authority should be fully included in it. Call this the *uniform treatment view*: democracy requires treating all those subject to the state's authority uniformly, regardless of whether they are temporary or permanent residents.

The problem with the uniform treatment view is that it is too sweeping in its blanket opposition to group-differentiated rights.[22] As critics of "difference blindness" have emphasized, certain forms of group-differentiated rights are consistent with, even required by, ideals of justice and democracy. Consider pregnancy leave for women, language rights for linguistic minorities, religious exemptions from generally applicable laws, and a discount on public transportation for those over sixty-five years old.[23] We need to inquire into the purpose, justification, and context of particular cases of group-differentiated policies to see whether they are consistent with the demands of justice and democracy. When it comes to guest-worker programs, I think there is an alternative to the all-or-nothing choice suggested by Walzer to either include guest workers as full members or tolerate their exploitation. Instead of viewing rights as an all-or-nothing bundle attached to citizenship status, we should consider an approach that *disaggregates* certain rights from the formal status of citizenship and extends them to noncitizens in virtue of their territorial presence. I elaborate what this might look like in chapter 10.

My central point here is that temporary-worker programs are morally permissible so long as the duration of workers' stay is genuinely temporary and they have rights protections of the kind discussed here. Temporary migrant workers are vulnerable to exploitation, but the answer is not to do away with temporary labor programs. We should instead insist on more robust rights protections for temporary workers and much greater government oversight and enforcement of the terms of their contracts. I believe that if such protections are put in place, temporary-worker programs can be consistent with justice.

Criteria of Exclusion

I turn now to consider criteria for selecting migrants for permanent residence. States have used a number of different criteria to exclude and include migrants for admission. Criteria of exclusion and criteria of admission are often different sides of the same coin: excluding members of group X goes hand in hand with admitting people who are not X. Nonetheless, it is important to analyze criteria of exclusion and admission separately, for two reasons. First, those who are excluded on the basis of some explicit criteria are often only a small subset of those who are not included. Second, the criteria of exclusion and inclusion are often based on distinctive normative rationales, which would be obscured by treating them as one. I begin with criteria of exclusion.

When a state refuses prospective migrants admission, it must provide good reasons for doing so. What kinds of reasons might justify excluding prospective migrants?

If we look to the history of immigration policy in liberal democratic countries, we find that states have explicitly sought to exclude migrants on the basis of race, ethnicity, national origin, and religion. Some prominent examples in the United States are the 1882 Chinese Exclusion Act and the 1924 National Origins Act aimed at excluding migrants from southern and eastern Europe. The United States has also enacted sexuality-based exclusions.[24] Such exclusions are morally indefensible because they violate a basic norm of equality. Many regard it as uncontroversial that a norm of equal treatment applies to members of democratic societies. Why should we think that this norm applies to how states treat people outside their borders, including prospective migrants?

There are several reasons. First, we can appeal to a human right against discrimination, which finds support from an overlapping consensus of different moral and religious traditions around the world. Article 26 of the International Covenant on Civil and Political Rights prohibits discrimination on grounds of "race, color, sex, language, religion, political or other opinion, national or social origin, property, birth or other status."[25] Interpretation of this right depends on context. For example, we think hiring someone because of a language skill when the skill is relevant to the job or giving priority to women where they are underrepresented is sometimes justified. The human right against discrimination, then, should be understood as a right against being treated on the basis of grounds that are *irrelevant* to the benefit or opportunity in question.[26] Proponents of racial exclusions, as we saw in chapter 2 in discussing public debates over Chinese exclusion, don't simply assert that some groups are racially superior or inferior to others; they claim that race is a relevant criterion in immigration policy because members of particular groups pose a threat to the "public safety" or "morals" of the country. To overturn this argument, we cannot simply appeal to the human right against discrimination; we need to challenge claims based on it as false or irrelevant. I will say more about such claims in discussing the national security criterion.

A second basis for rejecting categorical exclusions based on race, ethnicity, religion, and sexuality arises from a membership-based perspective: such exclusions deny equal respect to existing members who share the excluded group's identity. For example, the equal status of Muslim American citizens is undermined when politicians attempt to enact a "Muslim ban" restricting travel and immigration. This membership-based argument provides compelling reasons against discriminatory admissions policies in democratic societies: they violate core democratic values. But they have more limited application to countries that are ethnically homogenous and whose members wish to remain so. Another limit is that while the membership-based perspective captures the wrong race-based exclusions present toward existing members, it does not capture the wrong against nonmembers outside the state's territory. How might we understand the latter wrong?

A third reason for rejecting exclusions based on race, ethnicity, religion, and sexuality is the idea that all persons are owed equal respect. Equality does not require open borders, as I argued in chapter 5, but it does place constraints on the way states can exercise its power over immigration. Prospective migrants must be given some nonarbitrary reason for being denied entry. As Michael Blake has argued, the reasons states give for selective immigration policy must be "reasons that immigrants could not reasonably reject" assuming that the general aims of the policy are legitimate ones.[27] Excluding people on the basis of race, ethnicity, religion, or sexuality is unacceptable because such exclusions cannot be linked to any legitimate goals that democratic states might pursue.

Are any criteria of exclusion justifiable? In principle, states are justified in excluding people who pose a genuine threat to national security. National security and public safety are in the collective interest of the political community, and the state should act in defense of the public interest. The problem, however, is in how this principle has been implemented. In practice, the concept of "national security" has been abused; it has been interpreted in ways that discriminate based on race, ethnicity, religion, and sexuality instead of identifying genuine threats to national security. For example, American legislators and judges defended the exclusion of Chinese migrants in the late nineteenth century by appealing to concerns about "public safety" and the corrupting influence on "the manners of the citizens."[28]

A more recent example is Donald Trump's repeated call during his presidential campaign for "a total and complete shutdown of Muslims entering the United States."[29] In his first days as president, he issued an executive order halting travel to the United States by citizens of seven predominantly Muslim countries (Iran, Iraq, Libya, Somalia, Sudan, Syria, and Yemen) and suspending all refugee admissions. The rationale for the executive order is suggested by its title, "Protecting the Nation from Foreign Terrorist Entry into the United States."[30] When federal courts blocked parts of the order,

Trump invoked threats to national security in response: "When a country is no longer able to say who can, and who cannot, come in & out, especially for reasons of safety & security—big trouble!"[31] He issued a revised executive order, removing explicit references to religion and omitting Iraq from the list of countries.[32]

The Trump administration has insisted that the purpose of the ban is to protect national security, but it has not shown that the ban serves this goal. The executive order explained that each of the six countries either sponsored terrorism, was compromised by terrorist organizations, or contained active conflict zones, but it did not tie the nationals from these countries to terrorist organizations or provide any link between nationality and the likelihood of committing terrorism. Just as the Chinese Exclusion Act rested on a false link between public safety and race, the travel ban rests on a false link between public safety and religion. The ban excludes people we have no reason to suspect are connected to terrorism. The Department of Homeland Security's intelligence analysts found insufficient evidence that citizens of the seven Muslim-majority countries listed in Trump's initial travel ban posed a threat to the United States.[33] In fact, the order itself may endanger national security by fueling anti-American sentiment among Muslims in the United States and abroad and souring relations with the countries targeted by the ban.

Federal judges in Maryland and Hawaii blocked aspects of the revised order. In a 10-to-3 decision, the Fourth Circuit Court of Appeals affirmed the nationwide injunction against the order on the grounds that it violated the First Amendment's prohibition of government establishment of religion, writing that Trump's order "in text speaks with vague words of national security, but in context drips with religious intolerance, animus, and discrimination."[34] The Ninth Circuit Court of Appeals reached a similar conclusion by a different route. It held that Trump had exceeded the authority Congress grants the president to make national security judgments in the immigration context. The president defended the ban as necessary to preserve government resources and ensure adequate vetting standards, but he did not show that current vetting standards are inadequate. The Ninth Circuit also held that the revised order conflicted with another statutory provision barring discrimination based on national origin, enacted in 1965, when Congress ended the national origins quota system that had favored immigration from Western and Northern Europe. As the Ninth Circuit put it, "National security is not a 'talismanic incantation' that, once invoked, can support any and all exercise of executive power."[35] We should recognize the potential for abuse in implementing the national security criterion, but this does not mean doing away with the national security criterion altogether. Its principled use as a basis of exclusion is morally defensible; the continuing challenge is to determine what constitutes a genuine threat to national security.

Another criterion of exclusion used by states has to do with protecting public health. As a matter of principle, states have a legitimate claim to restrict immigration in cases where migrants pose clear and serious threats to public health. Yet, as with the national security criterion, health-based exclusions have been prejudicially constructed and applied in practice. In the United States, public health concerns have been used to exclude prostitutes, racial and ethnic minorities, the poor, and LGBT persons. Think of the many immigrants screened at Ellis Island, Angel Island, and the US-Mexico border by inspection officers looking for contagious disease, mental illness, and physical ability to earn a living.[36] In 1987, under pressure from President Reagan, the US Public Health Service added HIV/AIDS as a basis for exclusion, but as AIDS activists and public health officials emphasized, there was no scientific or medical basis for the ban. The ban was in effect for twenty-two years until President Obama lifted it in 2009 saying it was "rooted in fear rather than fact."[37] Democratic states must not apply the public-health criterion in ways that are arbitrary or discriminatory as was clearly the case in these examples.

Are exclusions based on public health ever morally permissible? As a matter of law, the US government currently excludes noncitizens suffering from a handful of communicable diseases, including active tuberculosis, gonorrhea, and leprosy.[38] If contagious disease is suspected, US border control officers must quarantine the individuals at the port of entry, transfer them to a federal detention facility to be placed in isolation, or repatriate them to the country of origin. In cases where prospective migrants pose genuine and serious risks to public health, the state is justified in restricting their movement, domestically and across borders, if doing so is necessary to protect public health.[39] The challenge is to identify serious threats to public health and implement regulations in a way that is not biased against particular groups. To guard against abuse, public-health-based restrictions should adhere to a set of standards, including evidence-based necessity and proportionality and a system of checks to ensure transparent, nonarbitrary implementation.

Another basis of exclusion has to do with the economic impact of immigration on receiving countries. One area of debate concerns the fiscal costs and benefits of immigration. States have historically designed their immigration laws to keep out the poor and admit people who can prove they are economically self-sufficient. Many countries stipulate that citizens and permanent residents who want to sponsor family members or refugees formally commit to financially supporting the newcomers. The concern about the fiscal impact of immigration obviously rests on answers to empirical questions, including how immigrants affect expenditures on welfare programs and how those expenditures compare to the taxes immigrants pay and the benefits they create by working. The answers to these questions are contested among scholars and policymakers.

On the first question, the Current Population Survey, the premier monthly survey of the US population, conducted by the Census Bureau, suggests that 37 percent of immigrant households used welfare programs, compared to 24 percent of native households. According to the Survey of Income and Program Participation, also conducted by the US Census Bureau, immigrants use welfare programs at higher rates than natives: nearly 46 percent of immigrant households used welfare programs, compared to 27 percent of native households. The higher rates of welfare use by immigrants have been attributed to immigrants being, on average, less skilled than natives and therefore doing more poorly in the labor market.[40]

but many of these immigrant households have children

What about the second question of whether the taxes immigrants pay cover the additional expenditures they benefit from? The National Academy of Sciences (NAS) gathered two panels of social scientists to examine the existing evidence and offer an answer. The first panel published a report in 1997; the second panel, in 2016. The panels estimated the fiscal impact of immigration in the short run and the long run. The short-run calculation examined the population in a particular state in a particular year and used available data to calculate the cost of the services provided to each person that year and to estimate how much each person paid in taxes, and then calculated the difference between the cost of services and taxes paid. The 1997 panel conducted this short-run calculation for California and New Jersey and found that immigration turned out to be a fiscal burden, particularly in California, which offers generous services to and has many low-skilled immigrants. Extrapolating the data from these two states nationwide implied that each native household paid about $300 per year (in inflation-adjusted 2015 dollars) to fund services provided to immigrants back in 1997.[41] The 2016 NAS panel estimated that the fiscal burden would be even larger if the expansion in state and local government services since 1997 were taken into account.

There are, however, two conceptual problems with short-run comparisons between benefits received and taxes paid. First, though public benefits, such as education, are costly to provide to immigrants, they are also an investment that will generate fiscal benefits in the long run. Second, the short-run estimates ignore the aging of the domestic population and the inevitable fiscal problems that will result. The fertility rate of American women is below the replacement rate, which means that the population of taxpayers funding Social Security and Medicare is shrinking. In the long term, benefits will have to be drastically cut or taxes drastically increased, unless more taxpayers are added. Immigration offers a solution here.

These concerns led the 1997 NAS panel to estimate the long-run scenario by considering what might happen over a three-hundred-year period after an immigrant enters. The country initially bears some costs, but over time immigrants' tax contributions grow, and after their descendants receive an education, they will also work and pay taxes. The panel concluded that admitting one immigrant would generate a net gain of $80,000 when added up over three centuries. The main reason is that more immigration brings more taxpayers:

> The role immigrants play in bearing the cost of the aging of the baby-boom generations and of rising health costs, largely for the elderly, contributes very strongly to their overall positive impact, more so than does any other single factor.[42]

Long-run estimates are not without their problems, however. First, it is impossible to predict the future path of taxes and government spending or economic and demographic trends over a three-hundred-year period. To their credit, the 1997 NAS panel made projections based on shorter time frames. Over a twenty-five-year period, the $80,000 fiscal gain became an $18,000 loss. Over fifty years, the fiscal gain dropped to $11,000. Second, the panel made unjustifiable assumptions about future taxes and spending: that starting in 2016 and thereafter, the federal government would either substantially cut benefits or pass a huge tax increase so the debt does not worsen.

The 2016 NAS panel learned from the mistakes of the earlier panel. In particular, they recognized that the estimated fiscal impact of immigration is very sensitive to the assumed future path of taxes and spending, and that the impact changes if we allow for the possibility that immigrants increase the cost of providing public goods. Using a seventy-five-year time span for the long run, the 2016 panel provided several different scenarios. If we assume the future path of taxes and spending stipulated by the Congressional Budget Office, and if immigrants do not increase the cost of public goods, the long-run fiscal impact of the average immigrant is a gain of $58,000. But if we assume that the current path of taxes and spending will continue, and if immigrants increase the cost of public goods, then the long-run fiscal impact is a loss of $119,000.[43] It is hard to know which scenario is more likely, since we cannot predict the path of taxes and government spending. Considering these difficulties, Borjas concludes that the "most credible evidence" suggests that it is "not far-fetched to conclude that immigration is a net economic wash."[44] Given the difficulty of predicting the long-run fiscal impact of immigration, it is unreliable basis on which to argue for excluding or admitting migrants.

What about the economic impact of immigration on the labor market of destination countries? As a matter of law, governments require that attention is paid to the impact of immigration on domestic workers. For example, in the United States the immigration statute requires a labor certification process that is supposed to take seriously the impact of labor immigration on domestic workers:

> Any alien who seeks to enter the United States for the purpose of performing skilled or unskilled labor is inadmissible, unless the Secretary of Labor has determined and certified to the Secretary of State and the Attorney General that (1) there are not sufficient workers who are able, willing, qualified . . . and available at the time of application for a visa for admission to the United States and at the place where the alien is to perform such skilled or unskilled labor, and (2) the employment of such alien will not adversely affect the wages and working conditions of workers in the United States similarly employed.[45]

Whether immigrant workers "adversely affect the wages and working conditions of workers" already in the labor markets of receiving countries is a contested empirical question.

In an early influential study, the economist David Card analyzed the effect of immigration on wages by looking at what happened in Miami after the Mariel boatlift. In 1980, Fidel Castro said that Cubans wishing to move to the United States could leave. A few months later, over 100,000 Cubans had migrated and Miami's workforce had grown by about 8 percent. Card compared the changes in Miami's wages to what was going on in cities unaffected by the boatlift, selecting Atlanta, Houston, Los Angeles, and Tampa–St. Petersburg as the control group. Card concluded, "The distribution of non-Cubans' wages in the Miami labor market was remarkably stable between 1979 and 1985 . . . These data provide little evidence of a negative effect of the Mariel influx on the earnings of natives."[46] Card's study played an important role in shaping the narrative that immigration is good for everyone.

Many other researchers have since compared outcomes between cities where few immigrants live and ones where many immigrants live, and the evidence suggests that wages fall in cities with many immigrants, although the effect is small.

Based on a review of these studies, the economist George Borjas argues their findings are limited, for three reasons.[47] First, the geographic sorting of immigrants is not random. Immigrants are more likely to settle in high-wage cities than in cities with stagnant labor markets. This locational choice builds in a spurious correlation (higher pay, more immigrants) that makes it harder to detect when immigration lowers the wages of competing workers. Second, natives may respond to the supply shock by moving to other cities, relieving some of the wage pressure. Finally, employers may relocate to cities where immigration offers the potential for higher profits. All these responses help diffuse the economic impact of immigration.

In contrast to Card, Borjas contends that low-skilled immigration has a detrimental impact on low-skilled workers already living and working in the United States. Based on a decades-long tracking of specific skill groups and the Mariel supply shock, Borjas concludes that

> a skill group hit by a 10 percent increase in the number of workers probably faces a wage reduction of at least 3 percent, and perhaps even 10 percent if the unique Mariel experience could be generalized to the entire labor market. In the modern American context, this fact suggests that low-skill workers have paid much of the bill for whatever gains have accrued elsewhere.[48]

Borjas is making a claim about the unequal distributive impact of immigration—namely, that immigrant participation in the labor market redistributes wealth from those who compete with immigrants to those who employ or use immigrant labor.

Borjas's empirical claim is contested, but let's assume, for the sake of argument, that it is true. Liberal democratic countries would then face a genuine dilemma from the standpoint of the membership-based perspective developed in this book. On the one hand, liberal democratic states have special membership-based obligations to domestic workers. On the other hand, liberal democratic states have an obligation to take in foreigners fleeing persecution and family-based migrants and the discretion to admit migrants with particular skill sets who may compete with native workers for jobs. What might be done to address the dilemma?

One response is to restrict immigration in the name of protecting workers already in the labor market. This move is reflected in Trump's rhetoric of "America First" nationalism, which successfully combined racial and economic appeals to win him the presidency. He tapped into the discontent among working-class voters who have suffered the loss of manufacturing jobs and wage stagnation. By railing against trade deals with NAFTA and the Trans-Pacific Partnership, he managed to capture the progressive critique of the neoliberal economy. Democratic Party leaders handed Trump the opening to capture the globalization debate by pushing the Trans-Pacific Partnership despite widespread voter opposition to it. Trump combined economic nationalism with racial nationalism and built a narrative of globalization and deindustrialization that blamed immigrants and foreigners as the source of the problem.

We should resist Trump's racial nationalism but also recognize and respond to concerns about the economic impact of immigration on workers, including immigrant workers, in the domestic labor market. Immigration restrictions aimed at protecting domestic workers are sometimes justified, but closing the border is not the answer. We need policies that improve the lives of domestic workers rather than xenophobic rhetoric scapegoating immigrants and foreigners. Immigration proposals should be coupled with policies targeted at improving the well-being of poor and working-class Americans, including minimum wage laws, better working conditions, and health and social welfare policies. This is the approach adopted by some labor organizations that have stepped up alongside immigrant rights' advocates to press for better wages and working conditions for all workers.[49] Many agricultural and service companies have greatly benefited from employing low-skilled immigrants. Some of their profits could be used to compensate low-skilled domestic workers for their losses and help them receive the training needed to transition to new jobs and occupations. If Microsoft creates four new jobs for every H-1B visa granted, as Bill Gates claims, then it should use some of its profits to pay for these coveted visas, and those funds could be used to compensate and retrain domestic workers affected by the admission of migrant workers.[50]

There are no easy answers, but an appealing feature of the membership-based approach developed in this book is that it allows us to recognize that there is a genuine moral dilemma *if* immigration of low-skilled workers puts downward pressure on the wages of domestic workers. In contrast, a purely global perspective does not concern itself with the economic impact of immigration on less advantaged members of the political community.

Criteria of Admission

What criteria can states use in selecting immigrants for admission? Family relationships ground a compelling moral claim for admission. In chapter 8, I argued that given the fundamental importance of family relationships, these should be regarded as obligatory, not discretionary, admissions. I also argued for a more pluralistic approach to defining "family," focusing on the caregiving role family relationships provide and giving individuals a greater say in defining which relationships are most important to them. Core family relationships, as defined by those seeking to sponsor family members, should be regarded as obligatory admissions. For family relationships that are regarded as more peripheral, states have the discretion to prioritize such relationships if they wish to, but they are not required to.

What about selecting immigrants based on ethnicity? States have used race, ethnicity, and religion as grounds not only for exclusion but also for admission, such as Germany's *Aussiedler* policy and Israel's Law of Return. According to nationalist theories, the state's discretionary power over immigration is based on national self-determination, and it is a legitimate prerogative of the nation-state to favor particular ethnic and religious identities that constitute a core part of the national identity.[51] The state can say that such ethnic or religious favoritism has good reasons behind it: the maintenance of a cherished national identity that has a particular ethnic or religious identity at its core. Are these ways of prioritizing migrants for admission justifiable, and how are they different from the racial and ethnic exclusions discussed in the previous section?

The use of ethnicity in immigrant admissions is on its face problematic for reasons discussed earlier. This is especially so when the direct reason for ethnic selection is motivated by beliefs in the superiority of the favored group or by prejudice against the nonfavored groups, but even more benign uses of ethnic selection are morally troubling. Why?

The problem stems in part from the blurriness of the boundary between concepts of national culture, on the one hand, and ethnicity and religion, on the other. Consider Miller's argument for "cultural selection" in immigration. What does he mean by "culture"? In discussing how immigrants may disrupt existing cultural patterns, he refers to "new cuisines, new forms of dress, new languages, new religious practices, new ways of using public space." Immigrants "who speak a different language, practice a different religion, or have a different lifestyle from the majority" may pose two kinds of problems. The first involves the costs of incorporating them into the receiving country as equals, which will include language assistance, citizenship education, and other forms of assistance. The second potential problem is the impact of immigration on the national culture of the receiving country. A society that is already multicultural can more easily tackle the challenges of diversity, but "democracies are entitled to decide how far they wish to protect their inherited national cultures and how far to encourage cultural diversity within their borders."[52] On a nationalist account, preserving the national culture is a legitimate prerogative of the nation-state.

The problem, however, is that cultural selection may slide into ethnic and racial selection in countries whose national cultures have been historically defined in terms of ethnic and religious identities. For some, this is not a bug but an attractive feature of a nationalist account of self-determination. What are states for, if not the preservation of distinctive national cultures?[53] What is troubling is that by privileging a particular group over others for reasons of ethnic identity alone, the state signals that the nonfavored groups are second-class, undermining the basic norm of equal respect for all members. For example, under the *Aussiedler* policy, Germany granted citizenship to co-ethnics returning to Germany but continued to deny access to citizenship to Turkish "guest workers" who had lived and worked for many years in Germany and their descendants who were born and raised in Germany, sending the message that full membership was reserved for ethnic Germans.

One circumstance in which the use of ethnicity may be defensible is when co-ethnics abroad are being discriminated against because of their ethnic identity. The rationale here is not just the state's valuing a particular ethnic identity but that it has a remedial responsibility to assist co-ethnics who suffer persecution and discrimination, as in the case of refugees. This rationale offers support for Israel's Law of Return and Germany's *Aussiedler* policy. The latter had a more convincing justification in the wake of World II when people of German descent in the Soviet Union and Eastern Europe were subject to violence and discrimination. The remedial argument for the *Aussiedlier* policy had lost its force by the end of the twentieth century.

Ethnic selection may also be defensible when some valued part of the national culture needs reinforcing. Language policy offers a concrete example. Canada gives some weight to prospective migrants who already speak English and French, Canada's official languages. Quebec is permitted to give priority to French speakers in making its immigration decisions; such a policy is defensible in the context in which French is a minority language in a country where English is dominant. Using language as one criterion among others is a mutually beneficial arrangement: migrants who speak French and English will have an easier time integrating into Canadian society. The ability to speak a language is not based on ascriptive characteristics in the way racial and ethnic exclusions are; anyone who makes some effort can learn a new language.[54] It is hard to think of a reason states should not be able to give some weight to language competence in selecting immigrants for admission.

Another criterion of admission is the potential economic contribution of prospective migrants. Under the Canadian "points system," applicants are given a numerical value based on the applicant's level of education, professional experience, and language skills, all of which are proxies for the skills migrants will bring to the host country. The points system originated in Canada and has since been adopted in other countries, including Australia, Denmark, and the United Kingdom. In contrast to earlier immigration policies that had "selected by origin" based on applicants' racial and ethnic backgrounds, the points system marks a shift toward "selecting by merit."[55] From the standpoint of the receiving states, prioritizing high-skilled immigrants serves the national interest. High-skilled immigrants will contribute to economic growth and are less likely to depend on public support. For these reasons, Borjas has argued that the United States should follow Canada and Australia in prioritizing high-skilled applicants. But economic growth is only one goal among many in liberal democratic countries. They have the discretion to prioritize high-skilled immigrants, but that must be weighed against other goals and obligations, including toward refugees and family-based migrants. Even Borjas, a strong proponent of high-skilled immigration, argues, "I truly buy into the exceptional role that our country [the US] has played by offering hope to the poor abroad."[56]

While high-skilled immigration is advantageous for receiving countries and for migrants themselves, the departure of high-skilled migrants may be bad for sending countries. This chapter has focused on how receiving countries should exercise their discretionary power over immigration, but do they have any responsibilities vis-à-vis sending countries when it comes to attracting high-skilled immigrants? This issue here is the problem of brain drain.[57] When high-skilled individuals move from poor to rich countries, the poor countries lose not only their economic investments in educating and training those workers but also the future contributions of these workers to developing and improving institutions at home. The brain-drain objection rests on empirical claims that are contested. Some scholars have found that the migration of high-skilled individuals is not so harmful, whereas others have found serious negative impacts on the sending countries.[58] If the more optimistic empirical story is correct, then the concern about brain drain loses force. Wealthy countries' practice of admitting high-skilled immigrants is morally permissible. If, however, the departure of high-skilled migrants does leave sending countries much worse off, then what should wealthy countries do?

I argue in chapter 6 that individuals have a strong right of exit, but some constraints on emigration are justifiable. In particular, those individuals who have been educated at public expense have a duty to pay back the cost of their education before they can leave. Sending countries cannot prevent skilled professionals from leaving once they have met that condition. Receiving countries also have a responsibility to address the losses experienced by sending countries. Receiving countries might compensate sending countries for the loss of their skilled workers through investments in infrastructure, education, health, and anticorruption efforts, but such investment would not directly make up for the shortfall in medical or other skilled professionals created by high-skilled emigration, at least in the short-term. Another response is to say that destination countries have a responsibility not to exacerbate brain drain by actively recruiting skilled professionals. For example, the United Kingdom's National Health Service has banned the recruitment of medical personnel from most developing countries. Such restrictions are within the discretionary power of receiving countries to adopt. Some argue that global justice *requires* wealthy countries to adopt such restrictions. For example, Miller has argued that having a skill set that can help meet the needs of one's compatriots, as medical professionals do, should be treated as a disqualifying condition in the eyes of the receiving country.[59]

Wealthy countries do have global obligations toward sending countries for reasons discussed in chapter 5, but I am not sure that receiving countries disqualifying high-skilled migrants is the best way to meet the obligations. The need for doctors and nurses in poor countries may be indefinite and might result in permanent restrictions on their mobility. How long would the emigration of skilled workers from the Democratic Republic of the Congo, one of the poorest countries in the world, need to be restricted before Congo caught up to destination countries and the restrictions became unnecessary?[60] In addition, some scholars suggest that the transfer of knowledge and skills is less unidirectional (from poor to rich countries) than is commonly assumed. If we look beyond the human-capital value of skilled migrants and examine their social capital, including their role as a transnational bridge between sending and receiving countries, it is possible to conceptualize global labor mobility in a way that is not necessarily zero-sum and is actually beneficial for the sending countries.[61] And there is the fact that global flows of remittances are rising toward $400 billion per year, a value that exceeds that of official development assistance.[62] High-skilled migration exposes genuine tensions between the interests of migrants, sending countries, and receiving countries, showing once again that there are no easy answers when it comes to migration.

Conclusion

This chapter has explored discretionary admissions in immigrant-receiving countries. I argue that temporary-worker programs are permissible if robust rights protections for migrant workers can be put in place and enforced. Turning to consider criteria for selecting migrants for permanent residence, I argue that categorical exclusion of migrants based on race, ethnicity, religion, and sexuality is morally impermissible. Such exclusions violate the basic norm of equality and cannot be tied to any legitimate policy goal. Principled exclusions on grounds of national security, public health, and economic impact are permissible, but they have been subject to abuse in practice. This suggests that the burden of proof should be placed on defenders of the exclusion requiring them to demonstrate that there is a genuine public interest that would be served by the exclusion.

When it comes to criteria for admitting migrants, it is in the interest of receiving countries to prioritize high-skilled workers for permanent admission and allow low-skilled workers for temporary admission to meet short-term labor shortages. By contrast, sending countries will usually prefer to send low-skilled workers abroad and hang on to high-skilled workers. All migrants stand to benefit from migrating from low-wage to high-wage countries. There is thus a genuine dilemma between what is best for migrants, for sending countries, and for receiving countries. Each perspective must be taken seriously and considered alongside the others in debating immigrant admissions policy. Where prospective migrants have urgent interests in moving, these may trump the less weighty interests of receiving countries. Where the basic interests of prospective migrants are not at stake, however, governments are justified in restricting their movement if it is necessary for protecting the important interests of their members.

10

The Rights of Noncitizens
in the Territory

THE PRECEDING THREE chapters considered immigrant admissions and explored the different grounds on which states may admit or exclude prospective migrants. This chapter turns to examine what is owed to migrants who are already present in the territory of democratic countries. I focus on three groups of noncitizens: those admitted on a temporary basis, those who have been granted permanent residence, and those who have overstayed their temporary visas or entered the territory without authorization. What legal rights are these different groups of noncitizens morally entitled to? How should their claims be weighed against the claim of states to control immigration?

Temporary Migrants

Temporary migrants include tourists, visiting students, diplomats, temporary workers, and other sojourners who enter a state's territory after agreeing to a short-term stay. States have an obligation to protect the *human rights* of all persons present in their territory. The list of human rights includes the rights to personal security, to due process and equality before the law, and to freedom from religious persecution and discrimination. For the purposes here, the precise list of human rights is less important than the point that there are certain basic rights to which all persons are entitled.[1] Citizenship status should not matter for whether one is protected by laws against murder and assault or whether one has the right to a fair trial when accused of a crime. Such laws should apply equally to tourists, long-term noncitizen residents, and citizens.

The obligation to protect a person's human rights falls on the particular state where the person happens to be. Why? Partly because that state is best positioned to provide the protection. It is also because the state has a duty toward all who are subject to its coercive power. This is the *coercion principle*. It says because state coercion always infringes on personal autonomy, all persons subject to state coercion are owed some form of justification. If we take the view that the type of justification required is hypothetical, we must ask what kind of treatment a person would consent to, ex ante, under some appropriate method of modeling rational consent.[2] It is plausible to think that, at minimum, the appropriate treatment of noncitizens must be nonarbitrary and include equal protection of their human rights.

This idea has been incorporated into the domestic law of some states. In 1886 the US Supreme Court first acknowledged that basic rights should be extended to *all persons* within the territory, regardless of their citizenship status: "[Fundamental rights] are not confined to the protection of citizens . . . These provisions are universal in their application to all persons within the territorial jurisdiction, without regard to any differences of race, of color, or of nationality."[3] The claim is that all persons within the territorial jurisdiction are entitled to the basic rights and benefits that citizens enjoy, a doctrine that Linda Bosniak has called "territorial personhood."[4]

Temporary workers are different from tourists and other short-term visitors because they have been admitted to work. This makes them vulnerable to exploitation by employers, especially if their work visa binds them to a particular employer. As I argued in chapter 9, admitting migrants to work on a temporary basis is morally permissible if their stay is truly temporary and they have access to a robust set of rights. In addition to civil rights and basic public goods, temporary workers should have access to labor rights, including the right to change employers and occupations, to participate in collective bargaining, and to be protected by workplace health and safety standards. They should also have access to basic social rights, including rights to housing and medical care, and be exempt from long-term social-insurance schemes since they cannot expect to benefit from them.

One important objection to a scheme of limited rights for temporary migrant workers arises from democratic theory's strong presumption in favor of equality. This view has been forcefully developed by Walzer: "Men and women are either subject to the state's authority, or they are not; and if they are subject, they must be given a say, and ultimately an equal say, in what that authority does."[5] He was writing in reference to temporary migrant workers—in particular, the metics of ancient Greece and "guest workers" in Germany.

He concluded that they "must be set on the road to citizenship." Admission into the territory must eventually come with admission into citizenship. I engaged Walzer's argument in chapter 9. Here I will just add that there is an alternative to the either/or choice presented by Walzer.

Rather than view rights as an all-or-nothing bundle attached to citizenship status, we should consider an approach that disaggregates certain rights from the status of citizenship and extends them to noncitizens in virtue of their territorial presence. I think this disaggregated rights approach has some advantages over Walzer's approach. First, it does not demand blanket opposition to group-differentiated rights, which some political theorists regard as required by justice. We need to inquire into the purpose and justification of particular cases of group-differentiated policies to see whether they are consistent with justice. As I argued in chapter 9, in the case of temporary migrants, granting basic rights protections, not the full rights of citizenship, is justifiable if their stay is truly temporary. Second, a disaggregated rights approach may offer a more practical alternative aimed at protecting vulnerable groups from domination. On Walzer's approach, the only options for guest workers are to accept the status quo or to gain admission to citizenship. The disaggregated rights approach offers an intermediate position that argues for extending a range of legal rights in virtue of territorial presence.

Temporary migrants may seek to renew their visas. If states agree to such renewals, they must do so knowing that a migrant's claim to settle in the country strengthens over time. Democratic states cannot keep a group of people in a state of permanent alienage. The question of when exactly migrants acquire a moral right to permanent residence is not one that philosophical reflection can answer precisely; instead, we can offer reasons that support some threshold beyond which migrants have the right to stay. In such cases, the claims of temporary migrants look like the claims of long-term residents.

Permanent Residents

What, if anything, justifies treating permanent residents differently from temporary migrants? All noncitizens are entitled to human rights protections, but are permanent residents entitled to a more extensive set of rights? Permanent residents are migrants who have been admitted to reside in a state's territory and who typically enter with the intent to settle. The longer a person lives in a state's territory, the greater that person's moral claim to a more extensive set of legal rights. The length of time serves as a proxy for something else. What might that be? Two distinct principles justify treating long-term

noncitizen residents differently from short-term migrants: social membership and fair play.

The *social membership* principle has been developed by a number of political theorists, including Ruth Rubio-Marín and Joseph Carens. It consists of
both a factual claim and a normative claim. The factual claim is that "membership is first, and above all, a social fact, determined by social factors such as
living, working or raising a family and participating in the social and cultural
life of a community."[6] One becomes a member by developing "a dense network
of relationships and associations."[7] Residence and time serve as proxies for social membership. Once individuals have settled in a place for an extended period, they acquire social membership. Carens suggests one or two years is not
enough, but "five years of settled residence without any criminal convictions"
is sufficient "to establish anyone as a responsible member of society."[8]

The normative claim is that "social membership gives rise to moral claims
in relation to the political community."[9] Rubio-Marín argues for full inclusion into citizenship: "[A]ll those who live on a permanent basis in a liberal
democratic state ought to be considered members of that democracy and
thus share in the sphere of civic equality with the equal recognition of rights
and duties."[10] Putting the factual and normative claims together, the social
membership principle says that long-term permanent residents are entitled to
many of the same rights as citizens and ultimately to citizenship itself. Social
membership is, in Carens's words, "normatively prior to" and "more fundamental" than citizenship in the sense that it "provides the foundation upon
which moral claims to citizenship normally rest."[11]

What grounds social membership? Carens refers to "membership-specific
human rights," which are universal human rights but "protect particular
connections to particular communities rather than generic human interests."
Most people develop "deep and rich networks of relationships in the place
where they live."[12] But the places where people live, the sites in which
they develop relationships, tend to be local settings—our homes, schools,
workplaces, and neighborhoods. Yet it is the political community, not a social
group or local community, in which immigrants seek inclusion. The theory of
social membership presupposes a theory of political membership. We need
an account of the nature and significance of political membership in order to
respond to a migrant's claim to be included in it.[13]

What is special about the relationship among members of a political community as opposed to other kinds of community? As I argued in chapter 4, we
should view the political community as "a people" engaged in a cooperative
political project that aspires to collective self-determination. One becomes a

member in virtue of participating in and bearing the burdens of the cooperative endeavor. This is the idea of *fair play*: that all those who participate in a cooperative scheme are entitled to the benefits and must bear the burdens of that scheme.[14] The modern state is perhaps the most consequential scheme of social and political cooperation humans have developed. The purpose of political institutions is to make, enforce, and interpret laws to govern our interactions with one another; they are supposed to ensure our security and survival and enable collective self-determination.

The fair play principle is distinct from the social membership principle in emphasizing the participation and contributions of noncitizens in shared institutions rather than social ties. The fair play principle provides equally compelling grounds for noncitizens' claims to many of the rights that citizens enjoy. Noncitizens shoulder the burdens of the cooperative scheme in a variety of ways. They do difficult, grueling work that many citizens do not want to do at the wages currently on offer. They pay taxes. Some immigrants contribute through military service.[15] They also contribute in their neighborhoods and local communities. All these contributions help sustain public institutions and the public goods they provide. Time also matters for the fair play principle: the longer one contributes to the cooperative scheme, the stronger one's claim to a share of the benefits of that scheme.

It is important to note that many liberal democratic states already grant migrants admitted for permanent residence many of the same rights that citizens enjoy. A number of scholars have documented the ways in which the legal distinctions between citizens and noncitizen permanent residents have been reduced with civil, social, and political rights increasingly predicated on residency, not citizenship status.[16] We should be careful not to overstate the extent or permanence of these legal changes. There are vocal opponents of this convergence between the rights of citizens and noncitizen residents. In addition, there are several areas in which legal differences between citizens and permanent residents remain.

One critical difference between citizens and noncitizen residents is that the latter can be deported if convicted of certain criminal offenses. Contrary to their legal categorization as "permanent residents," their residence may be cut short. US immigration law allows the federal government to deport lawful permanent residents found guilty of "aggravated felonies," which include battery, forging checks, and selling drugs. In deportation proceedings, some weight is given to how long a lawful permanent resident has lived in the United States. If they have lived for at least five years in the country, have seven years of continuous residence, and have not committed an aggravated felony, they may appeal to an immigration judge to cancel the deportation order.[17] But there is no guarantee that such factors will prevail over the deportation order.

Among the most morally troubling cases are those involving immigrants who were adopted as children but never naturalized into citizenship. Consider the story of Adam Crapser. He was born in South Korea and adopted by an American family at the age of three. He was abandoned by his first adoptive parents and abused by his second. After being kicked out of the house at sixteen, he tried to break in to get some of his possessions. He was arrested and pleaded guilty to burglary, serving twenty-five months in prison. He accumulated a criminal record, including unlawful possession of a firearm and an assault conviction after a fight with a roommate. He sought to get his life on track, working as a barber and an auto-insurance claims estimator. He married and became a father. He was finally able to get his adoption paperwork from his first adoptive family and in 2012 applied for a green card, which triggered background checks by the Department of Homeland Security. He was placed in deportation proceedings and in 2016, was deported back to South Korea, a country where he did not know anyone or speak the language.

Crapser's case is not unique. According to the Adoptee Rights Campaign, 35,000 adult adoptees in the United States may lack citizenship. At least three dozen other international adoptees have faced deportation charges or been deported in recent years.[18] Some did not know they lacked citizenship status until they applied for federal student loans, tried to get a passport, or registered to vote. In 2000, Congress passed the Child Citizenship Act, which granted automatic citizenship to children under the age of eighteen, but the law does not cover adult adoptees.

Deporting lawful permanent residents, including those who've been convicted of criminal offenses like Adam Crapser, is morally wrong. Noncitizen residents should have the right to reside permanently in the territory of their adopted state, for three reasons. The first has to do with social membership. They have built lives in their adopted country and become a part of a dense web of social connections with family, friends, neighbors, and co-workers. This is especially true of migrants who arrive as children and grow up in their adopted countries. Interviewed after he was deported, Crapser put it this way, "As a child, I didn't ask to be sent to the United States. I didn't ask to learn the English language. I didn't ask to be a culturalized American. And now I was forced back to Korea, and I lost my American family."[19]

The second argument against the deportation of noncitizen residents has to do with the harm it causes to family members. In Crapser's case, his appeal to family ties was not sufficient to convince the immigration judge to cancel his deportation order, but significant family ties are a compelling reason against deportation. The law has given some weight to family ties in the context of deportation proceedings. Discretionary relief from deportation originated in the 1930s when critics of deportation called attention to the broken families and economic hardship caused by deportation.[20] For reasons I discussed in Chapter 8 about the importance of family, keeping families together offers a compelling rationale for protecting migrants against deportation.

A third argument against the deportation of lawful permanent residents derives from the fair play principle. They participate in the labor market, pay taxes, and contribute to their local communities. In return, they are entitled to many of the legal rights and protections as citizens, including the right to reside permanently in the country. Some argue that by committing a crime, noncitizen residents fail to shoulder the responsibilities of the cooperative scheme. In response, it is important to emphasize that noncitizens who commit criminal offenses are subject to the criminal laws just as citizens are. Crapser served his time for his criminal convictions. His deportation constituted additional punishment on top of the punishment he had already received.[21]

Another area where permanent residents and citizens are treated differently is in access to social-welfare programs and public-sector employment. Immigrants' access to social-welfare programs is especially controversial in our polarized political climate, and some claim that immigrants are a "fiscal drain" on taxpayers.[22] For reasons of fair play, permanent residents should have access to the same social rights and opportunities that citizens have. The logic of fair play has been central to some prominent court cases extending access to social welfare programs to noncitizen residents. In the 1970 case *Graham v. Richardson,* the US Supreme Court struck down Arizona and Pennsylvania laws that conditioned the receipt of public assistance on being a US citizen or having resided in the US for at least fifteen years. Both states justified their restrictions on the basis of a "special public interest" in favoring their citizens over noncitizens in the distribution of scarce resources. The court acknowledged that a state has "a valid interest in preserving the fiscal integrity of its programs" but argued that a concern for fiscal integrity did not justify the use of "invidious distinctions" between aliens and citizens:

Aliens like citizens pay taxes and may be called into the armed forces . . . aliens may live within a state for many years, work in the state and contribute to the economic growth of the state . . . There can be no "special public interest" in tax revenues to which aliens have contributed on an equal basis with the residents of the States.[23]

The logic of fair play was also at work in cases that have extended access to public-sector jobs to noncitizen residents. In striking down a New York law that restricted state jobs to citizens, the US Supreme Court held, "A resident alien may reside lawfully in New York for a long period of time. He must pay taxes. And he is subject to service in this country's Armed Forces."[24] It may be reasonable to restrict public-sector jobs that involve national security or major policymaking responsibility to citizens, but in most public-sector jobs, there is no functional relationship between citizenship status and the skills necessary for the job. To use the language of employment discrimination law, citizenship has not been shown to be a "bona fide occupational qualification" for most public-sector jobs. These cases were decided in the 1970s. Today, federal laws in the United States prohibit noncitizens from receiving public assistance and from working in certain public-sector jobs.[25] I think the earlier court cases got it right: in virtue of living, working, and contributing to their adopted country, permanent residents should be entitled to social-welfare benefits and to most public-sector jobs.

A final area of difference between permanent residents and citizens is political rights. In the United States, one must be a citizen to vote in most local and all state and federal elections.[26] Other countries have been more open to extending the franchise to noncitizens. Since 1993, Ireland, the Netherlands, and all the Scandinavian countries have introduced universal local franchise for all residents, regardless of their citizenship. New Zealand has the most inclusive policy of all: local and national voting rights after one year of legal residence.[27] I think reasons of fair play and coercion support giving long-term noncitizen residents the right to vote in local and national elections. Long-term noncitizen residents contribute to the cooperative scheme, and they are subject to all the policies of the state in which they live, and such participation and coercion generate claims for their having a voice in collective decision-making.[28] On the other hand, it is within the legitimate power of democratic states to restrict voting rights to citizens. Voting is the most direct way in which members of the political community can direct their future; in this regard, it is at the core of citizenship. Citizenship involves not only rights but also duties, including the duty to consider the interests of other members when in engaging in political debate and when voting in favor of certain policies. It takes time for immigrants to integrate into society and acquire civic knowledge. Permanent residents can become citizens, and where

but then why become a citizen?

naturalization tests focus on knowledge of civics and history, the process of naturalization can serve a useful purpose in preparing noncitizen residents to exercise their political rights.[29]

Unauthorized Migrants

The preceding discussion of temporary migrants and lawful permanent residents does not address the distinctive situation of unauthorized migrants. It is important to note that the category "unauthorized migrants" encompasses a wide range of migrants. Although contemporary public debate often focuses on those who enter the territory without authorization, the more common way migrants become "unauthorized," "undocumented," or "illegal" is by overstaying their temporary visas or remaining after their asylum application is denied.[30] In all these cases, migrants who settle in the territory without authorization have not gone through the regular immigrant admissions process discussed in chapter 9. In this sense they have not been "selected" for admission by the state. What is the proper response to the situation of unauthorized migrants?

Some argue that the proper response is to deport all unauthorized migrants. By overstaying their temporary visas or entering without authorization, they have violated immigration laws. The core violation is residing in the territory without the consent of the political community. As Ryan Pevnick has argued, "In the case of illegal immigrants, by entering the country illicitly such individuals took their place in the community without the consent of the citizenry. Although it is true that—after a number of years—such individuals are . . . subject to the law and have an important stake in the future shape of the political community, it is important that they put themselves in this situation without the consent of the citizenry."[31] Pevnick's position (discussed further in chapter 3) is that states are justified in removing unauthorized migrants unless they qualify for refugee status or are children who are not responsible for their unauthorized status.

Two responses can be made against this consent argument. The first challenges the claim that the state has not consented to unauthorized migration. The state, together with politically powerful employers, has played a role in facilitating unauthorized migration in order to meet the demand for low-skilled labor. Its enforcement efforts have been inconsistent, suggesting some ambivalence about unauthorized migration. As Rubio-Marín puts it, "The alleged lack of consent becomes suspicious, when there has not been any serious attempt to prevent illegal entry or to deport illegal aliens before they

consolidate their existence in the new society."[32] The state-complicity argument certainly strengthens the case for extending rights, including the right
to remain, to unauthorized migrants, but it is a limited argument for three
reasons. It assumes that the state has the capacity to stop unauthorized migration, but insofar as structural factors beyond the state's control shape unauthorized migration, the state cannot be held responsible for failing to prevent
all unauthorized migration. In addition, we cannot infer the consent of the
political community from the fact that some employers have encouraged unauthorized migration and some state officials have tolerated it.[33] Finally, the
state-complicity argument loses force during periods of ramped-up immigration enforcement, as was the case in the United States during the Obama administration and is even more so during the Trump administration.

I think the better response to the consent argument is what we might call
the *supersession argument*: unauthorized migrants' violation of immigration
law is overridden or superseded by countervailing moral considerations.[34] As
I have emphasized throughout the book, democratic states are constrained in
how they can exercise the right to control immigration. They must do so in
ways that are consistent with democratic values. Even though unauthorized
migrants are present in the territory in violation of immigration law, their
presence entitles them to basic rights and over time, they acquire the right to
remain.

Consider first the claim about basic rights. Democratic states have an obligation to protect the human rights of all persons present in the territory,
including unauthorized migrants. This is the same human rights rationale
that applies to temporary migrants and lawful permanent residents. All
noncitizens present in the territory are morally entitled to basic rights, including the right to personal security, freedom of expression and association,
and basic public goods such as emergency medical care. The US Supreme
Court has developed this basic rights rationale in the doctrine of "territorial personhood." This doctrine stands for the proposition that, in Bosniak's
words, "when it comes to the alien's relationship with the government, the
government's immigration power does not occupy the entire terrain."[35]
Noncitizens are entitled to certain basic protections in virtue of their territorial presence.

Of course, there is a difference between having rights "on the books"
and really being able to exercise them. Unauthorized migrants face barriers
to accessing basic rights that lawful permanent residents do not: the fear
of being discovered by immigration authorities reduces the likelihood that
they will seek the legal protections to which they are entitled. For example,

unauthorized migrants who are victims of or witnesses to a crime may not go to the police out of fear that they will be reported to immigration enforcement officials. They may avoid seeking care in medical emergencies because they worry about being detained and deported. What might be done?

As Carens has argued, democratic states can and should build a "firewall" between the protection of human rights and the enforcement of immigration law.[36] The firewall takes the form of the legal principle that no information gathered by agents charged with protecting immigrants' basic rights can be used for the purposes of immigration enforcement. This means that police officers would not have to alert immigration authorities when unauthorized migrants come to them to report a crime and hospital workers would not be required to report unauthorized migrants who seek emergency medical care. The firewall idea is reflected in "sanctuary-city" policies, which instruct police and other city employees not to inquire about an individual's immigration status and which do not devote local resources to enforcing federal immigration laws. The firewall allows migrants to pursue their basic rights without exposing themselves to detention and deportation.

Beyond the person's rights to security and to emergency medical care, what other rights should unauthorized migrants have access to? Public education is critical. Children are an especially vulnerable group of unauthorized migrants because of their dependence on others for their well-being. The law has recognized their special vulnerability. For example, in the 1982 case *Plyler v. Doe*, the US Supreme Court struck down a Texas statute barring the children of unauthorized migrants from attending public schools. The court built on earlier decisions that created some separation between the government's immigration authority and noncitizens' access to basic rights protections. The court emphasized the harm of denying public education to children: "The inability to read and write will handicap the individual deprived of a basic education each and every day of his life." Depriving them of education will have an "inestimable toll . . . on the social, economic, intellectual and psychological well-being of the individual." The court also pointed to the costs to the host society: "We cannot ignore the significant social costs borne by our Nation when select groups are denied the means to absorb the values and skills upon which our social order rests . . . It is difficult to understand precisely what the State hopes to achieve by promoting the creation and perpetuation of a subclass of illiterates within our boundaries, surely adding to the problems and costs of unemployment, welfare and crime."[37] Given the fundamental importance of education in a child's life, unauthorized migrant children should have access to public education.

Another example of singling out children for special protection is the Deferred Action for Childhood Arrivals (DACA) program initiated by the Obama administration in 2012. In the absence of legislative action on comprehensive immigration reform, President Obama took executive action to defer the deportation of unauthorized migrants who had entered the United States before the age of sixteen and fulfilled certain educational or military service criteria. The benefits of DACA include receiving protection from deportation and permission to live and work lawfully in the United States for a two-year period, subject to renewal. Nearly 800,000 immigrant youth have been able to hold jobs, receive a social security number, and in nearly all states, receive a state-issued identification card or driver's license.[38] Recipients of DACA report that the program has given them stability in their daily lives and enabled them to pursue educational and professional goals without fear of detection and deportation.[39] The DACA program is rooted in an acknowledgment of the special vulnerability of children and the fact they had no responsibility for their unauthorized status.

What about unauthorized migrant adults? The narrative of "innocent children" has tended to go hand in hand with casting their parents or guardians as guilty "lawbreakers," with sharply contrasting implications for their access to basic rights. For example, in the *Plyler* decision, the court showed compassion for noncitizen children but not for their parents. Indeed, the innocence of children was seen to hinge on their parents' culpability. It is the parents who, in the court's words, "elect to enter our territory by stealth and in violation of our law" and who "should be prepared to bear the consequences, including, but not limited, to deportation." Had the case involved the denial of public goods to adults, not children, and involved some other right, not educational rights, the outcome might well have been different. The consent argument I discussed earlier was at work in the *Plyler* decision. As Justice Brennan put it, "Persuasive arguments support the view that a State may withhold its beneficence from those whose very presence within the United States is the product of their own unlawful conduct."[40]

The view of unauthorized adults as "lawbreakers" has fueled opposition to another deferred-action program initiated by the Obama administration. While DACA has received the most attention, deferred action is a tool that has existed in the United States immigration system for decades, and it has been extended not only to children but also to adults for largely humanitarian reasons, including parents, breadwinners, and victims of domestic violence. In 2014, President Obama released a program known as Deferred Action for Parents of Americans and Lawful Permanent Residents (DAPA), which would have enabled unauthorized parents of American citizens and perma-nent residents who have lived in the United States for a substantial period of time to qualify for deferred action. Roughly 3.7 million migrants would have qualified for the program. The program was stopped by a lawsuit brought by the state of Texas and twenty-five other states. The case went to the US Supreme Court and ended in a 4 to 4 ruling, leaving in place a federal district court decision blocking the program. In June 2017, the Trump administration rescinded DAPA.[41]

Let's examine the logic behind the opposition to deferred action and other measures that extend some rights to unauthorized migrant adults. It is morally wrong to argue that by violating immigration law unauthorized migrant adults have lost any claim to basic rights protections. Their presence may be regarded as wrong or unfair in certain respects—because they were not admitted through regular channels or because they bypassed prospective migrants who have been waiting for years to be admitted—and their violation may have to be redeemed in some way, as I consider later in the chapter. But unauthorized migrant adults are nonetheless morally entitled to basic rights protections for the same reason children are: they have fundamental interests that are at stake.

Work-related rights are especially important. In the United States there are roughly 11 million unauthorized migrants. Eight million of them work in the civilian workforce.[42] They should have the right to be paid for the work they do. Some argue that they should not have this right on the grounds that states should not enforce contracts that are against public policies, such as a contract that discriminates based on race or religion or a contract involving le-gally banned activities like drug dealing. But the vast majority of unauthorized migrants are not engaged in such activities; they are doing productive work that is often "dirty, dangerous, and difficult" and which many domestic workers do not want to do at the wages on offer. It is morally wrong for the state to let employers get away with not paying workers for labor they have performed.

I want to turn now to consider the conditions under which unauthorized migrants might be morally entitled to acquire legal residence status. In my view, the longer unauthorized migrants remain in the territory, the stronger their claim for legal residence status. Once unauthorized migrants have settled in a country, we should regard their violation of immigration law as having been overridden by countervailing factors. What might these coun-tervailing factors be?

The first is the social membership principle. Applying the principle di-rectly to the case of unauthorized migrants, Carens argues: "People who live and work and raise their families in a society become members, whatever their legal status. That is why we find it hard to expel them when they are discovered. Their presence may be against the law, but they are not criminals like thieves and murderers."[43] He points to the example of Marguerite Grimmond, a woman who was born in the United States but moved to Scotland as a young child. At the age of eighty, she traveled outside the United Kingdom for the first time on a family vacation to Australia. Because she was not a British citizen, she had acquired a US passport for the trip. When she returned, she was told she was not legally entitled to remain in the United Kingdom and had four weeks to leave for the United States. Her cause received widespread media attention, and Grimmond was ultimately permitted to remain in her adopted country. Grimmond had a moral right to stay because she had arrived at a young age and had stayed a very long time.[44] Most unauthorized migrants in the United States today have not been there as long as Grimmond had lived in the United Kingdom, but about 66 percent have lived in the United States for at least a decade, and 86 percent have lived in the United States for at least five years.[45] They would be covered by the five-to-seven year threshold Carens has suggested should be the point at which unauthorized migrants acquire the right of permanent residence.[46]

What is significant about the passage of time? Over time many unauthorized migrants have formed families. As we have seen, the right to family life is recognized as a basic human right, and grounds a claim not to be deported away from our families and to be reunited with family members separated from us by borders.[47] In the United States there are 1.7 million unauthorized adults with spouses who are US citizens or lawful permanent residents, and 3.8 million unauthorized adults with children who are US citizens. A total of 16.6 million people in the United States, citizens and noncitizens, are members of such "mixed status" families.[48] The federal judges and administrative judges who decide immigration cases used to have broad authority to prevent the removal of otherwise deportable noncitizens. Federal trial court judges could make a "judicial recommendation against deportation" (JRAD) when disposing of a federal criminal case brought against an immigrant. Immigration judges had similar powers under the immigration statute if the immigrant could show that her individual circumstances warranted reprieve, such as having lived for a long time in the United States or facing "extreme hardship" if deported.[49] Since the 1990s, Congress has made the deportation system more categorical, eliminating the judicial recommendation against deportation and many statutory forms of deportation relief. Yet keeping families together remains a strong moral rationale for protecting migrants against deportation. Ronald Reagan's 1987 "family fairness" program recognized this by protecting otherwise deportable unauthorized immigrants because of their family connections. The year before, Congress had passed the Immigration Reform and Control Act, which created a large-scale legalization program for unauthorized immigrants who had lived in the United States for years, but it did not extend the same protection to the spouses and children of those immigrants. The Reagan administration granted these family members deferrals of removal, which were continued and expanded by George H. W. Bush, until Congress passed legislation providing a statutory path to legalization for this group.[50]

What about unauthorized migrants who have not formed families and therefore may have weaker claims to social membership? A second principle supporting unauthorized migrants' claims for legal residence status is fair play. Most unauthorized migrants labor in the civilian workforce. They work on industrial farms and construction jobs, they clean people's houses and tend to gardens, and they care for the young, the ill, and the elderly. They pay taxes and contribute to their neighborhoods and local communities. Participation in these cooperative schemes generates associative obligations among all the participants. To deport noncitizens after they have become integrated in these cooperative schemes is a breach of associative obligations. Some argue that unauthorized migrants should be asked to perform part-time military or civilian service for a period of time as a way to redeem their immigration law violation and "earn" the right to remain.[51] Such a requirement is within the legitimate power of a state to impose, and it goes some way toward answering the consent argument discussed earlier. In my view, unauthorized migrants who have been settled for a period of time have already "earned" the right to remain in virtue of contributing their labor, paying taxes, and participating in their local communities.

In sum, time is significant for both the social membership and fair play principles. The greater the passage of time, the stronger the unauthorized migrant's claim to remain. This means those migrants who have been settled for a period of time acquire the right to remain, but it also means those who have just arrived or been present for only one or two years do not. It is within the legitimate exercise of the state's right to control immigration to deport unauthorized migrants who have not yet settled in the territory. There are constraints, however, on how democratic states can carry out removal.

Consider the current US immigration enforcement system. The weak procedural protections it currently provides fall far short of any reasonable standard of due process and are deeply troubling. Noncitizens facing deportation have no right to counsel, except at their own expense. The immigration judges who hear their cases face overwhelming caseloads. An immigration judge completes more than 1,500 cases per year on average, with one law clerk for every four judges. By contrast, the typical district court judge trying civil suits has a caseload of four hundred cases per year, with three law clerks for every judge.[52] Immigration judges are likely to face an even greater caseload in light of Trump's order repealing President Obama's Priority Enforcement Program, which had given top priority to deporting those convicted of criminal violations.

The basic idea behind Obama's program was that setting priorities is a reasonable exercise of prosecutorial discretion in immigration enforcement, not least because the government lacks the resources to carry out enforcement against every person who is legally deemed to be removable from the United States. When determining whether to apprehend, detain, or place someone in deportation proceedings, Immigration and Customs Enforcement (ICE) officials had to consider criteria including whether the person had a serious physical or mental illness; was disabled, elderly, pregnant or nursing; or could demonstrate that they were primary caretakers of children or other dependents. The Trump administration has put a stop to setting any priorities in whom it deports. A memo from an ICE official instructs ICE agents to "take enforcement action against all removable aliens encountered in the course of their duties." The agency "will no longer exempt classes or categories of removable aliens from potential enforcement."[53] The Trump administration also cancelled the annual training conference for immigration judges.[54] This combination of weak procedural protections for noncitizens, ramped-up enforcement, and untrained judges will deepen the existing injustices in immigration enforcement.

Conclusion

States have the right to control immigration, including the right to deport migrants who are present in their territory without authorization, but it is subject to a number of constraints. One constraint is the obligation of states to protect the human rights of all territorially present persons. The social membership and fair play principles also serve as constraints. The longer one lives in the territory, the stronger one's moral claim to a more extensive set of rights, including the right to remain. The time spent living in a place serves as a proxy for the social ties migrants have developed and for their contributions to collective life.

11

Conclusion

IMMIGRATION IS AN issue that generates strong disagreement and strange political bedfellows. Labor-market protectionists find themselves on the same side as restrictive nationalists in supporting immigration restrictions. On the other side, immigrant rights advocates are joined by proponents of the free market in their commitment to open borders. In the heat of the public debate about immigration, it may seem that the only positions are restrictive nationalism or radical cosmopolitanism, closed borders or open borders.

This book has offered an intermediate ethical position situated between these poles. In contrast to restrictive nationalists who favor closing borders, I do not believe states should regulate immigration solely in the interests of their own members. Although members of a political community have special obligations to one another, they also have an obligation to take the interests of prospective migrants into account alongside the interests of fellow members. Prospective migrants may have urgent reasons to move, and their interests may trump the less weighty interests of members. For example, refugees are migrants fleeing persecution and violence, and sometimes the only durable solution to their displacement is to make a new life in a new country. States with integrative capabilities have a duty to take them in.

At the same time, in contrast to proponents of open borders, I do not interpret the moral equality of all human beings as requiring us, in Carens's words, "to weigh the claims of those trying to get in equally with those who are already inside."[1] I believe political membership is morally significant, even if its distribution is morally arbitrary. Political membership grounds special rights and obligations, and a government may show some partiality toward the interests of its members. This means a government may deny prospective migrants admission if their basic interests are protected in their home countries and doing so protects important interests of its constituents. For example, a government is justified in excluding prospective migrants who want to move to pursue higher wages above an already decent level if doing so protects important interests such as sustaining social welfare programs and assisting the domestic poor.

What is required is not closed borders or open borders but controlled borders and open doors. The idea of collective self-determination grounds the right of political communities to control immigration, but this right of immigration control is qualified, not absolute. Countries must open their doors to those fleeing persecution and violence and those with family connections. Democratic states are also constrained by democratic principles. Democratic norms of equality and antidiscrimination limit the kinds of criteria that may be used in selecting prospective migrants. The norms of fair play and social membership also constrain the power of democratic states to remove noncitizens from their territories. When the basic interests of prospective migrants are not at stake, however, governments are justified in restricting their movement for the sake of protecting the important interests of their members.

As critics will point out, this moderate position embraces commitments that pull in opposing directions, an ethic of membership and an ethic of universalism. The ethic of membership says we have special obligations to members of our own country. The ethic of universalism says we have obligations to all human beings. I do not think either ethic should be relinquished; we must pursue both. The tensions between them may never be entirely eliminated, but they can be managed and reduced by recognizing that our membership-based obligations and our global obligations are mutually constraining.

In Part III, I elaborated a number of the policy implications this theory has for democratic societies. Can anything more be said about the specific content of immigration policy? I want to conclude by considering the question of priorities in immigration policy. How should states prioritize among different claims for admission, including the claims of forcibly displaced migrants, those with family ties, and those with economic skills? In the preceding chapters, I have considered the normative grounds and limits of each of these claims but not how the different claims might be weighed against one another.

As discussed in chapter 8, family-based immigration makes up a large share of the admissions for permanent residence in many democratic countries. For example, in 2015, the percentage of migrants admitted to the United States for permanent residence because of family ties was 65 percent of total admissions. By contrast, refugees and asylum seekers made up only 14 percent and employment-based preferences, 14 percent.[2] Some defend the current immigration system that prioritizes family ties. Others argue that we should reduce family immigration so that we can take in a greater number of refugees because the latter are at risk of serious harm in a way that many family migrants are not. Still others argue that it is in a country's best interests to prioritize high-skilled migrants over family migrants because of the contributions the former will make and because the latter are said to negatively impact the wages of low-skilled workers already in the domestic labor market.[3] Which priorities are the right priorities?

This is a question that must be answered by members of democratic societies. Political philosophy can provide analysis of the values and principles that might guide public debate about immigration policy, but it cannot deliver a comprehensive immigration reform proposal. This is not just because policymaking requires context-sensitive political judgments but also because the power to regulate immigration is a legitimate power of members of democratic societies. Part III offered a number of principles that might guide public deliberation about immigration. What serves the interests of the political community is surely one consideration, but there are also humanitarian and democratic commitments that must be honored.

Even critics of family-based immigration who favor high-skilled immigration, such as the Cuban-born American economist George Borjas, take pride in belonging to a country that has provided refuge to the world's persecuted and poor. Borjas stops short of recommending that the United States change its admission rules to select only high-skilled migrants, saying, "But I still feel that it is a good thing to give some of the poor and huddled masses, people who face so many hardships, a chance to experience the incredible opportunities that our country has to offer."[4] In other words, cost-benefit analyses of specific policy options are not the only things that matter. Values and principles also matter. When we engage in debate with others, we appeal not just to facts and numbers but also to our values. When people protest with signs that say "Refugees Welcome" and "Shame" in response to their political leader's decision to cut the number of refugee admissions by more than half, they are invoking values.

This appeal to values and principles is especially important in democratic societies in which political power is the collective power of the people who must ultimately authorize the decisions made in our name. Because political power belongs to all members, we owe one another reasons for the exercise of that power. Of course, we don't always argue that way but that is the promise of democracy: to show respect for others by debating pressing political issues with reasoned arguments. We may not reach agreement on a single solution to the challenges of immigration but, as this book has tried to do, we can identify the basic principles that an acceptable solution must satisfy. It is up to us, in our role as members of democratic political communities, to debate immigration in light of the values we hold dear and to press our political leaders to aspire to them.

Notes

CHAPTER I

1. United Nations Department of Economic and Social Affairs, Population Division (2016), *International Migration Report 2015: Highlights*, http://www.un.org/en/development/desa/population/migration/publications/migrationreport/docs/MigrationReport2015_Highlights.pdf. The UN defines an "international migrant" as a person living in a country other than his or her country of birth, a category that includes those registered as refugees by the UN Refugee Agency. In 2014, refugees comprised about 8 percent of all international migrants.

2. Alex Tabarrok, "The Case for Getting Rid of Borders," *The Atlantic*, October 10, 2015.

3. "Editorial: In Praise of Huddled Masses," *Wall Street Journal*, July 3, 1984, 1; and Robert L. Bartley, "Thinking Things Over: Open NAFTA Borders? Why Not?," *Wall Street Journal*, July 2, 2001.

4. See, e.g., Samuel Huntington, *Who Are We? The Challenges to America's National Identity* (New York: Simon and Schuster, 2005); and Ann Coulter, *Adios, America: The Left's Plan to Turn Our Country into a Third World Hellhole* (Washington, DC: Regnery Publishing, 2015).

5. Ezra Klein, "Bernie Sanders: The Vox Conversation," *Vox*, July 28, 2015, https://www.vox.com/2015/7/28/9014491/bernie-sanders-vox-conversation.

6. George Borjas, "The Immigration Debate We Need," *New York Times*, February 27, 2017, https://www.nytimes.com/2017/02/27/opinion/the-immigration-debate-we-need.html.

7. I take this idea from Rawls: "By showing how the social world may realize the features of a realistic utopia, political philosophy provides a long-term goal of political endeavor, and in working toward it gives meaning to what we can do today." See Rawls, *The Law of Peoples* (Cambridge, MA: Harvard University Press, 1993), 128.

8. My discussion here draws on Daniel J. Tichenor, *Dividing Lines: The Politics of Immigration Control in America* (Princeton, NJ: Princeton University Press, 2002); James Hampshire *The Politics of Immigration* (Cambridge, UK: Polity Press, 2013).

9. Bradley Jones, "Americans' Views of Immigrants Marked by Widening Partisan, Generational Divides," Pew Research Center, April 15, 2016, http://www.pewresearch.org/fact-tank/2016/04/15/americans-views-of-immigrants-marked-by-widening-partisan-generational-divides/.

10. "Europe's Rising Far Right: A Guide to the Most Prominent Parties," *New York Times*, December 4, 2016, https://nyti.ms/2jDwLVm.

11. Gary Freeman, *Immigrant Labor and Racial Conflict in Industrial Societies: The French and British Experience, 1945–1975* (Princeton, NJ: Princeton University Press, 1979), 3.

12. Gary Freeman, "Modes of Immigration Politics in Liberal Democratic States," *International Migration Review* 24 (1995): 881–902; and Gary Freeman, "National Models, Policy Types, and the Politics of Immigration in Liberal Democracies," *West European Politics* 29 (2006): 227–47.

13. Hampshire, *Politics of Immigration*, 44.

14. Virginie Guiraudon and Christian Joppke refer to the role of the courts in upholding liberal norms to protect the rights of vulnerable migrants as a case of "self-limited" sovereignty. Guiraudon and Joppke, "Controlling a New Migration World," in *Controlling a New Migration World*, ed. Virginie Guiraudon and Christian Joppke (London: Routledge, 2001), 12.

15. George J. Borjas, *We Wanted Workers: Unraveling the Immigration Narrative* (New York: W. W. Norton, 2016), 210.

16. Joseph H. Carens, "Aliens and Citizens: The Case for Open Borders," *Review of Politics* 49, no. 2 (1987): 252. See also Carens, *The Ethics of Immigration* (Oxford: Oxford University Press, 2013).

17. John Rawls, *A Theory of Justice* (Cambridge, MA: Belknap Press of Harvard University Press, 1971), 72.

18. Carens, "Aliens and Citizens," 252. He reiterates his case for open borders in his 2013 book: "[I]n principle, borders should generally be open and people should normally be free to leave their country of origin and settle in another." Carens, *Ethics of Immigration*, 225.

19. Here I draw on Samuel Scheffler, "Liberalism, Nationalism, and Egalitarianism," in *Boundaries and Allegiances: Problems of Justice and Responsibility in Liberal Thought* (Oxford: Oxford University Press, 2001), 66–67; and Scheffler, "Membership and Political Obligation," *Journal of Political Philosophy* 26, no. 1 (2018): 3–23.

20. David Miller, *Strangers in Our Midst: The Political Philosophy of Immigration* (Cambridge, MA: Harvard University Press, 2016), 27.

21. Linda Bosniak, "Immigration Ethics and the Context of Justice," *Ethics and International Affairs* 31, no. 1 (2017): 97.

22. Michael Walzer, *Spheres of Justice: A Defense of Pluralism and Equality* (New York: Basic Books, 1983); and David Miller, *National Responsibility and Global Justice* (Oxford: Oxford University Press, 2007).
23. Ryan Pevnick, *Immigration and the Constraints of Justice: Between Open Borders and Absolute Sovereignty* (Cambridge: Cambridge University Press, 2011).
24. Christopher Heath Wellman, "Immigration and Freedom of Association," *Ethics* 119, no. 1 (2008): 109–41.
25. Michael Blake, "Immigration, Jurisdiction, and Exclusion," *Philosophy and Public Affairs* 41, no. 2 (2013): 103–30.

CHAPTER 2

1. Chae Chan Ping v. United States (*Chinese Exclusion Case*), 130 U.S. 581 (1889). In Canada, the pivotal case articulating inherent, virtually absolute sovereign control over immigration is the 1906 Privy Council decision in Canada (Attorney General) v. Cain, A.C. 542 (1906). For discussion of the Canadian case, see Colin Grey, "The Rights of Migration," *Legal Theory* 20, no. 1 (2014): 27.
2. See Rogers M. Smith, "Beyond Sovereignty and Uniformity: The Challenges for Equal Citizenship in the Twenty-First Century," *Harvard Law Review* 122, no. 3 (2009): 919. For other scholars who interpret these early cases as novel assertions of virtually unfettered national sovereignty, see Stephen H. Legomsky, "Immigration Law and the Principle of Plenary Congressional Power," *Supreme Court Review* 1984 (1984): 267; Stephen H. Legomsky, *Immigration and the Judiciary: Law and Politics in Britain and America* (Oxford: Oxford University Press, 1987), 177–222; Louis Henkin, "The Constitution and United States Sovereignty: A Century of 'Chinese Exclusion' and Its Progeny," *Harvard Law Review* 100, no. 4 (1987): 862–63; Sarah H. Cleveland, "Powers Inherent in Sovereignty: Indians, Aliens, Territories, and the Nineteenth Century Origins of Plenary Power over Foreign Affairs," *Texas Law Review* 81, no. 1 (2002): 1–284; and Linda Bosniak, *The Citizen and the Alien: Dilemmas of Contemporary Membership* (Princeton, NJ: Princeton University Press, 2006), 51.
3. See Cleveland, "Powers Inherent in Sovereignty"; and Rogers M. Smith, *Civic Ideals: Conflicting Visions of Citizenship in U.S. History* (New Haven, CT: Yale University Press, 1997), 357–69.
4. Nishimura Ekiu v. United States, 142 U.S. 651 (1892); and Fong Yue Ting v. United States, 149 U.S. 698 (1893). Stephen Legomsky identifies these two cases and the *Chinese Exclusion Case* as the three "principal building blocks" of the plenary power doctrine. See Legomsky, "Immigration Law," 289.
5. Legomsky, "Immigration Law," 291.
6. Matthew J. Lindsay, "Immigration as Invasion: Sovereignty, Security, and the Origins of the Federal Immigration Power," *Harvard Civil Rights–Civil Liberties Law Review* 45 (2010): 3–4.

7. Lucy E. Salyer, *Laws Harsh as Tigers: Chinese Immigrants and the Shaping of Modern Immigration Law* (Chapel Hill: University of North Carolina Press, 1995), 8–12.

8. The Chinese Exclusion Act was formally known as An Act: To Execute Certain Treaty Stipulations Relating to Chinese, 22 Stat. 58 (1882).

9. Smith, *Civic Ideals*, 359.

10. An Act: To Amend an Act Entitled "An Act to Execute Certain Treaty Stipulations Relating to Chinese," approved May Sixth, Eighteen Hundred and Eighty-Two, 23 Stat. 115 (1884).

11. Briefs for Appellant by Attorneys Houndly and Carter, *Chae Chan Ping v. United States*, 130 U.S. 581 (1889) (No. 1446), at 34. See also Cleveland, "Powers Inherent in Sovereignty," 124-5.

12. *Chinese Exclusion Case* at 595.

13. *Chinese Exclusion Case* at 603–4, quoting The Schooner Exchange v. Mcfaddon & Others, 11 U.S. 116, 136 (1812).

14. *Chinese Exclusion Case* at 606, emphasis added.

15. As Susan Coutin, Justin Richland, and Véronique Fortin put it, "Declaring that the United States has plenary power in certain areas of law is an illocutionary legal act: it brings this power into being by calling it forth." See Coutin, Richland, and Fortin, "Routine Exceptionality: The Plenary Power Doctrine, Immigrants, and the Indigenous under U.S. Law," *UC Irvine Law Review* 4 (2014): 103.

16. *Chinese Exclusion Case* at 609.

17. As Hiroshi Motomura observes, this was an era of constitutional law when equal protection was on its way toward "separate but equal," and judicial recognition of the substantive and procedural rights of individuals was "far beyond the constitutional horizon." See Motomura, "Immigration Law after a Century of Plenary Power: Phantom Constitutional Norms and Statutory Interpretation," *Yale Law Journal* 100 (1990): 551.

18. Nishimura Ekiu v. United States, 142 U.S. 651 (1892). The case involved the Immigration Act of 1882, the general immigration statute that had authorized immigration commissioners to exclude any individuals "liable to become a public charge." While the habeas petition was pending, the immigration inspector upheld Nishimura's exclusion based on a later statute, An Act in Amendment to the Various Acts Relative to Immigration and the Importation of Aliens under Contract or Agreement to Perform Labor, 22 Stat. 1084 (1891).

19. *Nishimura Ekiu v. United States* at 659, citing Emer de Vattel, *The Law of Nations, or, Principles of the Law of Nature, Applied to the Conduct and Affairs of Nations and Sovereigns, with Three Early Essays on the Origin and Nature of Natural Law and on Luxury*, ed. Béla Kapossy and Richard Whatmore (Indianapolis, IN: Liberty Fund, 2008), bk. 2, ch. 7, §§ 94, 100. Justice Gray paraphrases Vattel; here is what Vattel states in the passages cited by Justice Gray: "The sovereign may forbid the entrance of his territory either to foreigners in general, or in particular cases, or to certain persons, or for certain particular purposes, according as he may think it

advantageous to the state. There is nothing in all this, that does not flow from the rights of domain and sovereignty" (§ 94). Also: "Since the lord of the territory may, whenever he thinks proper, forbid its being entered, he has no doubt a power to annex what conditions he pleases to the permission to enter" (§ 100).

20. Motomura, "Immigration Law after a Century of Plenary Power," 552.
21. *Fong Yue Ting v. United States.*
22. An Act to Prohibit the Coming of Chinese Persons into the United States, 27 Stat. 25 (1892).
23. *Fong Yue Ting v. United States* at 705, 13. Justice Gray also rejected the claim that deportation constitutes punishment: "The order of deportation is not a punishment for crime. It is not a banishment, in the sense in which that word is often applied to the expulsion of a citizen from his country by way of punishment" (730).
24. *Fong Yue Ting v. United States* at 707–8, citing Vattel, *Law of Nations*, bk. 2, ch. 19, § 230; bk. 1, ch. 19, § 31.
25. *Fong Yue Ting v. United States* at 711.
26. *Fong Yue Ting v. United States* at 711. See also Smith, *Civic Ideals*, 368.
27. *Fong Yue Ting v. United States* at 736–39, 744–46, 754–56.
28. Ten years after *Fong Yue Ting*, in Yamataya v. Fisher, 189 U.S. 86 (1903), the court suggested that a noncitizen already inside the United States who challenged deportation procedures might have some success. The government had arrested and tried to deport Yamataya four days after she had landed. Although the court left the plenary power doctrine untouched, it refused to permit Yamataya's deportation on two grounds: first, that noncitizens *inside* the United States can invoke more constitutional safeguards than noncitizens outside the territory; and second, that courts reviewing deportation orders should examine procedural due process questions more closely than substantive immigration rules and that aliens present in the territory were entitled to some procedural protections. Motomura, "Immigration Law after a Century of Plenary Power," 554. In a series of cases in the early to mid-twentieth century, instead of softening the plenary power doctrine's harshest aspects with respect to the treatment of noncitizens present in the US territory, the court upheld the US government's power to exclude such noncitizens. See, e.g., United States *ex rel*. Knauff v. Shaughnessy, 163 U.S. 537 (1896); Shaughnessy v. United States *ex rel*. Mezei, 345 U.S. 206 (1953); and Harisiades v. Shaughnessy, 342 U.S. 580 (1952).
29. Cleveland, "Powers Inherent in Sovereignty," 133–34.
30. In the *Head Money Cases*, the US Supreme Court for the first time considered the constitutionality of a federal immigration statute, the 1882 Act to Regulate Immigration, which had imposed a fifty-cent head tax for each immigrant on board ships arriving in the United States. See *Head Money Cases*, 112 U.S. 580 (1884); the consolidated cases were *Edye v. Robertson* and *Cunard Steamship Co. v. Robertson.* Shipmasters challenged the federal law on the grounds that the Constitution did not give Congress the power to tax immigrants. The solicitor general argued that

the power of Congress to regulate immigration was "implied in [the] very existence of independent government anterior to the adoption of a constitution" and
that constitutional provisions relevant to that power were "merely in recognition,
and not in creation thereof." See Brief for the United States at 2, *Edye v. Robertson*
(No. 772). Writing for a unanimous court, Justice Miller held that exclusive federal authority over immigration rested on the Commerce Clause, suggesting that
immigration regulation was primarily an *economic* matter intended to protect the
nation's prosperity.

31. Smith, *Civic Ideals*, 368. See also Daniel Kanstroom, *Deportation Nation: Outsiders
    in American History* (Cambridge, MA: Harvard University Press, 2007), 95–
    130; Gerald L. Neuman, *Strangers to the Constitution: Immigrants, Borders, and
    Fundamental Law* (Princeton, NJ: Princeton University Press, 1996), 119, 23–24;
    and Legomsky, "Immigration Law," 289.

32. *Chinese Exclusion Case* at 606.

33. F. H. Hinsley, *Sovereignty*, 2nd ed. (Cambridge: Cambridge University Press,
    1986), 186, 201.

34. Arthur Nussbaum, *A Concise History of the Law of Nations*, rev. ed.
    (New York: Macmillan, 1954), 160–61; and Vincent Chetail, "Vattel and the
    American Dream: An Inquiry into the Reception of *Law of Nations* in the United
    States," in *The Roots of International Law*, ed. Vincent Chetail and Pierre-Marie
    Dupuy (Leiden, NL: Martinus-Nijhoff, 2013), 263–66.

35. In the preface to the *Law of Nations*, Vattel acknowledged that his aim was to pop-
    ularize Christian Wolff's less accessible work *Jus Gentium*, although Vattel says
    he followed his own plan and drew selectively on Wolff's work so that his work
    "differed greatly" from Wolff's. See Charles G. Fenwick, "The Authority of Vattel,"
    American Political Science Review 7, no. 3 (1913): 395–410.

36. Wolff's naturalism was influenced by Aristotle and had antecedents in Aquinas,
    Grotius, and Leibniz. In this tradition, nature exhibits an order and teleology to
    which the faculty of reason gives human beings privileged access. Wolff gave this
    teleological vision unqualified support. See Nicholas Greenwood Onuf, "Civitas
    Maxima: Wolff, Vattel and the Fate of Republicanism," *American Journal of
    International Law* 88, no. 2 (1994): 283.

37. Fredrick G. Whelan, "Vattel's Doctrine of State," *History of Political Thought* 9, no.
    1 (1988): 76–81.

38. Stephen D. Krasner, *Sovereignty: Organized Hypocrisy* (Princeton, NJ: Princeton
    University Press, 1999), 20. Many scholars of international relations locate the de-
    finitive beginnings of the sovereign state in the Peace of Westphalia that ended
    the Thirty Years' War in 1648 and placed each state in control of its internal and
    external affairs. See, for example, Hedley Bull, *The Anarchical Society: A Study of
    Order in World Politics* (New York: Columbia University Press, 1977); and Adam
    Watson, *The Evolution of International Society: A Comparative Historical Analysis*
    (London: Routledge, 1992). Other scholars have come to reject this idea as the

"Westphalian myth": instead of beginning a new era of independent relations between states, the Peace of Westphalia codified a process that had its start in European courts and schools of law in the twelfth century. Stéphane Beaulac, *The Power of Language in the Making of International Law: The Word "Sovereignty" in Bodin and Vattel and the Myth of Westphalia* (Boston: Martinus Nijhoff, 2004); Hinsley, *Sovereignty*; and Derek Croxton, "The Peace of Westphalia of 1648 and the Origins of Sovereignty," *International History Review* 21, no. 3 (1999): 569–91.

39. Nussbaum, *Concise History of the Law of Nations*, 150–51; Hinsley, *Sovereignty*, 192–93; Onuf, "Civitas Maxima," 297–301; and Georg Cavallar, *The Rights of Strangers: Theories of International Hospitality, the Global Community, and Political Justice since Vitoria* (Burlington, VT: Ashgate, 2002), 307.

40. After World War I, Vattel was viewed as an unconditional supporter of reason of state, a doctrine that refers to the right of rulers to act against natural and positive law for the sake of preserving and expanding state power, who "disguised his evil intentions through words of sublime charity." Béla Kapossy and Richard Whatmore, introduction to Vattel, *Law of Nations*, xiv–xvi. By contrast, other interpreters of Vattel maintain that his approach is "more humanitarian, more cosmopolitan, and, in a measure, even democratic." See Nussbaum, *Concise History of the Law of Nations*, 157.

41. Hedley Bull, "Society and Anarchy in International Relations," in *Diplomatic Investigations: Essays in the Theory of International Politics*, ed. Herbert Butterfield and Martin Wright (London: Allen and Unwin, 1966), 35-60. See also Charles R. Beitz, "The Moral Standing of States Revisited," *Ethics and International Affairs* 23, no. 4 (2009): 329.

42. Christian Wolff, *Jus Gentium Methodo Scientifica Pertractatum*, trans. Joseph H. Drake (Oxford: Clarendon Press, 1934), sec. 2, pp. 9, 16.

43. See Charles R. Beitz, *Political Theory and International Relations* (Princeton, NJ: Princeton University Press, 1979), 81.

CHAPTER 3

1. Michael Walzer, *Spheres of Justice: A Defense of Pluralism and Equality* (New York: Basic Books, 1983), 29, 32.

2. Walzer, *Spheres of Justice*, 42.

3. Walzer, 39.

4. Walzer, 62, emphasis in original.

5. Michael Walzer, *Just and Unjust Wars: A Moral Argument with Historical Illustrations* (New York: Basic Books, 1977), 88.

6. Michael Walzer, "The Moral Standing of States: A Response to Four Critics," *Philosophy and Public Affairs* 9, no. 3 (1980): 210–11.

7. On the contrast between the traditional view of the global normative order and Walzer's revisionist view, see Beitz, "Moral Standing of States Revisited," 329–33.

8. My discussion here engages with David Miller, *On Nationality* (Oxford: Clarendon Press, 1995); Miller, "Territorial Rights: Concept and Justification," *Political Studies* 60, no. 2 (2012): 252–68; and Miller, *Strangers in Our Midst*.

9. Miller, *On Nationality*, 27.

10. Miller, *National Responsibility*, 218.

11. Miller, "Territorial Rights: Concept and Justification," 263.

12. Miller, *National Responsibility*, 218–19. Tamar Meisels has also developed a nationalist theory of territorial rights based on the concept of "settlement." "Settlement" refers not only to the physical presence of individuals on a piece of land but also to "the existence of a permanent physical infrastructure" that members of the nation have constructed. Sometimes such settlements are built in a conscious, premeditated manner, but more often they "simply evolve over time" as people settle in a given place. As in Miller's account, what is critical is the expressive element of labor: people shape the territory "so as to coincide with a particular way of life." Tamar Meisels, *Territorial Rights*, 2nd ed. (Dordrecht, NL: Springer, 2009), 118, 26–27.

13. Miller, *Strangers in Our Midst*, 63.

14. Miller, 26. He suggests only the nationalist account of political community can constitute a properly functioning state or explain why members of a political community would resist the dismemberment of their state via secession. If the political relationship among compatriots were simply about economic cooperation or political participation, "there is no obvious reason to resist the breakup (28).

15. Miller, 64–65.

16. Miller, *On Nationality*, 26.

17. David Miller, "Immigration: The Case for Limits," in *Contemporary Debates in Applied Ethics*, ed. Andrew I. Cohen and Christopher Heath Wellman (Malden, MA: Wiley-Blackwell, 2014), 204.

18. See Salyer, *Laws Harsh as Tigers*.; Smith, *Civic Ideals*; Leti Volpp, "The Citizen and the Terrorist," *UCLA Law Review* 49 (2002): 1575–1600; Mae M. Ngai, *Impossible Subjects: Illegal Aliens and the Making of Modern America* (Princeton, NJ: Princeton University Press, 2004).

19. Walzer, *Spheres of Justice*, 46–47.

20. International Social Survey Programme–National Identity reports I (1995), II (2003), and III (2013), https://www.gesis.org/issp/modules/issp-modules-by-topic/national-identity/.

21. John Locke, *Second Treatise of Government*, ed. C. B. Macpherson (Indianapolis, IN: Hackett, 1980), ch. 5.

22. A. John Simmons, *The Lockean Theory of Rights* (Princeton, NJ: Princeton University Press, 1992), 223.

23. Locke, *Second Treatise of Government*, ch. 8, § 120, p. 64.

24. A. John Simmons, *Boundaries of Authority* (Oxford: Oxford University Press, 2016).

25. I will say more about the connection between rightful occupancy and territorial rights in chapter 4.

26. My critique of Lockean theories is indebted to Margaret Moore, *A Political Theory of Territory* (Oxford: Oxford University Press, 2015), ch. 2; and Anna Stilz, "Why Do States Have Territorial Rights?," *International Theory* 1, no. 2 (2009): 185–213.

27. Robert Nozick, *Anarchy, State, and Utopia* (New York: Basic Books, 1974), 114–15.

28. Nozick, *Anarchy, State, and Utopia*, chs. 4–5.

29. Nozick, 33.

30. Hillel Steiner, "Territorial Justice," in *National Rights, International Obligations*, ed. Simon Caney, David George, and Peter Jones (Boulder, CO: Westview, 1996), 144.

31. For elaboration of this critique, see Cara Nine, "A Lockean Theory of Territory," *Political Studies* 56, no. 1 (2008): 150–54.

32. Locke, *Second Treatise of Government*, ch. 8, § 95, p. 52. Locke himself did not directly address the aspect of territorial rights pertaining to control over the movement of people and goods across borders. It is interesting to note that Locke has been a source for both property-based defenses of a state's right to control immigration and contemporary libertarian arguments in favor of open borders. I examine the latter in chapter 6.

33. A. John Simmons, "On the Territorial Rights of States," *Philosophical Issues* 11 (2001): 313.

34. Simmons, 313. "On the Territorial Rights."

35. Moore, *Political Theory of Territory*, 21.

36. Ryan Pevnick, *Immigration and the Constraints of Justice: Between Open Borders and Absolute Sovereignty* (Cambridge: Cambridge University Press, 2011), 33.

37. Pevnick, *Immigration and the Constraints of Justice*, 38.

38. Pevnick, 44.

39. Pevnick, 43–44. See also Jeremy Waldron, "Property and Ownership," *Stanford Encyclopedia of Philosophy*, first published 2004, https://plato.stanford.edu/archives/spr2012/entries/property/.

40. See also Allen Buchanan, "The Making and Unmaking of Boundaries: What Liberalism Has to Say," in *States, Nations, and Borders: The Ethics of Making Boundaries*, ed. Allen Buchanan and Margaret Moore (Cambridge: Cambridge University Press, 2003), 233.

41. In contrast to many neo-Lockeans, Locke distinguished between jurisdiction and ownership. He was influenced by Grotius, who distinguished sovereignty *(imperium)* from ownership *(dominium)*. Citing Seneca, Grotius characterized the distinction as follows: "To kings belongs the power over all things; to individuals, proprietorship." Grotius also draws on Dio Chrysostom: "The territory belongs to the state, but nonetheless on that account does each person in it have his own property." See Grotius, *On the Law of War and Peace*, ed. Stephen C. Neff (Cambridge: Cambridge University Press, 2012), bk. 2, ch. 3, § 4. I am grateful to

Dan Lee for pointing me to Grotius and for discussion of the differences between
Locke and neo-Lockeans.

42. For this line of critique, see Avery Kolers, *Land, Conflict, and Justice: A Political
Theory of Territory* (Cambridge: Cambridge University Press, 2009), 27–29.

43. Pevnick, *Immigration and the Constraints of Justice*, 164–65.

44. In contemporary political discourse, immigrant rights activists have emphasized the
role of *immigrant labor* (as opposed to citizen labor) to argue for greater openness
toward immigration and the inclusion of immigrants in the political community.
For example, the New York Hotel and Model Trades Council of the AFL-CIO
(American Federation of Labor and Congress of Industrial Organizations)
emphasized the legacy of Irish and other immigrant laborers in helping to construct buildings and build cities in the United States. See New York Hotel and
Motel Trades Council, "We Built This City: Immigrant Labor and the Fight for
a Democratic NY," New York Hotel and Motel Trades Council website, April 12,
2013, http://hotelworkers.org/article/we-built-this-city. Similarly, Pope Francis
remarked during his visit to the United States, "As the son of an immigrant family,
I am happy to be a guest in this country, which was largely built by such families."
See Elise Foley, "Pope Francis: U.S. 'Was Largely Built by' Immigrant Families,"
Huffington Post, September 23, 2015, http://www.huffingtonpost.com/entry/
pope-francis-immigration-refugees_us_5602ccа0e4b00310edf9740b.

45. See Shelley Wilcox, review of *Immigration and the Constraints of Justice: Between
Open Borders and Absolute Sovereignty* by Ryan Pevnick, *Ethics* 122, no. 3
(2012): 617-622.

46. Christopher Heath Wellman, "In Defense of the Right to Exclude," in *Debating
the Ethics of Immigration: Is There a Right to Exclude?*, ed. Christopher Heath
Wellman and Phillip Cole (Oxford: Oxford University Press, 2011), 25.

47. Stuart White, "Freedom of Association and the Right to Exclude," *Journal of
Political Philosophy* 5, no. 4 (1997): 360–61. Walzer analogized countries with
"clubs" in his discussion of membership, suggesting that countries are like clubs in
having "admissions committees"—in the United States, Congress functions as such
a committee. Walzer, *Spheres of Justice*, 40.

48. Christopher Heath Wellman, "In Defense of the Right to Exclude," in Wellman
and Cole, *Debating the Ethics of Immigration*, 37.

49. Christopher Heath Wellman, "Immigration and Freedom of Association," *Ethics*
119, no. 1 (2008): 109.

50. Wellman, "Immigration and Freedom of Association," 135.

51. In writing about secession elsewhere, Wellman does suggest that states must be
"sufficiently territorially contiguous" to fulfill their purposes and that this territorial contiguity requirement justifies a state's coercion of all inhabitants within
its territory. However, though this requirement might support the state's claim to
coerce those individuals already inside its borders, it has no bearing on the state's
right to exclude foreigners outside its territory who wish to enter. See Christopher

Heath Wellman, *A Theory of Secession: The Case for Political Self-Determination* (Cambridge: Cambridge University Press, 2005), 16–17. See also Sarah Fine, "Freedom of Association Is Not the Answer," *Ethics* 120, no. 2 (2010): 355.

52. White, "Freedom of Association and the Right to Exclude," 381, quoted in Wellman, "In Defense of the Right to Exclude," 32, emphasis added.

53. Fine, "Freedom of Association Is Not the Answer," 349–50.

54. Wellman, "Immigration and Freedom of Association," 114.

55. John Rawls, *Justice as Fairness: A Restatement*, ed. Erin Kelly (Cambridge, MA: Belknap Press of Harvard University Press, 2001), 4.

56. This is not to deny that in some contexts, exclusion from a golf club or other voluntary associations, such as the Jaycees or Boy Scouts, can result in significant harms to those excluded. See, e.g., Roberts v. US Jaycees, 468 U.S. 609 (1984); and Boy Scouts of America et al. v. Dale, 530 U.S. 640 (2000). Context-sensitive judgments are necessary to determine whether the harms are sufficiently significant to require constraints on the association's right to exclude.

57. I am grateful to Paul Gowder for discussion of the differences between clubs and states.

58. Michael Blake, "Immigration, Jurisdiction, and Exclusion," *Philosophy and Public Affairs* 41, no. 2 (2013): 115.

59. Blake, "Immigration, Jurisdiction, and Exclusion," 110–11.

60. See Michael Blake, "Distributive Justice, State Coercion, and Autonomy," *Philosophy and Public Affairs* 30, no. 3 (2001): 257–96.

61. Blake, "Immigration, Jurisdiction, and Exclusion," 113. Linda Bosniak calls this the principle of "territorial personhood": by virtue of one's presence in a state's territory, one is entitled to have her basic rights protected and fulfilled by the institutions of that state. Linda Bosniak, "Being Here: Ethical Territoriality and the Rights of Immigrants," in *Theoretical Inquiries in Law* 8, no. 2 (2007): 389-410. I discuss the significance of territorial presence in chapter 10.

62. Bosniak, "Being Here," 109.

63. Thanks to Michael Blake for conversations on this point, which serves as the basis for my interpretation of his view. Kantian theories of territorial rights have been developed in Allen Buchanan, *Justice, Legitimacy, and Self-Determination: Moral Foundations for International Law* (Oxford: Oxford University Press, 2004); Stilz, "Why Do States Have Territorial Rights?"; Anna Stilz, "Nations, States, and Territory," *Ethics* 121, no. 3 (2011): 572–601; Jeremy Waldron, "Two Conceptions of Self-Determination," in *The Philosophy of International Law*, ed. Samantha Besson and John Tasioulas (Oxford: Oxford University Press, 2010); and Lea Ypi, "A Permissive Theory of Territorial Rights," *European Journal of Philosophy* 22, no. 2 (2014): 288–312.

64. Immanuel Kant, *The Metaphysics of Morals*, ed. Mary J. Gregor (Cambridge: Cambridge University Press, 1996), 86, § 42.

65. Waldron, "Two Conceptions of Self-Determination," 411–12.

66. Moore, *Political Theory of Territory*, 97–110.
67. Blake, "Immigration, Jurisdiction, and Exclusion," 115.
68. Blake, 114.
69. Blake, 120.
70. Michael Kates and Ryan Pevnick, "Immigration, Jurisdiction, and History," *Philosophy and Public Affairs* 42, no. 2 (2014): 114.
71. Blake, "Immigration, Jurisdiction, and Exclusion," 114.

CHAPTER 4

1. Another way of capturing the distinction is between pro tanto and conclusory reasons. *Pro tanto* reasons are genuine reasons for a particular action or position, which may be overridden by competing reasons that may also be in play, whereas *conclusory* reasons require us to act regardless of other considerations in play. See Charles R. Beitz, *The Idea of Human Rights* (Oxford: Oxford University Press, 2009), 116–17.
2. United Nations, The Charter of the United Nations, signed June 26, 1945, article 1, http://www.un.org/en/sections/un-charter/chapter-i/index.html.
3. United Nations, International Covenant on Civil and Political Rights, December 16, 1966, article 1, http://www.ohchr.org/en/professionalinterest/pages/ccpr.aspx.
4. Thomas M. Franck, "The Emerging Right to Democratic Governance," *American Journal of International Law* 86, no. 1 (1992): 54–55.
5. By "justice" I mean what Simmons refers to as theories of *justification* of the state (whether its qualities or virtues show it to be morally acceptable), which he constrasts with the *legitimacy* of states (whether it has the right to impose binding duties on any particular subject). See A. John Simmons, "Justification and Legitimacy," *Ethics* 109, no. 4 (1999): 739–71. See also Joshua Cohen, "Is There a Human Right to Democracy?," in *The Egalitarian Conscience: Essays in Honour of G. A. Cohen*, ed. Christine Sypnowich (Oxford: Oxford University Press, 2006), 234.
6. See, e.g., Allen Buchanan's *Justice, Legitimacy, and Self-Determination: Moral Foundations for International Law* (Oxford: Oxford University Press, 2004).
7. On the distinction between collective self-determination and democracy, see Cohen, "Is There a Human Right to Democracy?"; and Buchanan, *Justice, Legitimacy, and Self-Determination*, 146.
8. I cannot pursue the question of how minimal or extensive the list of protections should be; the threshold of decency captured by the Universal Declaration of Human Rights is a good place to start.
9. See, e.g., the law of nations theorists who regard the state as a "moral person" (discussed in chapter 2).
10. As Joseph Raz puts it, "[T]he explanation and justification of the goodness or badness of anything derives ultimately from its contribution, actual or possible, to

human life and its quality." Joseph Raz, "Rights-Based Moralities," in *Theories of Rights*, ed. Jeremy Waldron (Oxford: Oxford University Press, 1984), 183.

11. I borrow this formulation from Andrew Altman and Christopher Heath Wellman, *A Liberal Theory of International Justice* (Oxford: Oxford University Press, 2011).

12. Joseph Raz, *The Morality of Freedom* (Oxford: Oxford University Press, 1986), 208–9.

13. Rousseau distinguishes between "moral liberty" and "natural liberty," defining the latter as an individual's "unlimited right to everything that tempts him and that he can acquire." Moral liberty "alone makes man truly the master of himself," and it is only possible "in the civil state." See Jean-Jacques Rousseau, *On the Social Contract*, in *Basic Political Writings*, trans. and ed. Donald A. Cress (Indianapolis, IN: Hackett, 1987), bk. 1, ch. 8, pp. 150–51.

14. Recognition of this collective aspect of the right of self-determination is what is missing from the deontic arguments for the state's right to control immigration offered by Wellman and Blake, whom I discuss later in the chapter. See also chapter 3 for extended discussion of their theories.

15. See chapter 1 for discussion of the idea of associative obligations.

16. Ernest Renan, "What Is a Nation?" (1882) in *What Is a Nation? and Other Political Writings*, trans. and ed. M.F.N. Giglioli (New York: Columbia University Press, 2018). See also Benedict Anderson, *Imagined Communities: Reflections on the Origin and Spread of Nationalism*, rev. ed. (London: Verso, 1991); Miller, *On Nationality*; and Bernard Yack, *Nationalism and the Moral Psychology of Community* (Chicago: University of Chicago Press, 2012).

17. For a critique of attempts to distinguish political and cultural reasons in movements for collective autonomy and self-determination, see Will Kymlicka, "The Essentialist Critique of Multiculturalism: Theories, Policies, Ethos" (paper on file with author). I am grateful to Will for sharing his paper with me. I had already completed my manuscript by the time I read his paper and regret that I did not have enough time to reflect on his critique.

18. See, e.g., Michael Blake, who relies on a principle of state coercion to define the scope of political membership and the scope of distributive justice. Michael Blake, "Distributive Justice, State Coercion, and Autonomy," *Philosophy and Public Affairs* 30, no. 3 (2001): 257–96.

19. Rogers M. Smith, *Stories of Peoplehood: The Politics and Morals of Political Membership* (New York: Cambridge University Press, 2003), 20; and Smith, *Political Peoplehood: The Roles of Values, Interests, and Identities* (Chicago: University of Chicago Press, 2015), 2.

20. Smith explicitly excludes football clubs, singing groups, and Girl Scout troops, but that still leaves an expansive range of voluntary associations that count as "political peoples." Smith, *Stories of Peoplehood*, 20. Smith's broad definition is connected to the purpose of his study: to develop an explanatory and normative framework for

analyzing how people come to have the senses of political affiliation and allegiance that they have, how those senses change, and which ones are more desirable (4).

21. This is not to suggest that religious associations do not aspire to collective self-determination. Consider nineteenth-century Mormons, who migrated to Utah to establish not only a religious community but a political kingdom. My conception of peoplehood is open to a wide range of groups, including religious groups, but they must meet the three conditions outlined.

22. My discussion here is indebted to Margaret Moore, *A Political Theory of Territory* (Oxford University Press, 2015), ch. 3.

23. I am grateful to Joel Sati for discussion of this point. In chapter 10, I consider what is owed to different groups of noncitizens in liberal democratic countries.

24. On noncitizen voting, see Rainer Bauböck, "Expansive Citizenship: Voting beyond Territory and Membership," *Political Science and Politics* 38, no. 4 (2005): 683–87; and Sarah Song, "Democracy and Noncitizen Voting Rights," *Citizenship Studies* 13, no. 6 (2009): 607–20.

25. In his reading of David Walker's *Appeal to the Colored Citizens of the World* (1829), Melvin Rogers argues that by calling on fellow African Americans in the nineteenth century to "lay aside abject servility and be determined to act like men, and not brutes," Walker was calling into existence a political standing that was otherwise denied to them. By pointing to political activity, not legal status, Walker means to elicit from his black audience that they are judgment-making beings and, in that regard, equal citizens. See Melvin L. Rogers, "David Walker and the Political Power of the Appeal," *Political Theory* 43, no. 2 (2015): 208–33.

26. Moore, *Political Theory of Territory*, 50–52.

27. Rousseau, *On the Social Contract*, in *Basic Political Writings*, bk. 4, ch. 2, p. 205.

28. I thank George Rainbolt and Ying Chan for pressing this objection.

29. Hannah Arendt, *The Origins of Totalitarianism* (New York: Harcourt Brace, 1968), 296.

30. Even Rousseau acknowledged that such disagreements can run deep, from judgments about the appropriate form of government and which collective decision-making rules provide the most reasonable balance of deliberativeness and efficacy to the level of revenue needed by government to conduct its business. See Joshua Cohen, *Rousseau: A Free Community of Equals* (Oxford: Oxford University Press, 2010), 69.

31. Democracy is more normatively demanding than collective self-determination; it requires equal rights of participation. Where this condition is met, democracy provides strong institutional guarantees that people can authorize their government. I say more about democratic self-determination later in the chapter.

32. See Miller, "Territorial Rights: Concept and Justification," 252–68.

33. I am grateful to Chris Kutz for discussion of this point.

34. There is reasonable disagreement about whether legitimate states can provide a set of substantive goods that is defined more minimally than what is required by

justice. For example, Andrew Altman and Christopher Heath Wellman argue that the legitimacy of states rests in part on the protection of human rights, which they define as moral rights to the protections generally needed against standard and direct threats to leading a minimally decent human life. Altman and Wellman, *Liberal Theory of International Justice*, ch. 1. See also Buchanan, *Justice, Legitimacy, and Self-Determination*.

35. Here I draw on Anna Stilz, "Occupancy Rights and the Wrong of Removal," *Philosophy and Public Affairs* 41, no. 4 (2013): 327; and Moore, *Political Theory of Territory*, ch. 3. Occupancy rights are distinct from private property rights in that occupancy rights are not assigned exclusively to particular individuals or groups (i.e., many people can share occupancy in the same area), and occupancy includes rights of use and access to a particular geographical space but not a number of Hohfeldian incidents typically associated with private property (such as rights to derive income, to give, to sell, or to bequeath). See Wesley Newcomb Hohfeld and Walter Wheeler Cook, *Fundamental Legal Conceptions as Applied in Judicial Reasoning and Other Legal Essays* (New Haven, CT: Yale University Press, 1919).

36. Thomas Hobbes, *The Elements of Law, Natural and Politic*, ed. J. C. A. Gaskin (Oxford: Oxford University Press, 1994), 1.17.2, emphasis added.

37. It is interesting and puzzling to note that Walzer, who is most commonly interpreted as providing a cultural argument for the state's right to control immigration (see chapter 3), also says an individual's right to place is something the state owes to "its inhabitants simply, without reference to their collective or national identity." Walzer, *Spheres of Justice*, 43.

38. Stilz, "Occupancy Rights and the Wrong of Removal," 334–39; Moore, *Political Theory of Territory*, 38–39.

39. I draw here on my discussion of historical injustice and minority group rights in Song, *Justice, Gender, and the Politics of Multiculturalism* (Cambridge: Cambridge University Press, 2007), ch. 3.

40. Jeremy Waldron, "Superseding Historic Injustice," *Ethics* 103, no. 1 (1992): 4–28; Robert Nozick, *Anarchy, State, Utopia* (New York: Basic Books, 1974).

41. Here I draw on Iris Marion Young, "Responsibility and Global Labor Justice," *Journal of Political Philosophy* 12, no. 4 (2004): 365–88; and Young, *Responsibility for Justice* (Oxford University Press, 2011).

42. Kevin K. Washburn, "What the Future Holds: The Changing Landscape of Federal Indian Policy," *Harvard Law Review Forum* 130 (2017): 218, 213–14.

43. We should also consider the impact of migration on sending countries and on migrants themselves, which I take up in Part II.

44. See Santa Clara Pueblo v. Martinez, 436 U.S. 49 (1978). For discussion of this case, see Song, *Justice, Gender, and the Politics of Multiculturalism*, ch. 5.

45. Michael Blake, "Immigration, Jurisdiction, and Exclusion," *Philosophy and Public Affairs* 41, no. 2 (2013): 119–20.

46. Blake, "Immigration, Jurisdiction, and Exclusion," 117.

47. Blake, 120.

48. I am not suggesting that would-be immigrants cannot offer good reasons that may override the claims of the political community to exclude them. I consider the claims of refugees (chapter 7), the claims of family (chapter 8), and the claims of noncitizens residing in the territory of liberal democratic states (chapter 10).

49. As Rousseau put it, "Since a thousand events can change the relationships of a people, not only can different governments be good for different peoples, but also for the same people at different times." Rousseau, *On the Social Contract*, in *Basic Political Writings* bk. 3, ch. 1. In his view, every legitimate government is republican, but republican government is compatible with nondemocratic forms of government, including monarchy and aristocracy (bk. 2, ch. 6).

50. See, e.g., Robert A. Dahl, *Democracy and Its Critics* (New Haven, CT: Yale University Press, 1989).

51. Joshua Cohen, *Philosophy, Politics, Democracy: Selected Essays* (Cambridge, MA: Harvard University Press, 2009), 7, emphasis added.

52. Jeremy Waldron, *Law and Disagreement* (Oxford: Clarendon Press, 1999), 114–15.

53. Charles Tilly, *Democracy* (New York: Cambridge University Press, 2007), 74.

54. For example, Robert Putnam argues that the decline in social trust and civic participation in the United States is strongly correlated with racial and ethnic diversity. Robert D Putnam, "E Pluribus Unum: Diversity and Community in the Twenty-First Century: The 2006 Johan Skytte Prize Lecture," *Scandinavian Political Studies* 30, no. 2 (2007): 137–74. Rodney Hero has shown that the more racial and ethnic heterogeneity in a state, the more restrictive the state-level welfare programs are. Rodney E. Hero, *Faces of Inequality: Social Diversity in American Politics* (Oxford: Oxford University Press, 1998); Rodney E. Hero and Robert R. Preuhs, "Multiculturalism and Welfare Policies in the USA: A State-Level Comparative Analysis," in *Multiculturalism and the Welfare State: Recognition and Redistribution in Contemporary Democracies*, ed. Will Kymlicka and Keith G. Banting (Oxford: Oxford University Press, 2006). Cross-national analyses suggest that differences in racial diversity are a significant part of the reason the United States has not developed a European-style welfare state. Alberto Alesina and Edward L. Glaeser, *Fighting Poverty in the US and Europe: A World of Difference* (Oxford: Oxford University Press, 2004).

55. Will Kymlicka and Keith Banting, "Immigration, Multiculturalism, and the Welfare State," *Ethics and International Affairs* 20, no. 3 (2006): 287.

56. David Miller and Sundas Ali, "Testing the National Identity Argument," *European Political Science Review* 6, no. 2 (2014): 237–59.

57. Barbara Arneil, *Diverse Communities: The Problem with Social Capital* (Cambridge: Cambridge University Press, 2006).

58. Arash Abizadeh, "Democratic Theory and Border Coercion: No Right to Unilaterally Control Your Own Borders," *Political Theory* 36, no. 1 (2008): 48.

59. David Miller, "Democracy's Domain," *Philosophy and Public Affairs* 37, no. 3 (2009): 224.

60. Miller, *Strangers in Our Midst*, 74. Miller insists on the distinction between coercion and prevention even in the case of refugees. Prevention requires justification "especially in cases where preventing somebody will have dire consequences" but he argues this is not a reason to conflate coercion and prevention (189, n. 33).

61. Joshua Cohen, "Procedure and Substance in Deliberative Democracy," in *Deliberative Democracy: Essays on Reason and Politics*, ed. James Bohman and William Rehg (Cambridge, MA: MIT Press, 1997), 407.

62. See, e.g., Alfred Mele, *Autonomous Agents: From Self-Control to Autonomy* (Oxford: Oxford University Press, 2001); and Michael Bratman, *Structures of Agency* (Oxford: Oxford University Press, 2007).

63. Bas van der Vossen, "Immigration and Self-Determination," *Politics, Philosophy, and Economics* 14, no. 3 (2015): 283, emphasis in original.

CHAPTER 5

1. Rawls, *Theory of Justice*, 8.

2. Proponents of open borders include Arash Abizadeh, "Democratic Theory and Border Coercion, 37–65; Bruce A. Ackerman, *Social Justice in the Liberal State* (New Haven, CT: Yale University Press, 1980); Carens, "Aliens and Citizens"; Carens, "Migration and Morality: A Liberal Egalitarian Perspective," in *Free Movement: Ethical Issues in the Transnational Migration of People and of Money*, ed. Brian Barry and Robert E. Goodin (University Park: Pennsylvania State University Press, 1992), 25–47; Carens, *Ethics of Immigration*; Phillip Cole, *Philosophies of Exclusion: Liberal Political Theory and Immigration* (Edinburgh: Edinburgh University Press, 2000); Michael A. E. Dummett, *On Immigration and Refugees* (London: Routledge, 2001); Loren Lomasky, "Toward a Liberal Theory of National Boundaries," in *Boundaries and Justice: Diverse Ethical Perspectives*, ed. David Miller and Sohail H. Hashmi (Princeton, NJ: Princeton University Press, 2001); Darrel Moellendorf, *Cosmopolitan Justice* (Boulder, CO: Westview, 2002); Kieran Oberman, "Immigration as a Human Right," in *Migration in Political Theory: The Ethics of Movement and Membership*, ed. Sarah Fine and Lea Ypi (Oxford: Oxford University Press, 2016); and Lant Pritchett, *Let Their People Come: Breaking the Gridlock on International Labor Mobility* (Washington, DC: Center for Global Development, 2006).

3. Carens, "Migration and Morality," 26.

4. Carens, 26.

5. United Nations Development Programme (UNDP), *Human Development Report 2009: Overcoming Barriers: Human Mobility and Development* (Basingstoke, UK: Palgrave MacMillan, 2009), 21–24.

6. Carens, *Ethics of Immigration*, 235, 311.

7. Ayelet Shachar, *The Birthright Lottery: Citizenship and Global Inequality* (Cambridge, MA: Harvard University Press, 2009), 11.

8. See Simon Caney, "Cosmopolitan Justice and Equalizing Opportunities," in *Global Justice*, ed. Thomas Pogge (Oxford: Blackwell, 2001); and Moellendorf, *Cosmopolitan Justice*, ch. 4.

9. Rawls, *Theory of Justice*, 73, emphasis added.

10. Rawls, *Theory of Justice*, 8.

11. Moellendorf, *Cosmopolitan Justice*, 49.

12. For elaboration of this critique, see Miller, *National Responsibility*, 63.

13. For relational views of equality and justice, see Elizabeth S Anderson, "What Is the Point of Equality?," *Ethics* 109, no. 2 (1999): 287–337; and Michael Blake, "Global Distributive Justice: Why Political Philosophy Needs Political Science," *Annual Review of Political Science* 15 (2012): 121–36.

14. My understanding of inequality and its relationship to injustice is indebted to Thomas M. Scanlon, *The Diversity of Objections to Inequality*, Lindley Lecture (University of Kansas Department of Philosophy, 1996); Scanlon, "When Does Equality Matter?," (paper on file with author); and Rawls, *Justice as Fairness*, which draws on Scanlon.

15. See Jeremy Waldron, "Superseding Historic Injustice"; Christopher Kutz, "Justice in Reparations: The Cost of Memory and the Value of Talk," *Philosophy and Public Affairs* 32, no. 3 (2004): 277–312; Duncan Ivison, "Historical Injustice," in *The Oxford Handbook of Political Theory*, ed. John S. Dryzek, Bonnie Honig, and Anne Phillips (Oxford: Oxford University Press, 2008): 507–27; Jeff Spinner-Halev, *Enduring Injustice* (Cambridge: Cambridge University Press, 2012).

16. Walzer, *Spheres of Justice*, 48–49.

17. Rogers M. Smith, "The Principle of Constituted Identities and the Obligation to Include," *Ethics and Global Politics* 1, no. 3 (2008): 139–53. See also James Souter, "Towards a Theory of Asylum as Reparation for Past Injustice," *Political Studies* 62, no. 2 (2014): 326–42.

18. Thomas Pogge, *World Poverty and Human Rights: Cosmopolitan Responsibilities and Reforms*, 2nd ed. (Cambridge, UK: Polity Press, 2008).

19. Pogge challenges the legitimacy of the state system in *World Poverty and Human Rights*. For critical discussion, see Mathias Risse, "What We Owe to the Global Poor," *Journal of Ethics* 9, no. 1–2 (2005): 81–117.

20. Citizens United v. Federal Election Commission, 558 U.S. 310 (2010).

21. John Rawls, *Political Liberalism* (New York: Columbia University Press, 1996), 357.

22. Scanlon, "When Does Equality Matter?," 9.

23. Rawls, *Justice as Fairness*, 131.

24. Carens, "Aliens and Citizens."

25. World Health Organization, "Sanitation," fact sheet, World Health Organization website, updated July 2017, http://www.who.int/mediacentre/factsheets/fs392/en/.

26. World Hunger Education Service, "2016 World Hunger and Poverty Facts and Statistics," *Hunger Notes*, 2016, http://www.worldhunger.org/2015-world-hunger-and-poverty-facts-and-statistics/.

27. UNICEF, "Water and Sanitation," updated December 16, 2016, https://www.unicef.org/supply/index_cpe_water.html.

28. Habitat for Humanity, "Habitat for Humanity to Celebrate World Habitat Day," Habitat for Humanity website, Setpember, 27, 2011, http://www.habitat.org/newsroom/09-27-2011-hfh-celebrate-world-habitat-day.

29. Scanlon, "Diversity of Objections to Inequality," 2.

30. Harry Frankfurt, "Equality as a Moral Ideal," *Ethics* 98, no. 1 (1987): 21.

31. Carens, "Migration and Morality," 26 (emphasis added).

32. Carens, "Aliens and Citizens," 251.

33. Carens, Ethics of Immigration, 235.

34. Devesh Kapur and John McHale, "What Is Wrong with Plan B? International Migration as an Alternative to Development Assistance," in *Brookings Trade Forum 2006: Global Labor Markets?* ed. Susan M. Collins and Carol Graham (Washington, DC: Brookings Institution Press, 2006), 167–68.

35. Although discussions of migration tend to focus on the movement from developing to developed countries, only 37 percent of international migration is from developing to developed countries. Most migration occurs between countries in the same category of development: about 60 percent move either between developing or between developed countries. Even in the case of migration within developing countries, differences in living standards are important: three-quarter of international migrants move to a country with a higher HDI than their country of origin; among those from developing countries, this share exceeds 80 percent. United Nations Development Programme, *Human Development Report 2009: Overcoming Barriers: Human Mobility and Development* (Basingstoke, UK: Palgrave Macmillan, 2009), 22–23.

36. United Nations Development Programme, *Human Development Report 2009*, 24–25. See also Filiz Garip, "Discovering Diverse Mechanisms of Migration: The Mexico-US Stream 1970–2000," *Population and Development Review* 38, no. 3 (2012); and Alberto Palloni, Douglas S. Massey, Miguel Ceballos, Kristin Espinosa, and Michael Spittel, "Social Capital and International Migration: A Test Using Information on Family Networks," *American Journal of Sociology* 106, no. 5 (2001): 1262-98.

37. United Nations Development Programme, *Human Development Report 2009*, 18.

38. Kapur and McHale, "What Is Wrong with Plan B?," in Collins and Graham, *Brookings Trade Forum 2006*, 159–67. I discuss concerns about brain drain at greater length in chapters 6 and 9.

39. Rainer Bauböck, "Citizenship and Free Movement," in *Citizenship, Borders, and Human Needs*, ed. Rogers Smith (Philadelphia: University of Pennsylvania Press, 2011), 355.

40. Carens, *Ethics of Immigration*, 235.
41. See chapter 7.
42. Mathias Risse, "How Does the Global Order Harm the Poor?," *Philosophy and Public Affairs* 33, no. 4 (2005): 372. Scholars of development are divided on the significance of geography, as opposed to institutions or market integration, as direct determinants of growth and prosperity. Dani Rodrik, Arvind Subramanian, and Francesco Trebbi argue that institutions trump everything else, whereas Jeffrey Frankel and David Roemer point to world market integration, and still others point to geographic factors, such as location, climate, endowment of resources, and agricultural productivity. See Dani Rodrik, Arvind Subramanian, and Francesco Trebbi, "Institutions Rule: The Primacy of Institutions over Geography and Integration in Economic Development," *Journal of Economic Growth* 9, no. 2 (2004): 131–65; Jeffrey A. Frankel and David Romer, "Does Trade Cause Growth?," *American Economic Review* 89, no. 3 (1999): 379–99; John Luke Gallup, Jeffrey D. Sachs, and Andrew D. Mellinger, "Geography and Economic Development" (NBER Working Paper Series No. 6849, National Bureau of Economic Research, Cambridge, MA, 1998); and Jeffrey D. Sachs, "Tropical Underdevelopment" (Working Paper Series No. 8119, National Bureau of Economic Research, Cambridge, MA, 2001).

CHAPTER 6

1. See, e.g., Carens, *Ethics of Immigration*, 238.
2. Moellendorf, *Cosmopolitan Justice*, 62.
3. Carens, "Migration and Morality," 36–37, 25.
4. Oberman, "Immigration as a Human Right," 32.
5. On Joseph Raz's interest-based theory of rights, " 'X has a right' if and only if X can have rights, and other things being equal, an aspect of X's well-being (his interest) is a sufficient reason for holding some other person(s) to be under a duty." Raz, *Morality of Freedom*, 166. Oberman explicitly grounds his argument on an interest account of human rights, citing John Tasioulas, "The Moral Reality of Human Rights," in *Freedom from Poverty as a Human Right: Who Owes What to the Very Poor?*, ed. Thomas Pogge (Oxford: Oxford University Press, 2007).
6. This list is drawn from Buchanan, *Justice, Legitimacy, and Self-Determination*, 128. My aim here is not to stipulate this list as the proper content of human rights. I use it to illustrate what is commonly included in a list of basic human rights.
7. Oberman, "Immigration as a Human Right," 35.
8. Oberman, 40.
9. This concern informs Rawls's claim that his first principle of justice ensures an "adequate scheme" of basic liberties, not a maximal scheme. See Rawls, *Political Liberalism*, 293.
10. Miller, *National Responsibility*, 206; see also Miller, *Strangers in Our Midst*, 52.
11. Joseph Raz, *Morality of Freedom*, 154–55.

12. Both Oberman ("Immigration as a Human Right," 39) and Carens (*Ethics of Immigration*, 244) raise this objection.
13. Carens, *Ethics of Immigration*, 249.
14. United Nations Development Programme, *Human Development Report 2009*, 15.
15. United Nations Development Programme, *Human Development Report 2009*, 17, emphasis added.
16. I am grateful to Michael Blake for discussion of this example.
17. Carens, *Ethics of Immigration*, 237.
18. Carens, 239.
19. *Passenger Cases*, 7 How. 283, 492 (1849).
20. United States v. Guest, 383 U.S. 745, 758 (1966).
21. *Slaughterhouse Cases*, 83 U.S. 36, 55–57 (1872).
22. Shapiro v. Thompson, 394 U.S. 618, 643 (1969) (concurring opinion).
23. Carens, "Aliens and Citizens," 251–52.
24. Carens, 251.
25. *Slaughterhouse Cases* at 53.
26. Saenz v. Roe 526 U.S. 489, 511 (1999).
27. Walzer, *Spheres of Justice*, 62. For further discussion of Walzer's view, see chapter 3.
28. *Slaughter-House Cases* at 53.
29. Carens, "Aliens and Citizens," 266–67.
30. Cole, *Philosophies of Exclusion*, 46.
31. Cole, 52–53.
32. Michael Blake, "The Right to Leave and What Remains," in *Debating Brain Drain: May Governments Restrict Emigration?*, ed. Gillian Brock and Michael Blake (Oxford: Oxford University Press, 2015), 197–98, 204.
33. David C. Hendrickson, "Migration in Law and Ethics: A Realist Perspective," in Barry and Goodin, *Free Movement*, 173.
34. Kapur and McHale, "What Is Wrong with Plan B?," in Collins and Graham, *Brookings Trade Forum 2006*, 166–68.
35. See Michael A. Clemens, "Economics and Emigration: Trillion-Dollar Bills on the Sidewalk?," *Journal of Economic Perspectives* 25, no. 3 (2011): 90–91. I discuss the brain drain thesis further in chapter 9.
36. Jagdish Bhagwati and William Dellalfar, "The Brain Drain and Income Taxation," *World Development* 1, no. 1–2 (1973): 94–101. See also Jagdish N. Bhagwati and Martin Partington, eds., *Taxing the Brain Drain*, 2 vols. (Amsterdam: North Holland Publishing Company, 1976).
37. Kapur and McHale, "What Is Wrong with Plan B?," 171.
38. Brock offers other grounds for the emigrant's responsibility to his home country: redress for the creation of disadvantage, thwarting governments' attempts to discharge their duties, thwarting citizens' abilities to support their governments, and duties of loyalty. She suggests these are jointly sufficient to build a case that emigrating citizens bear a duty to compensate for the resulting losses. Gillian Brock, "Part I,"

in *Debating Brain Drain: May Governments Restrict Emigration?*, ed. Gillian Brock and Michael Blake (Oxford: Oxford University Press, 2015), 65–68.

39. Blake also adopts the liberal asymmetry position, arguing for a strong right of exit in "The Right to Leave and What Remains" while also defending the right of states to restrict entry. See Blake, "Immigration, Jurisdiction, and Exclusion." For discussion of Blake's argument for the state's right to restrict entry, see chapter 3.

40. "In Praise of Huddled Masses," editorial, *Wall Street Journal*, July 3, 1984, 1; Robert L. Bartley, "Thinking Things Over: Open NAFTA Borders? Why Not?," *Wall Street Journal*, July 2, 2001. See also the book by a member of the *Wall Street Journal* editorial board: Jason Riley, *Let Them In: The Case for Open Borders* (New York: Gotham, 2008).

41. Clemens, "Economics and Emigration," 84–89.

42. Borjas, *We Wanted Workers*, 42. I engage empirical studies about the effects of immigration at greater length in chapter 9.

43. Commenting on the European experience with millions of guest workers, the Swiss playwright and novelist Max Frisch said, "We wanted workers, but we got people instead."See Ulas Sunata, *Highly Skilled Labor Migration: The Case of ICT Specialists from Turkey in Germany* (Berlin: Lit Verlag, 2011), 275.

44. Carens develops such an interpretation of Nozick in "Aliens and Citizens."

45. Locke, *Second Treatise of Government*, ch. 2, § 6, p. 9.

46. Locke, ch. 5, § 25, p. 18.

47. Hillel Steiner, "Libertarianism and the Transnational Migration of People," in Barry and Goodin, *Free Movement*, 89.

48. Steiner, "Libertarianism and the Transnational Migration of People," 91.

49. Locke, *Second Treatise of Government*, ch. 7, § 117, pp. 62–63.

50. Steiner, "Libertarianism and the Transnational Migration of People," 91–93.

51. Onora O'Neill develops this argument in "Commentary: Magic Associations and Imperfect People," in Barry and Goodin, *Free Movement*, 115-24.

PART III

1. Here I follow Joseph Carens's distinction between obligatory and discretionary admissions, in *Ethics of Immigration*, ch. 9. See also Michael Blake, "Discretionary Immigration," *Philosophical Topics* 30, no. 2 (2002): 273–89.

2. My discussion here draws on Douglass S. Massey, Jorge Durand, and Nolan J. Malone, *Beyond Smoke and Mirrors: Mexican Immigration in an Era of Economic Integration* (New York: Russell Sage, 2002), ch. 2.

3. Immanuel Wallerstein, *The Modern World System I: Capitalist Agriculture and the Origins of the European World Economy in the Sixteenth Century* (New York: Academic Press, 1974); and Saskia Sassen, *The Mobility of Labor and Capital: A Study in International Investment and Labor Flow* (Cambridge: Cambridge University Press, 1988).

4. Michael J. Piore, *Birds of Passage: Migrant Labor in Industrial Societies* (Cambridge: Cambridge University Press, 1979).

5. Massey, Durand, and Malone, *Beyond Smoke and Mirrors*, 20.

CHAPTER 7

1. Hannah Arendt, *The Origins of Totalitarianism* (New York: Harcourt Brace, 1968), 293, 296-97.

2. United Nations High Commissioner for Refugees, *Global Trends: Forced Displacement in 2016* (Geneva: United Nations High Commissioner for Refugees, 2017), 2–3 (hereafter cited as "UNHCR"), http://www.unhcr.org/en-us/statistics/unhcrstats/5943e8a34/global-trends-forced-displacement-2016.html?query=global%20trends%20forced%20displacement.

3. For discussion of a variety of deterrence measures used by states, see Thomas Gammeltoft-Hansen and Nikolas F. Tan, "The End of the Deterrence Paradigm? Future Directions for Global Refugee Policy," *Journal on Migration and Human Security* 5, no. 1 (2017): 28–56.

4. UNHCR, *Convention and Protocal Relating to the Status of Refugees* (Geneva: Communications and Public Information Service, UNHCR), http://www.unhcr.org/en-us/3b66c2aa10.

5. UNHCR, *The State of the World's Refugees: In Search of Solidarity*" (UNHCR Summary, Geneva: UNHCR, 2012), 2, 5, http://www.unhcr.org/4fc5ceca9.html.

6. For elaboration of a reparative theory of asylum, see Souter, "Towards a Theory of Asylum as Reparation for Past Injustice."

7. Walzer, *Spheres of Justice*, 49.

8. Rogers Smith develops a similar "principle of coercively constituted identities" in the context of arguing for special obligations of the United States toward Mexican immigrants. See Rogers M. Smith, "The American 'Promiseland' and Mexican Immigrants," in *Political Peoplehood: The Roles of Values, Interests, and Identities* (Chicago: University of Chicago Press, 2015), 219–46. Sara Amighetti and Alasia Nutti have also developed an identity-based argument that former colonizing nations have an obligation to admit members from former colonies because of the "pervasive cultural impact of colonialism on the national identity" of both the former colonizing and the colonized nations. See Sara Amighetti and Alasia Nutti, "A Nation's Right to Exclude and the Colonies," *Political Theory* 44, no. 4 (2016): 541–66.

9. On the analogy with the duty of rescue, see Miller, *Strangers in Our Midst*, 78.

10. Niraj Chokshi and Nicholas Fandos, "Demonstrators in Streets, and at Airports, Protest Immigration Order," *New York Times*, January 29, 2017.

11. See Miller, *National Responsibility*, ch. 4.

12. I have benefited from reflecting on the exchange between Anna Stilz and David Miller, "Review Symposium: Strangers in Our Midst," *European Political Science* (2017), https://doi.org/10.1057/s41304-016-0095-2.

13. See Matthew J. Gibney, "Kosovo and Beyond: Popular and Unpopular Refugees," *Forced Migration Review* 5 (1999): 29.

14. Dane Bowker, "Forget the Syrian Refugees: America Needs to Bring Its Afghan and Iraqi Interpreters Here First," *Washington Post*, September 17, 2015, http://wapo.st/1LiSdGv?tid=ss_mail&utm_term=.265dce4bd72a (last accessed January 20, 2018).

15. UNHCR, Convention and Protocol Relating to the Status of Refugees, (1951), chap. 1, art. 1, http://www.unhcr.org/3b66c2aa10.html.

16. See Guy S. Goodwin-Gill, "The Dynamic of International Refugee Law," *International Journal of Refugee Law* 25, no. 4 (2013): 651–66.

17. Andrew E. Shacknove, "Who Is a Refugee?," *Ethics* 95, no. 2 (1985): 277. Scholars who have advanced a broader definition of refugees include Matthew J. Gibney, *The Ethics and Politics of Asylum: Liberal Democracy and the Response to Refugees* (Cambridge: Cambridge University Press, 2004); Alexander Betts, *Survival Migration: Failed Governance and the Crisis of Displacement* (Ithaca, NY: Cornell University Press, 2013); and Carens, *Ethics of Immigration*, ch. 10; Miller, *Strangers in Our Midst*, ch. 5.

18. UNHCR, *Global Trends: Forced Displacement in 2015*, 2.

19. Matthew J. Gibney, "Refugees and Justice between States," *European Journal of Political Theory* 14, no. 4 (2015): 6–8.

20. Shacknove, "Who Is a Refugee?," 277.

21. Matthew Lister, "Who Are Refugees?," *Law and Philosophy* 32 (2013): 648.

22. My argument here about the significance of persecution in determining refugee status is a contingent one, based on asylum being the only way a person's basic needs can be met. By contrast, in defending the focus on persecution in the convention's definition of a refugee, Matthew Price posits an essential connection between the harm of persecution and asylum: the asylum-granting state expresses political condemnation of the persecuting state. See Matthew E. Price, *Rethinking Asylum: History, Purpose, and Limits* (Cambridge: Cambridge University Press, 2009).

23. See chapter 5, where I argue that emergency aid and development assistance are more effective tools for alleviating global poverty than open borders.

24. Based on fieldwork in Bangladesh, Jane McAdam found that those displaced by temporary environmental problems expressed strong preferences to return to their homes. She also suggests that most climate-change-related migration is likely to be internal, not international. If people are able to relocate in their own countries, then asylum as a remedy becomes less pressing if aid is provided within the country. See Jane McAdam, *Climate Change, Forced Migration, and International Law* (Oxford: Oxford University Press, 2012).

25. Matthew Lister argues for extending the logic of the Refugee Convention definition to those suffering indefinite displacement because of environmental problems.

See Matthew Lister, "Climate Change Refugees," *Critical Review of International Social and Political Philosophy* 17 (2014): 618–34.

26. I take this term from Walzer who refers to "necessitous men and women, clamoring for entry" in his discussion of the White Australia policy. Walzer, *Spheres of Justice*, 46.

27. T. Alexander Aleinikoff, "The Mandate of the Office of the United Nations High Commissioner for Refugees," in *Research Handbook on International Law and Migration*, ed. Vincent Chetail and Céline Bauloz (Cheltenham, UK: Edward Elgar, 2014), 389–416.

28. In the remainder of the chapter, I focus on refugees while recognizing the need for a broader theory aimed at addressing the diverse needs of other forced migrants.

29. My discussion draws on UNHCR, *State of the World's Refugees*, ch. 3.

30. UNHCR, *State of the World's Refugees*, 12; UNHCR, "World at War: Global Trends: Forced Displacement in 2014" (Geneva: UNHCR, 2014), 3, http://www.unhcr.org/en-us/statistics/country/556725e69/unhcr-global-trends-2014.html; UNHCR, *Global Trends: Forced Displacement in 2015*, 2.

31. UNHCR, *Global Trends: Forced Displacement in 2015*, 20.

32. UNHCR, *Global Trends: Forced Displacement in 2015*, 2. GDP per capita allows the size of a refugee population to be compared to a host country's national economic development. By the end of 2015, thirty countries with the largest numbers of refugees per GDP per capita were all in developing regions. The only exception was the Russian Federation, which was in thirtieth place with twelve refugees per one US dollar GDP per capita. These thirty countries included twenty states classified as "least developed countries" (18).

33. UNHCR, *Global Trends: Forced Displacement in 2015*, 3.

34. James C. Hathaway, "A Global Solution to a Global Refugee Crisis," *European Papers: A Journal on Law and Integration* 1, no. 1 (2016): 95.

35. UNHCR, *Global Trends: Forced Displacement in 2015*, 3.

36. Gibney, "Refugees and Justice between States."

37. Gibney, 10.

38. Walzer, *Spheres of Justice*, 49.

39. Gil Loescher and John A. Scanlan, *Calculated Kindness: Refugees and America's Half-Open Door, 1945 to the Present* (New York: Free Press, 1986), 172.

40. Haitian Refugee Center v. Civiletti, 503 F.Supp. 442 (S.D.Fla. 1980).

41. "Protecting the Nation from Foreign Terrorist Entry into the United States," Exec. Order No. 82 F.R. 8977 (Jan. 27, 2017), https://www.federalregister.gov/documents/2017/02/01/2017-02281/protecting-the-nation-from-foreign-terrorist-entry-into-the-united-states; "Protecting the Nation from Foreign Terrorist Entry into the United States," Exec. Order No. 82 F.R. 13209 (Mar. 6, 2017), https://www.federalregister.gov/documents/2017/03/09/2017-04837/protecting-the-nation-from-foreign-terrorist-entry-into-the-united-states; State of Hawaii and Ismail

Elshikh vs. Donald J. Trump (March 15, 2017): (https://assets.documentcloud. org/documents/3518057/Order.pdf). International Refugee Assistance Project et al. v. Donald J. Trump (March 16, 2017): https://assets.documentcloud.org/ documents/3518169/Read-the-federal-judge-s-ruling-in-Md-on-Trump-s.pdf.

42. For discussion of these examples, see Gibney, *Ethics and Politics of Asylum*, 52–53.

43. Marc R. Rosenblum, "Unaccompanied Minor Migration to the United States: The Tension between Protection and Prevention" (report, Transatlantic Council on Migration and Migration Policy Institute, Washington DC, April 2015), 11.

44. TRAC Immigration, "Priority Immigration Court Cases: Women with Children," updated February 2018, http://trac.syr.edu/phptools/immigration/mwc/.

45. Debra Pressé and Jessie Thomson, "The Resettlement Challenge: Integration of Refugees from Protracted Refugee Situations," *Refuge: Canada's Journal on Refugees* 25, no. 1 (2008): 94–99. See also Tally Kritzman-Amir, "Not in My Backyard: On the Morality of Responsibility Sharing in Refugee Law," *Brooklyn Journal of International Law* 34 (2008): 388–89.

46. For a detailed proposal for how to strengthen the international refugee-protection system, see James C. Hathaway and R. Alexander Neve, "Making International Refugee Law Relevant Again: A Proposal for Collectivized and Solution-Oriented Protection," *Harvard Human Rights Journal* 10 (1997): 115–211.

47. Gammeltoft-Hansen and Tan, "End of the Deterrence Paradigm?," 45.

48. Operation Portal Refugee Situations, "Refugees/Migrants Emergency Response— Mediterranean," UNHCR Operation Portal website, http://data.unhcr.org/mediterranean/ (accessed January 20, 2018).

49. Gammeltoft-Hansen and Tan, "End of the Deterrence Paradigm?," 43; Peter Andreas, *Border Games: Policing the U.S.–Mexico Divide* (Ithaca, NY: Cornell University Press, 2000).

50. David Owen, "Global Justice, National Responsibility and Transnational Power," *Review of International Studies* 36, no. S1 (2010): 110; Carens, *Ethics of Immigration*, 216.

51. Peter H. Schuck, "Refugee Burden-Sharing: A Modest Proposal," *Yale Journal of International Law* 22 (1997): 243-97. See also Deborah Anker, Joan Fitzpatrick, and Andrew Shacknove, "Crisis and Cure: A Reply to Hathaway/Neve and Schuck," *Harvard Human Rights Journal* 11 (1998): 295-310.

52. In cases of family reunification, two distinct normative claims are at work: the claim of already settled refugees to sponsor their family members and the claim of overseas refugees to be reunited with family members. I discuss these distinct perspectives in chapter 8.

53. Miller, *Strangers in Our Midst*, 93.

54. See chapter 4 for discussion of the special obligations of political membership.

55. Germany and Sweden have taken in many more asylum seekers than have other European countries in the wake of the European migration crisis, but I leave it open for debate whether Germany and Sweden have come close to reaching such a limit.

56. Operation Portal Refugee Situations, "Syrian Regional Refugee Response," UNHCR, Operation Portal website, last updated March 29, 2018, http://data. unhcr.org/syrianrefugees/regional.php.

57. Operation Portal Refugee Situations, "Resettlement and Other Admission Pathways for Syrian Refugees," UNHCR Operation Portal website, "Documents," April 30, 2017, http://data.unhcr.org/syrianrefugees/download.php?id=10772.

58. Operation Portal Refugee Situations, "Syrian Regional Refugee Response," http:// data.unhcr.org/syrianrefugees/asylum.php.

59. The definition of "refugee" in US immigration law is consonant with the international legal definition set forth in the 1951 Refugee Convention; see *Immigration and Nationality Act*. 8 U.S.C. 12 (2012). For refugee admissions statistics, see US State Department, "Cumulative Summary of Refugee Admissions" (summary report, Bureau of Population, Refugees, and Migration, December 31, 2015), https:// 2009-2017.state.gov/j/prm/releases/statistics/251288.htm.

60. Refugee Act of 1980, Pub. L. No. 96-212, 94 Stat. 102 (1980), codified at INA § 207(a)(2)–(3), 8 U.S.C. § 1157(a)(2)–(3) (2000); Julie Hirschfeld Davis and Miriam Jordan, "Trump Plans 45,000 Limit on Refugees Admitted to U.S.," *New York Times*, September 26, 2017, http://www.nytimes.com/2017/09/26/us/politics/ trump-plans-45000-limit-on-refugees-admitted-to-us.html.

61. Government of Canada, "2017 Annual Report to Parliament on Immigration" (report, Refugees and Asylum, Immigration and Citizenship), https://www.canada. ca/en/immigration-refugees-citizenship/corporate/publications-manuals/annual-report-parliament-immigration-2017.html; and "#WelcomeRefugees: Canada Resettled Syrian Refugees" (report, Refugees and Asylum, Immigration and Citizenship), updated January 29, 2017, https://www.canada.ca/en/immigration-refugees-citizenship/services/refugees/welcome-syrian-refugees.html.

CHAPTER 8

1. Organization for Economic Co-operation and Development, *International Migration Outlook 2007* (Paris: Organisation for Economic Co-operation and Development, 2007), http://www.oecd.org/els/mig/internationalmigrationoutl ook2007.htm.

2. Department of Homeland Security, *Yearbook of Immigration Statistics 2015*, 2015, https://www.dhs.gov/immigration-statistics/yearbook/2015. Family unity provisions have accounted for about 60 percent of authorized entries to the United States for the past two decades. See Catherine Lee, *Fictive Kinship: Family Reunification and the Meaning of Race and Nation in American Immigration* (New York: Russell Sage Foundation, 2013), 34–35.

3. George J. Borjas, *Heaven's Door: Immigration Policy and the American Economy* (Princeton, NJ: Princeton University Press, 1999), 192.

4. See Borjas's "Immigration Debate We Need" and *We Wanted Workers*.

5. Stephen Macedo, "The Moral Dilemma of U.S. Immigration Policy: Open Borders v. Social Justice?," in *Debating Immigration*, ed. Carol M. Swain (Cambridge: Cambridge University Press, 2007).

6. Julia Preston, "Beside a Path to Citizenship, a New Path on Immigration," *New York Times*, April 16, 2013.

7. Like the claims of refugees (see chapter 7), family immigration constitutes obligatory, not discretionary, admissions. I adopt the distinction from Carens, *Ethics of Immigration*, ch. 9. The claims of family discussed in chapter 8 of my book apply not only to admission for permanent residence but also to protection from deportation. I focus here on the role of family ties in immigrant admissions. Chapter 10 examines the role of family ties in protecting immigrants from deportation.

8. Universal Declaration of Human Rights, 1948, http://www.un.org/en/universal-declaration-human-rights/; United Nations, International Covenant on Civil and Political Rights, 1966, http://www.ohchr.org/en/professionalinterest/pages/ccpr.aspx. See also International Covenant on Economic, Social, and Cultural Rights, 1966, art. 10(1), http://www.ohchr.org/EN/ProfessionalInterest/Pages/CESCR.aspx; the European Convention of Human Rights, 1950, art. 8, https://www.echr.coe.int/Documents/Convention_ENG.pdf; and the African Charter on Human and People's Rights, 1981, art.18, http://www.achpr.org/files/instruments/achpr/banjul_charter.pdf.

9. See Elizabeth Brake, *Minimizing Marriage: Marriage, Morality, and the Law* (New York: Oxford University Press, 2012), 174.

10. White, "Freedom of Association and the Right to Exclude," 390.

11. I discovered Caleb Yong's "Caring Relationships and Family Migration Schemes," in *The Ethics and Politics of Immigration*, ed. Alex Sager (Lanham, MD: Rowman and Littlefield, 2016) after I had already written a draft of this chapter. I have benefited from his discussion of the moral significance of family relationships and share his view that family-based immigration should recognize caregiving relationships, not simply biological relationships or marriage.

12. See chapter 4, where I discuss the right of individuals to occupy a particular place.

13. Betty de Hart, "Love Thy Neighbour: Family Reunification and the Rights of Insiders," *European Journal of Migration and Law* 11 (2009): 235.

14. Matthew Lister, "Immigration, Association, and the Family," *Law and Philosophy* 29, no. 6 (2010): 717–45.

15. Rawls, *Justice as Fairness*, 163, and more generally, § 50, "The Family as a Basic Institution"; Rawls, *Theory of Justice*, § 71, "The Morality of Association."

16. Lister, "Immigration, Association, and the Family," 722.

17. Lister, 728, 742.

18. Wellman, "Immigration and Freedom of Association." See chapter 3 for a critical discussion of Wellman.

19. Lister, "Immigration, Association, and the Family," 741–42.

20. Lee, *Fictive Kinship*, ch. 3.

21. Ngai, *Impossible Subjects*, 27; Lee, *Fictive Kinship*, 75.
22. An Act: To Repeal the Chinese Exclusion Acts, to Establish Quotas, and for Other Purposes. 57 Stat. 600 (1943).
23. Lee, *Fictive Kinship*, 95.
24. Hiroshi Motomura, "The Family and Immigration: A Roadmap for the Ruritanian Lawmaker," *American Journal of Comparative Law* 43, no. 4 (1995): 513, 25. See also Lee, *Fictive Kinship*, 109.
25. This category only applies to sons and daughters who are age twenty-one years and over since those under twenty-one are regarded as "children" and therefore counted as "immediate relatives."
26. 8 U.S.C. § 203(a) (2012). Unlike "immediate relatives," the four family preferences are subject to annual numerical ceilings, and when applications outnumber admissions spaces, as has been the case since the 1990s, there are backlogs and long waiting periods.
27. Section 203(d) of the Immigration and Nationality Act provides that the spouse or child may be admitted in the same preference category as the "principal" immigrant and in the same spot on the waiting list if there is a backlog. Spouses and children are known as "derivative beneficiaries"; this includes those "accompanying" the principal immigrant or those "following to join" later. This provision extending derivative immigration status to spouses and minor children applies not only to the explicit family-sponsored preferences but also to other visa categories, including employment-based, refugee, and diversity visas.
28. My calculations are based on statistics provided by Department of Homeland Security, *Yearbook of Immigration Statistics 2015*, table 7, https://www.dhs.gov/immigration-statistics/yearbook/2015.
29. Mark Kirkorian, "Legal Immigration: What Is to Be Done?," in *Blueprints for an Ideal Legal Immigration Policy*, ed. Richard D. Lamm and Alan Simpson (report, Center for Immigration Studies, Washington, DC, 2001), http://cis.org/articles/2001/blueprints/krikorian.html.
30. 153 Cong. Rec. 13260–61 (2007). See Lee, *Fictive Kinship*, 110.
31. Jonathan Vespa, Jamie M. Lewis, and Rose M. Kreider, "America's Families and Living Arrangements: 2012" (report, US Census Bureau, Washington, DC, 2013), https://www.census.gov/prod/2013pubs/p20-570.pdf.
32. Vespa, Lewis, and Kreider, *America's Families and Living Arrangements: 2012*, 13.
33. Eric Klinenberg, *Going Solo: The Extraordinary Rise and Surprising Appeal of Living Alone* (New York: Penguin, 2012).
34. The US Census Bureau defines "multigenerational families" as including either a householder with both a parent and a child, a householder with both a child and grandchild, a householder with both a grandchild and a parent, or a four-generation household, such as a householder with a parent, child, and grandchild present. Vespa, Lewis, and Kreider, *America's Families and Living Arrangements: 2012*, 7–9.

35. European Migration Network, "Compilation Ad-Hoc Query on Family Reunification" (European Commission, Brussels, 2011), https://ec.europa.eu/home-affairs/sites/homeaffairs/files/what-we-do/networks/european_migration_network/reports/docs/ad-hoc-queries/family-reunification/316_emn_ad-hoc_query_family_reunification_28apr2011_wider_dissemination_en.pdf.

36. See Alan Desmond, "The Private Life of Family Matters: Curtailing Human Rights Protection for Migrants under Article 8 of the ECHR?" 29, no. 1 (2018), doi: 10.1093/ejil/chy008.

37. Martha C. Nussbaum, "Human Capabilities, Female Human Beings," in *Women, Culture and Development: A Study of Human Capabilities*, ed. Martha C. Nussbaum and Jonathan Glover (New York: Oxford University Press, 1995), 78. See also Nussbaum, *Women and Human Development: The Capabilities Approach*, John Robert Seeley Lectures (Cambridge: Cambridge University Press, 2000).

38. Eva Feder Kittay, *Love's Labor: Essays on Women, Equality, and Dependency* (New York: Routledge, 1999), 186.

39. Martha Fineman, *The Neutered Mother, the Sexual Family, and Other Twentieth Century Tragedies* (New York: Routledge, 1995), 226–36.

40. Iseult Honohan, "Reconsidering the Claim to Family Reunification in Migration," *Political Studies* 57, no. 4 (2009): 775.

41. Government of Canada, "Family Sponsorship," 2017, http://www.cic.gc.ca/english/immigrate/sponsor/index.asp.

42. Robert Trempe, "Not Just Numbers: A Canadian Framework for Future Immigration," (Ottawa, CAN: Immigration Legislative Review Advisory Group, Citizenship and Immigration Canada, 1997), 43, http://publications.gc.ca/site/eng/9.646801/publication.html. It is important to note that one way in which Canadian immigration law appears more restrictive involves siblings: adult siblings cannot be sponsored in Canada, except under special conditions, most commonly when they are dependent on parents residing in Canada. Also, on August 1, 2014, the age at which a child is considered a dependent was reduced from twenty-two to nineteen years of age. This contrasts with the US definition of child as being under twenty-one.

43. UNHCR, "Protecting the Family: Challenges in Implementing Policy in the Resettlement Context" (report, UNHCR, Geneva, June 2001), 2, http://www.refworld.org/docid/4ae9aca12.html.

44. Alice Ristroph and Melissa Murray, "Disestablishing the Family," *Yale Law Journal* 119 (2011): 1258–59. See also Tamara Metz, *Untying the Knot: Marriage, the State, and the Case for Their Divorce* (Princeton, NJ: Princeton University Press, 2010), who argues for the separation of marriage from the state and the creation of an alternative narrow legal status that recognizes all intimate caregiving unions.

45. Lawrence v. Texas, 539 U.S. 558 (2003). See also Griswold v. Connecticut, 381 U.S. 479 (1965); Eisenstadt v. Baird, 405 U.S. 438 (1972); Roe v. Wade, 410 U.S. 113 (1973).

46. For an egalitarian argument for cultural accommodation, see Will Kymlicka, *Multicultural Citizenship: A Liberal Theory of Minority Rights* (New York: Oxford University Press, 1996); and Song, *Justice, Gender, and the Politics of Multiculturalism*, ch. 3.

47. Wendy Brown, "After Marriage," in *Just Marriage*, ed. Mary Lyndon Shanley, Joshua Cohen, and Deborah Chasman (Oxford: Oxford University Press, 2004), 87-92.

48. Trempe, "Not Just Numbers," 43–48 (emphasis added), cited in Law Commission of Canada, "Beyond Conjugality," 45, https://ssrn.com/abstract=1720747.

49. Law Commission of Canada, "Beyond Conjugality," 45–46, emphasis added.

50. In March 2017, Canada did permit two best friends to become co-parents. Natasha Bakht and Lynda Collins, who are best friends but not lovers or "conjugal" partners, were legally recognized as co-parents to Bakht's biological son, Elaan. Collins had become a caregiver to Elaan and was Bakht's closest confidant. This case is a good example of moving beyond blood ties and marriage to publicly support a broader range of caretaking relationships. See "How Two Friends Fought to Be Legal 'Co-Mommas' to a 7-Year-Old Boy—and Won," CBC Radio, "The Current," July 17, 2017, http://www.cbc.ca/radio/thecurrent/the-current-for-february-21-2017-1.3991287/how-two-friends-fought-to-be-legal-co-mommas-to-a-7-year-old-boy-and-won-1.3991307.

51. Additional elements of the definition of "permanent partner" included age (at least eighteen years), financial interdependence, not already being in a similar relationship or marriage; inability to contract a marriage recognized under the INA; and not being a third degree or closer blood relation of the partner. See Permanent Partners Immigration Act of 2000. H.R. 3650, 106th Cong. (2000).

52. Obergefell v. Hodges, 135 S. Ct. 2584, 2590 (2015).

53. Melissa Murray, "*Obergefell v. Hodges* and Nonmarriage Inequality," *California Law Review* 104 (2016): 1210. For exploration of what marriage reveals about membership, see Sarah Song, "After *Obergefell*: On Marriage and Belonging in Carson McCullers' *Member of the Wedding*," *Looking for Law in All the Wrong Places*, ed. Marianne Constable, Leti Volpp, and Bryan Wagner (Fordham University Press, 2018).

54. I am grateful to Matt Lister for pressing me to address this particular concern during a panel on migration at the 2017 APA-Pacific meeting. I also have benefited from reflecting on "Note: Looking for a Family Resemblance: The Limits of the Functional Approach to the Legal Definition of Family," *Harvard Law Review* 104, no. 7 (1991): 1640-59.

55. Immigration Marriage Fraud Amendments of 1986, 100 Stat. 3537 (1986). This law subjects couples married for less than two years to considerably more scrutiny than other couples. Unlike spouses who gain admission in the "immediate relative" category, spouses in marriages that are less than two years old must wait an additional two years before they can obtain permanent residence, and they must demonstrate that the marriage is bona fide by showing that they did not enter into it for the purpose of evading the immigration laws.

56. Mary Anne Case, "Marriage Licenses," *Minnesota Law Review* 89 (2005): 1772–74.
57. In the United States all immigrants who use the "immediate family" or family preference categories and their US citizen or LPR sponsors are required to make a financial commitment to each other. Under the Immigration and Nationality Act, an immigrant is inadmissible if he is "likely at any time to become a public charge." See 8 U.S.C. § 212(a)(4)(A) (2012). Since 1997, an immigrant will be deemed likely to be a public charge unless the sponsoring relative signs an "affidavit of support," demonstrating that the sponsor can support the immigrant at an annual income that is not less than 125 percent of the federal poverty line.
58. I am grateful to Alex Sager for pressing this point at the 2017 APA-Pacific Division Meeting panel, where I presented this chapter.

CHAPTER 9

1. I adopt the distinction from Carens, *Ethics of Immigration*, ch. 9. A key difference between my discussion and Carens's is that he does not think state control over immigration is justifiable. He pursues the question of "who should get in" on the presumption that state discretion over immigration is legitimate, but he goes on to reject the presumption in favor of open borders. I believe this leaves his theory ill-equipped to explain the normative grounds of constraints on how democratic states exercise their power over immigration; he appeals to "democracy" and "democratic values" in discussing legitimate bases for excluding and admitting immigrants but those values have an uncertain role within his broader theory, which prioritizes the moral equality of all human beings. On my theory, members of democratic political communities have membership-based obligations, including the obligation to support democratic values, which must be balanced against global obligations to assist refugees and other necessitous migrants.
2. Ryan Baugh and Katherine Witsman, "U.S. Law Permanent Residents: 2015" (annual flow report, Office of Immigration Statistics, Washington, DC, March 2017), https://www.dhs.gov/sites/default/files/publications/Lawful_Permanent_Residents_2015.pdf.
3. Department of Homeland Security, "Table 25. Nonimmigrant Admissions by Class of Admission: Fiscal Years 2013 to 2015," in *Yearbook of Immigration Statistics 2015* (Washington, DC: Department of Homeland Security, last published date, December 15, 2016), https://www.dhs.gov/immigration-statistics/yearbook/2015/table25.
4. Cindy Hahamovitch, "Creating Perfect Immigrants: Guestworkers of the World in Historical Perspective," *Labor History* 44, no. 1 (2003): 72–73. See also Hahamovitch, *No Man's Land: Jamaican Guestworkers in America and the Global History of Deportable Labor* (Princeton, NJ: Princeton University Press, 2011).
5. See Martin Ruhs and Philip Martin, "Numbers vs. Rights: Trade-offs and Guest Worker Programs," *International Migration Review* 42, no. 1 (2008): 249–65;

Rhacel Salazar Parreñas, *Servants of Globalization: Women, Migration and Domestic Work* (Stanford, CA: Stanford University Press, 2001); and Rebecca Smith, "Guest Workers or Forced Labor?," *New Labor Forum* 16, no. 3–4 (2007): 70-78.

6. Walzer, *Spheres of Justice*, 61.

7. Walzer, 60.

8. Walzer, 60.

9. Patti Tamara Lenard and Christine Straehle, "Temporary Labor Migration, Global Redistribution, and Democratic Justice," *Politics, Philosophy, and Economics* 11, no. 2 (2011): 206–30 at 215.

10. For elaboration of the view that migration programs should take the "aspirations and projects of the migrants themselves" seriously, see Valeria Ottonelli and Tiziana Torresi, "Inclusivist Egalitarian Liberalism and Temporary Migration: A Dilemma," *Journal of Political Philosophy* 20, no. 2 (2012): 202–24 at 208.

11. Oded Galor and Oded Stark, "Migrants' Savings, the Probability of Return Migration and Migrants' Performance," *International Economic Review* 31 (1990), 463–67; and Massey, Durand, and Malone, *Beyond Smoke and Mirrors*.

12. As Lenard and Straehle put it, "[W]hat *is* temporary about the programs we advocate is the employment to which these migrants are committed, which may vary in length, not the migrants' status among us." Lenard and Straehle, "Temporary Labor Migration," 218.

13. As Lea Ypi argues, what makes guest-worker programs exploitative is that they contribute to a "global competition for labor driven by the desperate bidding of those who have only their labor to sell." Lea Ypi, "Taking Workers as a Class: The Moral Dilemmas of Guestworker Programs," *Migration in Political Theory: The Ethics of Movement and Membership* (Oxford: Oxford University Press, 2016), 168.

14. Hahamovitch identifies employers' power to deport as "the key problem" behind the deteriorating working and living conditions under the US Bracero Program that brought workers from Mexico and the West Indian farmworker program. Hahamovitch, "Creating Perfect Immigrants," 82–83. By contrast, guest workers in postwar Europe enjoyed more protection than they did elsewhere in large part because states, not employers, controlled who could come in and be made to leave. In most European countries, guest workers received separate work and residence permits, so losing one's job did not necessarily mean losing one's right to remain in the country (84–85).

15. Smith, "Guest Workers or Forced Labor?," 71.

16. Kalayaan, "Slavery by Another Name: The Tied Migrant Domestic Worker Visa," (London: Kalayaan, 2013), http://www.kalayaan.org.uk/wp-content/uploads/2014/09/Slavery-by-a-new-name-Briefing.pdf.

17. Kav LaOved Worker's Hotline v. Government of Israel, HCJ 4542/02, March 30, 2006.

18. I am indebted to Vasanthi Venkatesh for discussion of temporary foreign worker programs. In her comparative study of temporary foreign worker programs in

Israel, Canada, and Hong Kong, she attributes the greater rights protections for temporary foreign workers in Israel to their easier access to constitutional courts and the network of labor rights organizations dedicated to advocating on behalf of temporary foreign workers. See Vasanthi Venkatesh, "Rights Mobilization in Comparative Perspective," (PhD diss., University of California, Berkeley, 2018), on file with the author.

19. Hahamovitch, "Creating Perfect Immigrants," 81–82.

20. I agree with Carens that it is "blatantly unfair" to require people to pay into an insurance scheme if they are not eligible to benefit from it. Carens, *Ethics of Immigration*, 118.

21. Walzer, *Spheres of Justice*, 61. Lenard and Straehle characterize the denial of equal citizenship to temporary workers as a harm not only to temporary workers but to the receiving society itself: "[T]the existence of partial members, whose access to the political environment is restricted, is *our* failure to live up to the democratic principles we claim to uphold." Lenard and Straehle, "Temporary Labor Migration," 216.

22. Here I draw on Sarah Song, "The Significance of Territorial Presence and the Rights of Immigrants," in *Migration in Political Theory: The Ethics of Movement and Membership*, ed. Sarah Fine and Lea Ypi (Oxford: Oxford University Press, 2016), 225–48.

23. For a critique of difference blindness and defense of group-differentiated rights, see Iris Marion Young, *Justice and the Politics of Difference* (Princeton, NJ: Princeton University Press, 1990); and Kymlicka, *Multicultural Citizenship*.

24. For histories of exclusion based on race, ethnicity, and religion, see Smith, *Civic Ideals*; Aristide Zolberg, *A Nation by Design: Immigration Policy in the Fashioning of America* (Cambridge, MA: Harvard University Press, 2006); and Christian Joppke, *Selecting by Origin: Ethnic Migration and the Liberal State* (Cambridge, MA: Harvard University Press, 2005). For histories of exclusion focused on sexuality and gender identity, see Eithne Luibhéid, *Entry Denied: Controlling Sexuality at the Border* (Minneapolis: University of Minnesota Press, 2002); and Margot Canaday, *The Straight State: Sexuality and Citizenship in Twentieth-Century America* (Princeton, NJ: Princeton University Press, 2011).

25. UN Office of the High Commissioner, International Covenant on Civil and Political Rights, 1966, http://www.ohchr.org/EN/ProfessionalInterest/Pages/CCPR.aspx.

26. Here I draw on Miller, *Strangers in Our Midst*, 103–4.

27. Blake, "Immigration and Political Equality," 971; and Miller, *Strangers in Our Midst*, 105.

28. *Fong Yue Ting v. United States* at 707–8, citing Vattel, *Law of Nations*, bk. 1, ch. 19, §§ 230, 31. See chapter 2 for further discussion.

29. "Statement on Preventing Muslim Immigration" (December 7, 2015), cited in International Refugee Assistance Project et al. v. Donald J. Trump (2017), No. 17–1351, http://coop.ca4.uscourts.gov/171351.P.pdf.

30. "Protecting the Nation from Foreign Terrorist Entry into the United States," Exec. Order No. 82 F.R. 8977 (Jan. 27, 2017), https://www.federalregister. gov/documents/2017/02/01/2017-02281/protecting-the-nation-from-foreign-terrorist-entry-into-the-united-states.

31. Donald J. Trump @realDonaldTrump February 4, 2017.

32. "Protecting the Nation from Foreign Terrorist Entry into the United States," Exec. Order No. 82 F.R. 13209 (March 6, 2017), https://www.federalregister. gov/documents/2017/03/09/2017-04837/protecting-the-nation-from-foreign-terrorist-entry-into-the-united-states.

33. Department of Homeland Security, "Citizenship Likely an Unreliable Indicator of Terrorist Threat to the United States" (paper prepared for the DHS Acting Under Secretary of Intelligence and Analysis, Washington, DC), https://www.documentcloud.org/documents/3474730-DHS-intelligence-document-on-President-Donald.html (last accessed January 20, 2018). See also Vivian Salama and Alicia A. Caldwell, "AP Exclusive: DHS Report Disputes Threat from Banned Nations," *Associated Press*, February 24, 2017. http:// bigstory.ap.org/article/39f1f8e4ceed4a30a4570f693291c866/dhs-intel-report-disputes-threat-posed-travel-ban-nations.

34. International Refugee Assistance Project et al. v. Donald J. Trump, No. 17-1351 (2017), http://coop.ca4.uscourts.gov/171351.P.pdf.

35. State of Hawaii and Ismail Elshikh v. Donald J. Trump, No. 17-15589 (June 12, 2017), https://assets.documentcloud.org/documents/3863014/Read-the-Ninth-Court-of-Appeals-Ruling-on-Trump.pdf.

36. Alan M. Kraut, *Silent Travelers: Germs, Genes, and the Immigrant Menace* (Baltimore, MD: Johns Hopkins University Press, 1995); and Kraut, "Comment: Health, Disease, and Immigration Policy," *Journal of American Ethnic History* 24, no. 3 (2005): 54.

37. Julia Preston, "Obama Lifts a Ban on Entry into U.S. by HIV-Positive People," *New York Times*, October 30, 2009, http://www.nytimes.com/2009/10/31/us/politics/31travel.html.

38. Immigration and Nationality Act § 212(a)(1)(A)(i), 8 U.S.C. § 1182 (2013). The Department of Health and Human Services regulations at 42 C.F.R. 34.2(b) (2013) define "communicable disease of public health significance" as including (1) chancroid, (2) gonorrhea, (3) granuloma inguinale, (4) HIV infection, (5) infectious leprosy, (6) lymphogranuloma venereum, (7) infectious stage syphilis, and (8) active tuberculosis.

39. International health and human rights documents identify public-health-based restrictions on freedom of movement as acceptable. According to article 18(1) of the World Health Organization's International Health Regulations, states can (1) refuse entry of affected and suspected persons, (2) refuse entry of unaffected persons to affected areas, and (3) implement exit screening and/or restrictions on persons from affected areas. Article 12(1)–(4) of the International Covenant

on Civil and Political Rights allows for restrictions on movement on the basis of laws that are necessary for the protection of "national security, public order, public health or morals or the rights and freedoms of others."

40. Borjas, *We Wanted Workers*, 180–81.

41. James P. Smith and Barry Edmonston, eds., *The New Americans: Economic, Demographic, and Fiscal Effects of Immigration* (Washington, DC: National Academy Press, 1997), 292–93.

42. Smith and Edmonston, *New Americans*, 325.

43. Borjas, *We Wanted Workers*, 188–89.

44. Borjas, 191.

45. Immigration and Nationality Act, Sec. 212(a)(5)(A).

46. David Card, "The Impact of the Mariel Boatlift on the Miami Labor Market," *Industrial and Labor Relations Review* 43 (1990): 252.

47. Borjas, *We Wanted Workers*, 135.

48. Borjas, 152.

49. This includes temporary migrant workers. The two largest farmworker unions in the United States have sought to organize and represent the interests of H-2A agricultural workers. In 2004, the Farm Labor Organizing Committee signed a collective bargaining agreement covering H-2A workers employed by the North Carolina Grower's Association, giving them a grievance procedure to help enforce their H-2A contract rights. The committee also restored blacklisted employees to their jobs and corrected a recruitment fee scam by labor recruiters. See Smith, "Guest Workers or Forced Labor?," 74.

50. For discussion of these and other proposals, see Borjas, *We Wanted Workers*, 207–8.

51. Here I draw on my review of David Miller's book and his reply. See "Review Symposium: Strangers in Our Midst," *European Political Science* (2017), https://doi.org/10.1057/s41304-016-0095-2.

52. Miller, *Strangers in Our Midst*, 18, 107–8.

53. It is important to stress that Miller's conception of national culture is capacious and contested. It consists not only of languages, religions, modes of dress, and distinctive cultural practices and identities but also political values and principles. As I discussed in chapter 3, the challenge for liberal nationalists like Miller is to determine what ought to be done when a nation's commitment to preserving particular ethnic or religious identities conflicts with its commitment to cherished political principles such as equality.

54. Carens, *Ethics of Immigration*, 182–83.

55. See Ayelet Shachar, "Selecting by Merit: The Brave New World of Stratified Mobility," in *Migration in Political Theory: The Ethics of Movement and Membership*, ed. Sarah Fine and Lea Ypi (Oxford: Oxford University Press, 2016), 183; and Triadafilos Triadafilopoulos, "Dismantling White Canada: Race, Rights, and the Origins of the Points System," in ed., *Wanted and Welcome? Policies for Highly*

Skilled Immigrants in Comparative Perspective, ed. Triadafilos Triadafilopoulos (New York: Springer, 2013), 15–37.

56. Borjas, *We Wanted Workers*, 208.

57. See chapter 6 for discussion of brain drain in the context of considering constraints on the right of individuals to exit their native countries.

58. See Pritchett, *Let Their People Come*; Oded Stark, "Rethinking Brain Drain," *World Development* 32, no. 1 (2004): 15–22; Clemens, "Economics and Emigration"; and Kapur and McHale, "What's Wrong with Plan B?"

59. Miller, *Strangers in Our Midst*, 111.

60. I take this example from economist Michael Clemens. He argues for a new research agenda for economists studying emigration that goes beyond a focus on national welfare to consider "the gains to migrants" themselves. Clemens argues that economists' tendency to focus on brain drain and remittances in studying emigration goes back to Adam Smith's *Wealth of Nations* and the mercantilist tradition, where the goal of economic policy was to encourage national production and exports and discourage imports. He argues for opening up the research agenda to focus on economic gains to migrants themselves. Clemens, "Economics and Emigration," 99–101. In my view, he goes to the other extreme, neglecting the perspective of political communities and emphasizing the benefits of migration for migrants themselves.

61. Gi-Wook Shin and Joon Nak Choi, *Global Talent: Skilled Labor as Social Capital in Korea* (Stanford, CA: Stanford University Press, 2015).

62. Sanket Mohapatra, Dilip Ratha, and Ani Silwal, "Outlook for Remittance Flows 2011–13" (Migration and Development Brief 16, World Bank, Washington, DC, May 23, 2011).

CHAPTER 10

1. See chapter 6 for discussion of human rights.

2. I discuss the coercion principle in greater length in chapter 4.

3. Yick Wo v. Hopkins, 118 U.S. 356, 369 (1886). A decade later, in Wong Wing v. United States, 163 U.S. 228 (1896), the court ruled that noncitizen criminal defendants, like citizen defendants, are entitled to the protection of the Fifth and Sixth Amendments.

4. Linda Bosniak, *The Citizen and the Alien* (Princeton, NJ: Princeton University Press, 2006), 55.

5. Walzer, *Spheres of Justice*, 60–61.

6. Ruth Rubio-Marín, *Immigration as Democratic Challenge: Citizenship and Inclusion in Germany and the United States* (Cambridge: Cambridge University Press, 2000), 21.

7. Carens, *Ethics of Immigration*, 158, 164. See also Shachar, *Birthright Lottery*, which argues for social connection as a basis for membership, and Motomura, *Americans*

in Waiting: The Lost Story of Immigration and Citizenship in the United States (Oxford: Oxford University Press, 2007), which identifies "immigration as affiliation" as "the view that the treatment of lawful immigrants and other noncitizens should depend on the ties that they have formed in this country" (11).

8. Carens, *Immigrants and the Right to Stay*, 20–21.

9. Carens, *Ethics of Immigration*, 158.

10. Rubio-Marín, *Immigration as Democratic Challenge*, 6.

11. Carens, *Ethics of Immigration*, 160.

12. Carens, 161, 168.

13. I develop this critique in Sarah Song, "Immigration and Democratic Principles: On Carens' *Ethics of Immigration*," *Journal of Applied Philosophy* 33, no. 4 (2016): 450–56.

14. As Rawls put it, "We are not to gain from the cooperative labors of others without doing our fair share." Rawls, *Theory of Justice*, 4, 112. See also Rawls's "Legal Obligation and the Principle of Fair Play," in *Law and Philosophy: A Symposium*, ed. S. Hook (New York: New York University Press, 1964).

15. About 65,000 foreign-born persons serve in the US military, representing about 5 percent of all active-duty personnel; one-third of the foreign born serving in the military are not US citizens. See Jeanne Batalova, "Immigrants in the U.S. Armed Forces," Migration Policy Institute, May 28, 2008, http://www.migrationinformation.org/USFocus/display.cfm?ID=683.

16. See Yasemin Soysal, *Limits of Citizenship: Migrants and Postnational Membership in Europe* (Chicago: University of Chicago Press, 1994); David Jacobson, *Rights across Borders: Immigration and the Decline of Citizenship* (Baltimore, MD: Johns Hopkins University Press, 1996); Seyla Benhabib, *The Rights of Others: Aliens, Residents, and Citizens* (Cambridge: Cambridge University Press, 2004); Bosniak, *Citizen and the Alien*; and Saskia Sassen, *Territory, Authority, Rights* (Princeton, NJ: Princeton University Press, 2008).

17. Illegal Immigration Reform and Immigrant Responsibility Act of 1996, P.L. 104–208 § 240A(a), 8 U.S.C. 1229b(a) (2006).

18. Maggie Jones, "Adam Crapser's Bizarre Deportation Odyssey," *New York Times*, April 1, 2015, https://www.nytimes.com/2015/04/01/magazine/adam-crapsers-bizarre-deportation-odyssey.html.

19. Choe Sang-Hun, "Deportation a 'Death Sentence' to Adoptees after a Lifetime in the U.S." *New York Times*, July 2, 2017, https://www.nytimes.com/2017/07/02/world/asia/south-korea-adoptions-phillip-clay-adam-crapser.html.

20. Mae Ngai, *Impossible Subjects*, 76–82. Under current law, eligibility for a cancellation of removal requires a minimum period of continuous residence (seven years for LPRs; ten years for unauthorized migrants).

21. For discussion of the claim that deportation is punishment, see Gabriel "Jack" Chin, "Illegal Entry as Crime, Deportation as Punishment: Immigration Status and the Criminal Process," *UCLA Law Review* 58 (2011): 1417–59.

22. "Put bluntly, low-skill immigration is likely to be a drain on native taxpayers, while high-skill immigration is likely to be a boon." Borjas, *We Wanted Workers*, 175.
23. Graham v. Richardson, 403 U.S. 365, 374–76 (1970).
24. Sugarman v. Dougall, 413 U.S. 634, 645, 646 (1973).
25. For limits on lawful permanent residents' access to public assistance, see 8 U.S.C. 1611–1613, 1621–1622, 1631–1632 (2006), and for restrictions on employment opportunities for lawful permanent residents, see Cabell v. Chavez-Salido, 454 U.S. 432 (1982).
26. For a 150-year period in US history, ending in 1928, at least twenty-two states permitted white, male, property-owning noncitizens to vote in local, state, and federal elections. See L. E. Aylsworth, "The Passing of Alien Suffrage," *American Political Science Review* 25, no. 1 (1931): 114–16; and Alexander Keyssar, *The Right to Vote* (New York: Basic Books, 2000).
27. Bauböck, "Expansive Citizenship, 683–87.
28. See Song, "Democracy and Noncitizen Voting Rights," 607–20.
29. I argue in favor of naturalization tests that take a more "civic" form, focusing on basic knowledge of history and politics, in contrast to ethnocultural conditions, in Song, "Three Models of Civic Solidarity," *Citizenship, Borders, and Human Needs*, ed. Rogers M. Smith (Philadelphia: University of Pennsylvania Press, 2011), 192–207.
30. I use the term "unauthorized migrant" because it is not closely associated with a particular ideological position in the way that the terms "illegal immigrant" and "undocumented immigrant" are. Joel Sati makes a compelling case for using the term "illegalized migrant" in his paper, "Knowing Justice: On Illegalization, Epistemic Justice, and the Legal Person as Interlocutor" (on file with the author). See also Harald Bauder, "Why We Should Use the Term 'Illegalized' Refugee or Immigrant: A Commentary," *International Journal of Refugee Law* 26, no. 3 (2014): 327–32.
31. Ryan Pevnick, *Immigration and the Constraints of Justice*, 164–65.
32. Rubio-Marín, *Immigration as Democratic Challenge*, 83.
33. For critique of the state complicity argument, see Carens, *Ethics of Immigration*, 153. See also Pevnick, *Immigration and the Constraints of Justice*, 167.
34. I take the idea of supersession from Jeremy Waldron, "Superseding Historic Injustice."
35. Bosniak, *Citizen and the Alien*, 54–55.
36. Carens, *Ethics of Immigration*, 132–35.
37. Plyler v. Doe, 457 U.S. 202 at 272, 222, 221, 230. For further critical analysis of *Plyler*, see Bosniak, *Citizen and the Alien*, 65.
38. Consideration of Deferred Action for Childhood Arrivals (DACA), U.S. Citizenship and Immigration Services, 2018, https://www.uscis.gov/humanitarian/consideration-deferred-action-childhood-arrivals-daca.

39. Because it is a time-limited program and does not confer permanent resident status, it does not offer a long-term solution. For a study based on interviews with DACA recipients, see Laurel E. Fletcher, Roxanna Altholz, and the International Human Rights Law Clinic, Berkeley Law, "DREAMers at Cal: The Impact of Immigration Status on Undocumented Students at the University of California at Berkeley" (report, International Human Rights Law Clinic, University of California Berkeley School of Law, May 2015).
40. *Plyler* at 220, 219; Bosniak, *Citizen and the Alien*, 66.
41. Migration Policy Institute, "As Many as 3.7 Million Unauthorized Immigrants Could Get Relief from Deportation under Anticipated New Deferred Action Program," press release, November 19, 2014, http://www.migrationpolicy.org/news/mpi-many-37-million-unauthorized-immigrants-could-get-relief-deportation-under-anticipated-new; Shoba Sivaprasad Wadhia, "The Birth and Death of Deferred Action (and What the Future Holds)," *The Medium*, June 16, 2017, https://medium.com/@shobawadhia/the-birth-and-death-of-deferred-action-and-what-the-future-holds-168d138eb088.
42. Jens Manuel Krogstad, Jeffrey S. Passel, and D'Vera Cohn, "5 Facts about Illegal Immigration in the U.S." (Washington, DC: Pew Research Center April 27, 2017), http://www.pewresearch.org/fact-tank/2017/04/27/5-facts-about-illegal-immigration-in-the-u-s/.
43. Carens, *Ethics of Immigration*, 150.
44. Carens, 148.
45. Krogstad, Passel, and Cohn, "5 Facts about Illegal Immigration in the U.S.," http://www.pewresearch.org/fact-tank/2017/04/27/5-facts-about-illegal-immigration-in-the-u-s/.
46. Carens, *Ethics of Immigration*, 151.
47. See chapter 8 on family connections as a ground for immigrant admissions.
48. "The Facts of Immigration Today," Center for American Progress, October 23, 2014, https://www.americanprogress.org/issues/immigration/reports/2014/10/23/59040/the-facts-on-immigration-today-3/.
49. See, e.g., Cruz Rendon v. Holder, 604 F.3d 1104 (9th Cir. 2009) (minor child's specialized medical and educational needs offered as grounds for canceling the deportation order).
50. "INS Announces Limited Policy on Family Unity," 64 Interpreter release 1191, October 26, 1987.
51. Miller, *Strangers in Our Midst*, 126. On the idea of "earned citizenship," see Shachar, *Birthright Lottery*, 177–78.
52. National Association of Immigration Judges, "Improving Efficiency and Ensuring Justice in the Immigration Court System" (statement before the Senate Committee on the Judiciary), May 18, 2011, https://www.naij-usa.org/images/uploads/publications/Senate-Improving_Efficiency_and_Ensuring_Justice_in_the_Immigration_Court_System_5-18-11.pdf.

53. Memorandum for All ERO Employees, U.S. Immigration and Customs Enforcement, https://www.documentcloud.org/documents/3889695-doc00801320170 630123624.html.

54. Sarah Shermon-Stokes, "Immigration Judges Were Always Overworked: Now They'll Be Untrained, Too," *Washington Post*, July 11, 2017, http://wapo.st/ 2sMxpla?tid=ss_mail&utm_term=.417413743b58.

CHAPTER 11

1. Carens, "Migration and Morality," 37.

2. See Table 8.1 on p. 140. My calculation of percentages is based on data provided by the Department of Homeland Security, *2015 Yearbook of Immigration Statistics*, table 6, https://www.dhs.gov/immigration-statistics/yearbook/2015/table6.

3. Borjas, "The Immigration Debate We Need," *New York Times*, February 27, 2017, https://www.nytimes.com/2017/02/27/opinion/the-immigration-debate-we-need.html.

4. Borjas, *We Wanted Workers*, 205.

Index

Page numbers followed by *t* refer to tables.

p. 156 —

her point about great worker programs being shows seems in tension with someone self-determination/ membership in the policy being the highest order value

and she cited the Bracero program as example of good worker protections- Ngai shows us that wasn't the case

exclusion is just a form of privilege hoarding